Issue Politics in Congress

Do representatives and senators respond to the critiques raised by their challengers? This study, one of the first to explore how legislators' experiences as candidates shape their subsequent behavior as policy makers, demonstrates that they do. Winning legislators regularly take up their challengers' priority issues from the last campaign and act on them in office, a phenomenon called "issue uptake." This attentiveness to their challengers' issues reflects a widespread and systematic yet largely unrecognized mode of responsiveness in the U.S. Congress, but it is one with important benefits for the legislators who undertake it and for the health and legitimacy of the representative process. Because challengers focus their campaigns on their opponents' weaknesses, legislators' subsequent uptake of these issues helps to inoculate them against future attacks and brings new and salient issues to the congressional agenda. This book provides fresh insight into questions regarding the electoral connection in legislative behavior, the role of campaigns and elections, and the nature and quality of congressional representation.

Tracy Sulkin is an assistant professor in the departments of political science and speech communication at the University of Illinois, Urbana–Champaign. She received her Ph.D. from the University of Washington in 2002. Her work has appeared in the *American Political Science Review*, *Political Analysis*, *American Politics Research*, and *Political Psychology*. This book is based on her dissertation, which won APSA's Schattschneider Award in 2003.

Issue Politics in Congress

TRACY SULKIN

University of Illinois, Urbana-Champaign

CAMBRIDGE UNIVERSITY PRESS
Cambridge, New York, Melbourne, Madrid, Cape Town, Singapore, São Paulo

Cambridge University Press
40 West 20th Street, New York, NY 10011-4211, USA

www.cambridge.org
Information on this title: www.cambridge.org/9780521855211

© Tracy Sulkin 2005

First published 2005

Printed in the United States of America

A catalog record for this publication is available from the British Library.

Library of Congress Cataloging in Publication Data

Sulkin, Tracy.
Issue politics in Congress / Tracy Sulkin.
    p.   cm.
Includes bibliographical references and index.
ISBN 0-521-85521-7 (hardback) – ISBN 0-521-67132-9 (pbk.)
1. Political planning – United States.   2. Representative government and representation –
United States.   3. United States. Congress – Elections.   4. Legislators – United States –
Attitudes.   5. Public opinion – United States.   6. Political leadership – United States.
7. Political campaigns – United States.   I. Title.
JK468.P64S85   2005
328.73 – dc22   2005008116

ISBN-13   978-0-521-85521-1 hardback
ISBN-10   0-521-85521-7 hardback

ISBN-13   978-0-521-67132-3 paperback
ISBN-10   0-521-67132-9 paperback

Contents

Figures

Tables

Acknowledgments

Like all books, this one is the result of a number of years of work, and one of the many pleasures of bringing it to completion is the opportunity to thank those who have helped along the way.

This project began as my dissertation at the University of Washington, and my biggest debt is to my committee members there, Lance Bennett, Peter May, John Wilkerson, and especially my chair, Bryan Jones. The old saying about the job of journalists, that they ought to "comfort the afflicted and afflict the comfortable," also seems to describe the role played by the best graduate mentors. Bryan combined equal measures of enthusiasm for the project with the conviction that I could make it better. I am grateful to him for both, and for his continuing wise counsel on matters both big and small.

At the University of Illinois, Urbana-Champaign, I found a collegial and congenial place to complete the book. Many colleagues in the departments of political science and speech communication offered helpful suggestions and feedback. In particular, Jim Kuklinski, Peter Nardulli, and Scott Althaus all went above and beyond the call of duty on many occasions, and I thank them for their patience and advice. Kris Miler, Leanne Knobloch, and Lisa Asplen took time off from their own work to read and comment on mine, and I am fortunate to count them as good colleagues and as good friends.

Funding for the project came from a number of sources, including a National Science Foundation Graduate Research Fellowship, a Congressional Research Award from the Dirksen Congressional Center, and grants from the Center for American Politics and Public Policy at the University of Washington and the Campus Research Board at the University of Illinois. A number of undergraduate Fellows at the Center for American Politics and Public Policy at UW helped in coding data, and Jillian Evans at UIUC provided expert research assistance in the final stages of the project.

The analyses presented here would not have been possible without the generosity of a number of colleagues who graciously offered their data to me. Adam Simon provided his content analysis data on discourse in Senate campaigns and Brian Gaines his data on challenger quality. My deepest debt on this front, though, is to those affiliated with the Policy Agendas Project and particularly to John Wilkerson, who shared both the bill introductions data he collected with Scott Adler and, even more valuable, his expertise in working with it.

Finally, I am grateful for the support of a number of family members and friends. Special thanks to Carolyn McNeill, Heather Larsen-Price, Katy Stenger, Matt Sulkin, and Jaret and Kim Treber. Most of all, I thank my parents, Steve and Shelley Sulkin, for thirty years of love and guidance. I dedicate this book to them, and to the memory of my grandmother, Dorothy Sulkin, who passed away shortly before it was completed.

Issue Politics in Congress

Electoral Challenges and Legislative Responsiveness

Going into his first reelection campaign in 1992, Senator Bob Graham was about as secure as any incumbent facing a challenge could hope to be. Though new to the Senate, he had a long history in Florida politics, including many years of service in the state legislature and two terms as governor. Endorsed by a host of newspapers and interest groups, he was described by many as the state's most popular politician, largely as the result of his reputation for action on environmental and economic issues of interest to his constituents (Duncan 1993, 321). During his active and well-funded campaign, Graham further leveraged these strengths by highlighting his competence and interest in the economy, the environment, and the proper role of governmental regulation.

In contrast, his opponent, Republican representative Bill Grant, faced an even greater uphill battle than most challengers. Hurt by his record of overdrafts at the House bank and his recent switch from the Democratic to the Republican Party, Grant experienced considerable difficulty raising funds, eventually raising only $200,000 to Graham's $3 million. Characterized by *St. Petersburg Times* political reporter Bill Moss as having "drive, but no fuel," (1992, 1B) he nonetheless launched a spirited campaign against Graham, focusing on health care, economic issues, and the need for a balanced budget.

Not surprisingly, Graham won the race easily, netting nearly two-thirds of the vote. When he returned to Washington, he continued to pursue his interests in the environment and in general economic issues, introducing and cosponsoring legislation and serving on the Environment and Public Works and Banking, Housing, and Urban Affairs committees. More unexpectedly, perhaps, he also became much more active on Grant's priority

issues from the campaign. In the term following the election, he introduced twenty-three bills, resolutions, and amendments relating to health
issues (on topics ranging from public health and health education to ensuring emergency care and preventive health benefits to health maintenance
organization enrollees to regulating the quality of hospitals), more than
twice as many as he had introduced in the previous term. He also introduced thirteen measures on balancing the budget, more than four times
as many as he had before.[1]

Graham's attentiveness to Grant's issues is not a coincidence, nor is
it unusual. To the contrary, it reflects a widespread yet largely unrecognized mode of responsiveness in the U.S. Congress. Winning legislators
regularly take up their challengers' priority issues from the last campaign
and act on them in office, a phenomenon I call "issue uptake." Congressional campaigns thus have a clear legacy in the content of legislators' agendas, influencing the areas in which they choose to be active and
the intensity with which they pursue these activities. Moreover, as I will
show, the extent of this legacy varies in a predictable way across individual representatives and senators, across legislative activities, across time,
and across chambers of Congress. Understanding the factors leading to
variation in uptake therefore offers fresh insight into some of the most
important and enduring normative and empirical questions in American
politics regarding the electoral connection in legislative behavior, the role
of campaigns and elections, and the nature and quality of congressional
responsiveness.

Legislators' motivation for engaging in uptake behavior is simple; they
undertake it because they believe that doing so will help them to achieve
their electoral goals. Because challengers focus their campaigns on the
incumbent's weaknesses, their choices of campaign themes provide signals
to winning legislators about important issues that they may have previously neglected. To the extent that legislators act on these signals, taking
up salient issues and making them a part of their agendas, they can remedy any weaknesses, strengthening their records before the next campaign
and inoculating themselves against possible attacks. Uptake thus has the
potential to promote individual legislators' electoral goals as well as the
health and legitimacy of the representative process, as legislators adjust

---

[1] This change cannot be explained by an increase in introduction activity, since Graham actually introduced fewer measures in his second term (the 103rd through 105th Congresses)
than in his first (the 100th through 102nd Congresses). Nor can it be attributed to greater
overall congressional attention to these issues because roughly the same number of bills
and resolutions were introduced on health and the balanced budget across the two terms.

their activity in office in response to electoral challenges. The central theme of this book is to explore these possibilities by investigating the dynamics of uptake, explaining why it occurs, how it varies, what it reveals about legislators' motivations and decision making, and how it impacts the policymaking process.

Linking the Electoral and Legislative Arenas

The claim that legislators' behavior is influenced by their past campaign experiences seems perhaps intuitive, and it is certainly not new. As far back as 1960, in his work on norms and behaviors in the U.S. Senate, Donald Matthews noted that it was "difficult, really, to understand the senators, how they act and why, without considering what happens to them when they are running for office" (1960, 68). However, despite the central role given to elections in democratic theory, systematic examinations of how they influence legislative politics and policymaking remain remarkably absent in the literature. We know very little about how legislators' experiences as candidates shape their subsequent activity in office, even though the "reelection-oriented representative" lies at the core of our conception of legislative behavior.

Why is there such a dearth of knowledge about how campaigns influence legislative behavior? It is certainly not due to a lack of scholarly interest in campaign effects or representation and responsiveness, two research agendas that enjoy considerable attention in the literature on American politics. Nor is it likely due to disagreement among scholars working in these fields that the situation described earlier demonstrates a campaign effect or an instance of responsiveness. Instead, the lack of attention to these linkages is the natural result of the traditional divisions of labor in political science research that have limited our ability to recognize and address political phenomena that lie at the intersection of these divisions.

Within legislative studies, the major substantive division mirrors the general institutions–behavior divide of the American field as a whole, with some scholars focusing on the structures and processes of Congress as an institution and others studying the elections that bring representatives and senators to Washington in the first place. There is little overlap, and even those scholars who do research in both areas seldom address both in a single work. As a result, the idea of the "Two Congresses," originally developed as an analytical device to distinguish legislators' careers in Washington, D.C., from their careers in their districts or states, actually accurately describes the current state of research in the field.[2] Most research treats representatives' and senators' experiences as candidates as separate from their subsequent behavior as legislators even though the two are inextricably linked.

The most damaging result of the bifurcation between electoral and institutional studies is that we neglect many important questions about the representative process. Most studies of legislative behavior assume that representatives and senators are strategic and forward-looking, using their time in office to promote their future reelection prospects. Following Mayhew's (1974) lead, scholars have asked, "If legislators were proactive and concerned about reelection, what patterns of behavior would we expect to see?" Explorations of this question in a variety of settings have provided substantial insight into how electoral considerations influence incumbents' roll call voting decisions (Fiorina 1974; Kingdon 1989); their participation in committees (Fenno 1973; Hall 1996); their efforts at legislative entrepreneurship (Schiller 2000; Wawro 2000); their "home styles" in their districts or states (Fenno 1978); and their choices about casework and constituency service (Bond 1985; Johannes 1984; Parker 1980). What is missing in this literature is a retrospective approach investigating how past experiences influence legislators' current choices about their activities. If campaigns teach legislators which strategies work and which don't, and what their strengths and weaknesses are in the eyes of the constituency and of potential opponents, then they should play an important role in shaping responsive behavior in the next term. An approach to studying Congress that neglects this potentially important linkage between the electoral and legislative arenas yields a necessarily incomplete picture of legislative behavior.

Studies of congressional elections are similarly limited by their sole focus on a single stage in the representative process. In fact, perhaps the best illustration of the problems inherent in the separation of electoral and institutional behavior falls on the elections side in the debate about whether or not campaigns matter. The ongoing scholarly and popular concern about the quality of campaigns is predicated on the notion that they do, but empirical confirmation of these effects has proven more elusive. Fifty years of quantitative research on elections has confirmed

---

[2] This perspective is reflected in Polsby and Schickler's (2002) recent essay on the history of congressional studies over the past half century. Their discussion focuses exclusively on institutional research, omitting work on congressional elections, which they characterize as "an important literature in its own right" (333) but as distinct from research on Congress as an institution.

that, while campaigns generally increase voters' information levels, they rarely change many vote decisions (Campbell et al. 1960; Holbrook 1996; Lazarsfeld, Berelson, and Gaudet 1944; Miller and Shanks 1996; Nie, Verba, and Petrocik 1976). More evidence exists for their indirect influence on efficacy and turnout, but there is still considerable disagreement about the magnitude and importance of these effects (see, for example, Ansolabehere and Iyengar 1995; Freedman and Goldstein 1999; Wattenberg and Brians 1999). As a consequence, debates about the potential impacts of campaigns remain among the most vigorously contested in the literature on American politics.

Unfortunately, the scope of these discussions has been quite limited, focusing almost exclusively on how campaigns may or may not influence citizens' attitudes and vote choices. Whatever the eventual conclusion drawn from this research, a solely voter-centered approach to campaign effects can provide only a partial answer to the question of whether or not campaigns matter. The limits of this approach become clear when we consider that the outcomes of congressional elections are generally quite predictable – incumbents win the vast majority of the time. For this reason, any impact of campaigns on voters will be important only at the margins. By expanding our focus to include their potential influence on winners' behavior in office, we can get more analytical leverage. Specifically, if campaigns inform the content and intensity of legislators' subsequent legislative activity, then they clearly do matter, apart from any effect they may have on voters. To assess the true impact of campaigns, we must therefore look for effects that extend beyond Election Day. However, as Fenno noted in his recent work on representation, "for most political scientists most of the time, the study of elections has meant only the study of voters and their voting behavior" (1996, 76), a perspective that limits our conception of the role of campaigns and results in a great gulf in our understanding of the linkages between electoral and legislative politics.

Defining Uptake

By explicitly specifying the process through which legislators' activity in office is related to their campaign experiences, the study of uptake makes a significant advance in closing this gap. Though I focus on uptake as a mechanism for connecting campaigns to legislative behavior, it has its scholarly roots in other subfields of political science, particularly political communication and political theory. Scholars in these fields studying deliberation and discursive processes have been interested in determining the conditions under which ideas expressed by certain participants are incorporated into the arguments of others.[3] If, for example, in a discussion about the merits of a particular tax policy, one discussant raises the issue of its impact on the budget deficit, do other discussants also address this point? To the extent that they do, uptake has occurred, and the deliberative process itself can be judged to be more successful, at least from a procedural standpoint.

In the congressional setting, uptake is conceived of in a slightly different way, going beyond language to focus on other types of behavior, in particular, participation in the legislative process, including legislators' sponsorship and cosponsorship of bills, resolutions, and amendments and their statements on the floor about pending legislation. If a challenger focuses her campaign on agriculture, defense, and education, uptake is measured as the amount of attention the winning legislator devotes to these issues in his legislative activity when he returns to Congress. Graham's introduction of measures on health care and the balanced budget is thus evidence of his uptake of Grant's themes.

At its roots, then, uptake is fundamentally about legislative responsiveness, as representatives and senators use their time in office to respond to and address their previous challengers' critiques. Uptake levels provide an indicator of this responsiveness, both for individual legislators and for Congress as a whole. At the individual level, we can compare the rates of uptake across legislators to place an individual legislator's behavior in context. For example, we can determine whether Graham's level of attention to his challenger's themes is relatively high, relatively low, or somewhere in between. Such analyses also enable us to identify the factors that distinguish those legislators who are highly responsive to their challengers' critiques from those who are less so and to predict uptake levels based on characteristics of a legislator or his or her constituency. Similarly, aggregate uptake patterns across all legislators allow us to assess the strength of *institutional* responsiveness – the success of the institutions of representative democracy at transmitting issues from one stage of the process to another as issues are introduced in campaigns, incorporated into legislative activity, and translated into public policy. We can investigate whether the legacy of campaigns is stronger in certain types of activities than others, or at certain times within legislative terms, and use these findings to estimate the longevity of uptake effects. Although the opportunity to

---

[3] Bohman (1996) discusses uptake in small group settings, and Simon (2002) explores the level of dialogue between candidates in Senate campaigns.

study individual and institutional agenda-based responsiveness is in some ways a side consequence of modeling the linkages between campaigns and legislative behavior, it is a critically important one. By quantifying and measuring uptake levels, we gain a new perspective on the dynamics of the relationship between the electoral and legislative arenas as well as a more nuanced understanding of the nature of legislative responsiveness.

As may be obvious, my approach is greatly influenced by the agenda-setting tradition in public policy, political communication, and public opinion research. At the core of the agenda-setting paradigm is a focus on issues: how they arise, how they change, and how they are communicated and acted on by different actors in the political process. Within the public policy field, this tradition is exemplified by the work of scholars who have studied agenda formation and change at the national level (Baumgartner and Jones 1993; Cobb and Elder 1983; Downs 1972; Kingdon 1984). In political communication research, the focus has been on the micro-foundations of agenda-setting, examining in particular the relationship between the amount of media coverage given to issues and the extent to which they are perceived as important problems by the public (see, for example, Iyengar and Kinder 1987; McCombs and Shaw 1972). Public opinion scholars have, in turn, attempted to unite the insights of these two fields to focus on the relationships between the governmental, public, and media agendas (Erikson, MacKuen, and Stimson 2002; Page and Shapiro 1992).

The agenda-setting perspective is much less familiar to scholars of legislative behavior, where the focus has traditionally been not on legislators' relative attention to different issues, but on the positions they take on roll call votes, which are generally interpreted as manifestations of their underlying ideological preferences. This focus on preferences has informed nearly all of the literature on legislative representation and responsiveness (but see Hall 1996). An agenda-based approach like uptake thus constitutes a fundamentally different way of thinking about responsiveness. The leverage provided by this approach becomes most apparent when we compare it to the traditional way of conceptualizing representational linkages. As such, I begin with a review of the literature on representation and responsiveness in Congress.[4]

---

4 Although these terms are often used interchangeably, there are important theoretical distinctions between the two. Representation is generally a static concept, focusing on the relationship between legislators' and constituents' opinions or actions at any one point in time. Responsiveness has a more dynamic connotation, implying a change in legislators' behavior in response to changing circumstances. Uptake is therefore more about

Research on Legislative Responsiveness

Concerns about representation are as old as the history of democratic theory. As Pitkin (1967) notes, modern theorizing about the proper role of representatives is still largely centered on the work of classical theorists like Burke, Rousseau, and Mill, who all concerned themselves with the standards for representative legitimacy. For instance, should representatives act as delegates, letting their constituents' directives dictate their behavior? Or should they act as trustees, gathering information and making their own judgments as to which actions would be in the best interests of their districts or states? With the growth of quantitative political science, scholars became interested in operationalizing these concepts and determining whether or not legislators behaved as theorists prescribed. Research on representation has therefore enjoyed a central place in the study of American politics over the past fifty years.

Different studies propose slightly different conceptualizations of legislative representation, but most focus on a particular type, called "policy responsiveness."[5] The basic premise underlying policy responsiveness is that, in accordance with the delegate standard of representation, legislators' behavior in office should reflect the interests of their districts or states. If we ask what sorts of behavior might indicate such responsiveness on the part of legislators, a number of possibilities come to mind. For example, legislators' roll call voting decisions should reflect the preferences of their constituents on these matters, so their issue positions should serve as one important indicator of their responsiveness. Similarly, responsive legislators should devote attention to important issues, adjusting their agendas in response to outside events, the desires of the constituency, critiques from challengers, and the like. For the most part, however, the literature on policy responsiveness has focused solely on issue positions, an approach that can be traced back to one of the earliest and still most influential empirical studies of representation, Miller and Stokes's (1963) article, "Constituency Influence in Congress."

Miller and Stokes's primary goal in their now-classic piece was to assess the claim that constituents have considerable influence on or control over

---

responsiveness than about representation, though I will occasionally use the latter term when referring to it.

[5] Of course, policy representation is not the only thing constituents may want from their representatives. As Fenno (1978) notes, they may also desire "extrapolicy" benefits – access to their legislators, help in dealing with bureaucratic problems, and the like. Hence, there exists a large literature devoted to investigating the dynamics and effects of home style and casework (see, for example, Bond 1985; Fenno 1978; Johannes 1984; Parker 1980).

legislators' behavior, particularly their voting decisions. Though this is an assertion that would be strongly questioned today, it was, at the time of their writing, "commonly thought to be both a normative principle and a factual truth about American government" (1963, 45). Coining the term "policy congruence" to refer to the relationship between legislators' positions on issues and their constituents' opinions on those same issues, Miller and Stokes compared the results of district opinion polls to representatives' roll call voting records to assess the strength of the correlation between the two across three broad issue areas – social welfare, foreign affairs, and civil rights. Contrary to the expectations of the textbook models of representation, which predicted high levels of congruence, they found that the relationship between legislators' and constituents' positions was positive, but relatively weak, and varied markedly by issue area.

At least in part because of this surprising and somewhat disturbing conclusion, Miller and Stokes's work spawned a large number of studies examining the extent of constituency influence on legislators' vote decisions (for a review, see Bernstein 1989 or Jewell 1983). Some of these studies continued in their footprints, examining congruence within specific issue areas (see, for example, Page et al. 1984; Stone 1982) and further explicating the structure of the congruence relationship (Cnudde and McCrone 1966; McCrone and Stone 1986). Others took a different tack, attempting to tie variation in congruence to other factors like electoral vulnerability (Fiorina 1974; Kuklinski 1977; Sullivan and Uslaner 1978), legislators' role orientations (Jones 1973; Kuklinski and Elling 1977; McCrone and Kuklinski 1979), and proximity to the next election (Elling 1982; Kuklinski 1978). Still others offered methodological critiques of the measurement strategies used in assessing congruence and offered alternatives (Achen 1977, 1978; Erikson 1978; Stone 1979; Weissberg 1979). However, despite providing considerable refinement in how we think about policy congruence, these studies all generally reached the same conclusion: that responsiveness did exist, particularly on salient issues, but at lower levels and in more subtle and contingent ways than the framers might have wanted and the conventional wisdom pre–Miller and Stokes might have predicted.[6] Perhaps because of the consistency of these findings, scholarly attention to policy responsiveness waned throughout much of the 1980s.

---

[6] Some scholars offer a harsher interpretation of these findings. Arnold (1990), for example, argues that Miller and Stokes's major finding, "as yet unrefuted – was that such [congruence] linkages were weak" (37).

More recently, there has been a revival of interest in the subject, driven, at least in part, by the increased availability of data about public opinion and legislative voting and by widespread access to powerful software that enables scholars to explore more complicated models of policy congruence. Although these new studies have diverged from the approaches taken by the earlier work, they remain clearly influenced by Miller and Stokes's insights. For example, one important innovation in the recent literature on representation has been to take the policy congruence standard, but to apply it to Congress as an institution rather than to individual representatives. Most of the early empirical work on policy representation focused on *dyadic* representation, that is, the relationship between one representative and his or her constituency. However, as Weissberg (1978) noted, a different sort of policy representation was possible that focused on how well Congress represented the preferences of the public as a whole. Thus, even if dyadic representational linkages were relatively weak, strong *collective* representation could exist, a claim that was supported by Weissberg's preliminary analysis of the issue (but see Hurley 1982).

In the best-known examination of this sort of representation, Stimson, MacKuen, and Erikson's (1995) work on what they refer to as "dynamic" representation, the authors take up the issue of collective responsiveness, arguing that the cross-sectional nature of most representation research limits investigation into the process that produces the linkage between representatives and constituents (see also Erikson et al. 2002; Jacobs and Shapiro 2000; Page and Shapiro 1992). Process is important because the direction of the relationship is crucial for evaluating responsiveness – governmental action must *follow* public opinion. Stimson et al. (1995) advocate a time-series design that is capable of disentangling the reciprocal causal links between public opinion, policy activity, and policy outputs. This approach yields a more positive assessment of the linkage between Congress and the public, demonstrating that the ideological tenor of public policy does respond to changes in public opinion.[7]

These insights about the reciprocal nature of collective responsiveness have been taken up by another group of scholars, most notably Hill and Hurley (1999; Hurley and Hill 2003), who have sought to explore whether such reciprocal policy linkages exist at the dyadic level. While previous

---

[7] Importantly, however, in these models, responsiveness is generally viewed as achieved via replacement of current legislators by new ones. As such, they do not provide much insight into the ways in which individual representatives change in response to new circumstances.

congruence studies conceived of constituency opinion as an independent variable, Hill and Hurley revisited Miller and Stokes's original data to demonstrate that the linkages between constituents and legislators go in both directions. They conclude that legislators are influenced by public opinion but also mold it, which they suggest yields a more optimistic conclusion about the strength of representational linkages.

Reassessing Policy Responsiveness

Whether high levels of collective responsiveness or strong reciprocal policy linkages between legislators and constituents make up for weak direct congruence relationships largely depends on one's normative view of what legislative representation should look like. Importantly, though, *any* conclusion drawn from the studies discussed previously is based entirely on a single-dimensional conception of policy responsiveness – the congruence of positions between elites and the masses. In fact, the congruence standard has become so ingrained that, for many scholars, legislative representation *is* policy congruence. While there have been other critiques of this narrow focus, they have been mainly theoretical and have focused on the need to consider types of responsiveness other than policy responsiveness (e.g., Eulau and Karps 1977; Wahlke 1971). I agree with the spirit of these critiques but argue that there is still much to be learned about policy responsiveness, and that focusing on agendas as the target of this responsiveness offers substantial leverage in understanding representational linkages.

The expansion of the concept of policy-based responsiveness to include an agenda-based measure like uptake yields several clear theoretical benefits.[8] The value added becomes most apparent when we consider the choices that representatives and senators face in their legislative activity. As Hall (1996) notes in his study of participation in Congress, all legislators face three major decisions – how to vote, how active to be, and how to allocate their activity among different issue areas. Preference-based representation focuses only on the first and arguably the easiest of the three choices, and so neglects much of what legislators do in office (Schiller 2000). Limiting our conception of representation to the congruence of

---

[8] It is important to note that uptake is only one possible component of the broader notion of agenda-based responsiveness. This category of responsiveness could also include behaviors like keeping campaign promises about devoting increased attention to certain issues or responding to constituents' requests. I focus on uptake because my primary interest is in exploring the linkage between campaigns and legislative behavior.

preferences between representatives and constituents thus leads to an incomplete understanding of the ways in which legislators demonstrate responsiveness.

To illustrate why this is the case, imagine two hypothetical districts with identical characteristics and two legislators from these districts who cast the same votes on every roll call. The representational models based on preferences would lead us to the conclusion that these legislators are equally representative. However, what if, in addition to casting roll call votes, one was very active in setting the agenda, formulating and introducing bills on issues of interest to the constituency, gathering cosponsors, and speaking on the floor of Congress on behalf of them? It seems commonsensical that the active legislator was more intently advocating for the district's interests and so should be judged as more responsive, an intuition that is recognized from the perspective of uptake but is not captured by the preference model.[9]

The approach I propose thus reflects a broader, more entrepreneurial view of legislative behavior, going beyond the dichotomous vote choices that legislators face when presented with a roll call measure to investigate the entirety of their issue agendas. This expanded focus is important for at least two reasons. First, as Schiller (2000) argues, "if senators view their jobs as multidimensional and use the different legislative tools available to them to accomplish the task of representation, then congressional scholars have an obligation to study the full range of their activities" (162), a point that is particularly valid if one expects, as I do, that focusing on different activities might yield different conclusions. Second, a review of challengers' campaign strategies provides concrete evidence that voting records are not the only standard by which legislators are judged. For instance, Bill Grant's critique of Bob Graham's performance as a senator was not that he was voting against the interests of constituents on health issues or balanced budget policy, but that he wasn't being proactive enough in promoting them. Graham was thus being criticized not for his positions but for his lack of attention to important issues, a strategy that appears to be common among challengers. To give just a few examples, in the 1990 elections, Senator Nancy Kassebaum's (R-KS) challenger claimed that she paid "insufficient attention to health-care issues"

---

[9] Of course, a representative who was very active in introducing legislation that went against the constituency's expressed interests could not be judged responsive (though there is little reason to assume that strategic, reelection-oriented legislators would behave in this fashion), which is why agenda representation serves as a supplement to, rather than a replacement of, preference representation.

(Benenson 1990, 3310), Representative Pat Williams' (D-MT) criticized him for "failing to resolve the wilderness issue" (Kaplan 1990, 3327), and Representative John Miller's (R-WA) labeled him as "uninterested in the traffic congestion problems of the district" (Idelson 1990, 3354). In their next terms, all of these legislators increased the amount of attention they paid to these issues, responsiveness that is captured by the uptake standard but not by the policy congruence criterion.[10]

The other major theoretical benefit of the agenda-based approach is that it may more closely reflect political reality, incorporating what we know about how legislators actually approach politics. Policy congruence, as it has traditionally been measured, may be low because it often sets an unrealistic standard for responsiveness. Consider, for example, a Republican legislator who represents a district where the issue of health care rises in salience (as it did nationwide in the early 1990s). The legislator orders a poll taken in the district and finds that a majority of constituents support a government-funded universal health care system. How should he or she respond to this information? The policy congruence standard suggests that, if faced with a vote on this issue, a responsive representative would vote in support of universal health care.[11] Is it realistic to assume that a Republican representative could support this position? In most cases, the answer would be no, as he or she would immediately come under attack from both the party leadership and the base constituency in the district. As Jacobs and Shapiro (2000) argue, it is simply "infeasible for politicians to regularly change their positions in response to centrist [or district] opinion" (16). A better option might be for the legislator to recognize the underlying concern with health care availability indicated by the poll results and take action to address this concern, framing it in a way that is more broadly acceptable. For instance, he or she might introduce legislation to support the building of a new clinic in the district or to start a program to encourage more health professionals to practice in underserved areas. In short, since it is generally more politically feasible

---

[10] Kassebaum made twenty-four bill and resolution introductions on health in her next term, as compared to a single introduction on the issue in the term immediately preceding her challenge. Williams made five more introductions on the particular wilderness controversy raised by his challenger (a debate between logging interests and environmental interests), and Miller increased his attention to traffic issues by seven activities.

[11] The "if" is of critical importance here. According to the measurement standards of the preference representation approach, an issue must be the subject of a roll call vote in order for a legislator to demonstrate responsiveness (or lack thereof) to the interests of his or her constituents.

for a legislator to shift attention than to shift positions (Jones 1994), the agendas approach may more accurately capture how legislators actually demonstrate responsiveness, not by attempting to implement a particular policy proposal desired by constituents but by addressing the underlying policy problem indicated by their responses.

Agenda representation could constitute a weaker form of responsiveness than preference representation if we assumed that constituents are primarily concerned with issue positions – both their own and those of their elected representatives. Preference-based models (particularly those that focus on specific issues) are generally based on the notion that citizens have defined positions on the issues of the day and that they closely monitor the positions taken by elected officials. However, these are assumptions that much recent work has questioned. We know, for example, that citizens' knowledge of the particulars of politics and policy is generally fairly low. Because only about one-third of citizens can recall even the name of their member of the House of Representatives, it seems unreasonable to assume that most are aware of the specific positions taken by these legislators (Delli Carpini and Keeter 1996; Neuman 1986). Moreover, voters may not have positions of their own on public policy issues, and, even if they do express a position on an issue when asked to by an interviewer, this is not necessarily an indication of a stable opinion. Instead, as Zaller (1992) argues, many citizens construct an opinion off the top of their heads, using whatever considerations are foremost on their minds at the time of the interview. Thus, a lack of strong policy congruence may not be normatively troublesome, as long as district or state interests are being responded to in other ways.

Furthermore, it may not trouble constituents, who are generally characterized as being concerned with solving problems rather than advocating specific solutions, and who may not even perceive the connections between problems, proposed solutions, and outcomes (Arnold 1990; Bianco 1994). In an environment of asymmetric information about the effects of policy proposals, constituents may therefore be content to delegate decisions about the particulars of policy to their representatives. Put another way, to the extent that they trust their representatives to look after their interests (based, perhaps, on a positive retrospective evaluation of past performance), they give them leeway to vote as they see fit (Bianco 1994). For most constituents, on most issues, most of the time, it may therefore be enough that their representative is actively attending to important problems.

Agendas, Uptake, and Legislative Responsiveness

An agenda-based approach to understanding the linkages between campaigns and legislative behavior reflects a clear theoretical departure from previous research on Congress. Most fundamentally, it constitutes a major reconceptualization and expansion of the concept of responsiveness: in legislative behavior, in campaigns, and in congressional agenda-setting. By explicitly connecting all stages of the political process – legislators' experiences as candidates in campaigns, their subsequent activities in office, and the impact of these individual decisions on the content of public policy outcomes – into a single model, the uptake approach yields a broader and more nuanced conception of individual and institutional responsiveness.

At the level of the individual legislator, it shifts the expected locus of policy responsiveness, away from a sole focus on legislative voting decisions and toward the content of agendas. Responsive legislators are those who use their activity in office to demonstrate attentiveness to salient issues they may have previously neglected. By linking legislators' experiences as candidates to their behavior as policy makers, uptake also highlights the *process* of responsiveness, as legislators learn about potential issue weaknesses in campaigns and then adjust their behavior in response to this new information.

At the institutional level, uptake provides an indicator of collective responsiveness: how attentive Congress as a whole is to the issues raised in campaigns. As a consequence, the study of uptake offers new leverage into understanding how information is processed and agendas are set in Congress. A perennial topic of interest in policy research has been the dynamics of agenda change – how it is that new issues reach individual legislators' agendas and the broader congressional agenda (see Baumgartner and Jones 1993; Kingdon 1984). Schattschneider (1960) argued, for example, that agendas change when losers in the current status quo effectively introduce new cleavages and expand the scope of conflict. Although he was thinking of minority parties or pressure groups as the agents of change, in my formulation challengers fulfill this role. In their efforts to unseat incumbents, they highlight their issue weaknesses, which are then picked up by the winners and incorporated into their agendas in order to avoid difficulties in future elections. In looking out for their own electoral interests, legislators contribute (albeit unintentionally) to the process of agenda change in Congress.

This point underscores the need for a reassessment of the importance of campaigns and elections in general and the role of challengers in particular. From the perspective of uptake, congressional campaigns matter not just because they may influence voters, but because they *clearly* influence winners, shaping the content of their agendas in the next Congress. Previous challengers' campaigns provide the target for uptake, and the threat of future challengers provides the motivation for responsiveness. This conception is in contrast to past research on challengers, which has generally focused on defining what it means to be a "quality" challenger and on explaining the emergence of such challengers (Abramowitz 1980; Bond, Covington, and Fleisher 1985; Canon 1993; Hinckley 1980; Lublin 1994; Squire 1989, 1992). The basic argument in this literature is that challengers are important because of the role they can play in educating voters about differences between the candidates and because they occasionally upset incumbents, serving to promote accountability and possibly change the partisan composition of Congress. The uptake approach gives a new role to challengers – influencing the downstream policy agendas of winners. As such, it changes the location of incumbents' responsiveness to their challengers, away from the campaign and toward the floor of Congress. A growing literature in political communication focuses on dialogue and deliberation between candidates in campaigns (see, for example, Hart 2000; Simon 2002). Theorists and pundits alike often lament the lack of discussion and debate on the issues as a sign of unresponsiveness. However, even if candidates do not engage in a back-and-forth dialogue on the issues, incumbents can still respond to their challengers in an arguably more meaningful way, through the content of their activity in office.

Plan of the Book

In the pages to come, I address the questions and issues raised in the previous sections, beginning in Chapter 2 with a detailed theory of issue uptake. I describe more specifically why legislators should be motivated to take up their challengers' issues, their methods for doing so, and the potential payoffs of this responsiveness. I focus in particular on how legislators' strategic considerations regarding reelection shape both their uptake levels and their patterns of responsiveness, developing predictions about variation in uptake across individuals, across time, across legislative activities, and across chambers in Congress.

In Chapter 3, I discuss my strategies for assessing the content of campaign and legislative agendas and for measuring uptake. Drawing on data gathered from my sample – the issue content of 51 Senate campaigns from 1988 to 1992 and 422 House campaigns from 1988 to 1996, and the legislative activity of the winners of these races in the term following their election (a total of over 200,000 bill, resolution, and amendment introductions, cosponsorships, and floor statements in the 101st through 105th Congresses) – I describe what these agendas look like and how they vary. In the process, I dispel some common myths about agendas that have important consequences for uptake. For example, I demonstrate that congressional campaigns are not content-free, but in fact have clear issue foci, and, moreover, that there is a great deal of variation in choices of campaign themes across races, so that campaigns reflect more than just national trends in opinion. On the legislative activity side, I show that, contrary to the conventional wisdom, individual representatives' and senators' agendas vary widely in scope and are not overly constrained by their particular committee assignments, so that legislators enjoy considerable freedom in constructing their agendas.

Chapter 4 establishes the framework for comparing relative uptake levels across legislators. I present some basic descriptive information about uptake, including statistics about average levels of responsiveness and about the amount of variation we observe in this behavior. I also describe the factors that must be taken into account when making these comparisons and illustrate the uptake process using responsiveness on a single issue – health care.

The next two chapters seek to explain the substantial variation in uptake levels identified in Chapter 4. In Chapter 5, I focus on individual variation in responsiveness in the U.S. House of Representatives and Senate. I demonstrate that electoral vulnerability has a significant impact on uptake levels, but that the relationship between vulnerability and responsiveness is more complicated than is generally assumed. In addition, I explore some interesting and telling differences in uptake patterns between senators and representatives that yield insight into how institutional differences between the chambers influence the dynamics of responsiveness. Chapter 6 tests hypotheses about the location and timing of uptake in the political process, identifying the activities for which uptake levels are highest and describing the ebb and flow of uptake across legislators' terms.

In Chapter 7, I move away from cross-sectional examinations of variation in uptake to explore its effects over time. In particular, I examine the impact of responsiveness on legislators' electoral fortunes and their career decisions, evaluating whether the evidence supports my claim that engaging in uptake promotes reelection. Chapter 8 examines the policy implications of uptake, addressing the common assumption that activities that benefit legislators electorally must somehow be insincere and without consequences for policy. I explore the intensity with which legislators pursue their challenger-themed legislation compared to the other legislation in their portfolios and trace the eventual fates of both types of legislation, demonstrating that individual legislators' decisions about responsiveness have important downstream consequences for public policy. Finally, I conclude in Chapter 9 by summarizing the important results and returning to the normative implications of these findings for our understanding of representation and responsiveness, and of the linkages between campaigns and governance.

2

A Theory of Issue Uptake

The model of uptake described in Chapter 1 requires that legislators recognize and act on their challengers' campaign issues. I proposed that engaging in this behavior is a strategic choice, undertaken by legislators who believe that it will promote their reelection goals. Presumably, all other things being equal, legislators would not choose to act on their challengers' themes, as paying attention to these issues diverts attention from other issues that may be of more intrinsic interest to them. However, to the extent that doing so helps them to accomplish their electoral goals, they have a clear incentive to look to their previous campaign experiences when formulating their agendas. Of course, reelection is not legislators' only goal; they may also want, as Fenno (1973) noted, to make good public policy or to achieve influence in Congress. They may also wish to be good representatives, faithfully reflecting their constituency's interests, apart from any tangible benefit they may receive. Nonetheless, rational legislators should recognize that they cannot achieve these other goals unless they are able to remain in office, and so reelection is, for the majority, the most proximate goal.

This idea of the electoral connection, that, while in office, "congressmen must constantly engage in activities related to reelection" (Mayhew 1974, 49), has become central to the study of legislative behavior. The possible mechanisms for this connection are numerous and are discussed in more detail later. In general, though, the lesson that comes from this literature is that the optimal legislative strategy for reelection-oriented representatives and senators is to use their time in Congress to build on their strengths and shore up their weaknesses. Uptake helps them to do the latter, and so has the potential to promote the reelection goal in several ways. Most simply, constituents may recognize and reward responsive behavior on the part of their legislators, forming more positive evaluations of their performance in office and increasing their likelihood of reelecting them. However, even if constituents don't directly recognize and reward responsiveness, it may still pay off indirectly. If a legislator's next challenger raises some of the same issues, a record of uptake may help him or her to counter these critiques more effectively. The criticism that a representative does not pay enough attention to an issue like education or agriculture or the budget loses much of its punch if the legislator can point to recent activity on the issue. Perhaps the best possible benefit of a record of responsiveness, however, is that it may prevent potentially strong challengers from deciding to run in the first place, thus increasing the probability that the incumbent will be reelected.

The purpose of this chapter is to explore these possibilities and develop a theory of uptake behavior at the individual level. This "strategic motivation" theory explains why challengers' campaign themes serve as a particularly important and effective signal to legislators about their relative issue weaknesses, why legislators should be motivated to take up these signals, how they make choices about when and where to demonstrate their responsiveness, and the mechanism through which this behavior pays off for them. In the process, it points to a number of predictions about variation in uptake that have important implications for our assessments of the nature and quality of individual and institutional responsiveness.

Campaign Themes and Issue Salience

The general argument underlying my theory of uptake is that legislators stand to gain electorally by using their time in office to act on the "right" issues. Correctly identifying these issues is a critical task; because the size of their agendas is limited both by time and by resources, legislators simply can't be active in every realm of legislative activity or devote high levels of attention to every issue that might potentially be of interest to them or to their constituents (Bauer, Pool, and Dexter 1963). During the 1990s, for example, nearly 10,000 bills and resolutions were introduced in the House and Senate in each Congress on a myriad of issues, many more than an individual legislator could ever hope to address. When choosing their agenda priorities, legislators should therefore be very sensitive to signals about which issues have potentially high payoffs for them in future elections.

Although most research on the campaign as an information source focuses on voters (see, for instance, Abramowitz and Segal 1992; Franklin 1991; Kahn and Kenney 1999; Krasno 1994; Westlye 1991), campaigns also constitute an important source of information for legislators. Observing their challengers' selection of campaign themes provides a signal to incumbents about their relative strengths and weaknesses in the district or state. We know from previous work on candidate behavior that challengers are particularly strategic in their choice of issues – they carefully select those that they believe best highlight the incumbent's weaknesses (see Arnold 1990, 2004; Jacobson and Dimock 1994; Jacobson and Kernell 1983; Simon 2002). Arnold (1990) argues, for example, that it is not necessary for voters to search their representatives' records to look for possible weaknesses because challengers are more than happy to do this for them, "sift[ing] through incumbents' records ... and employ[ing] their newly discovered evidence to persuade citizens how poorly their current representatives have served their interests" (49).[1]

Challengers' incentives for adopting this strategy are clear. Most obviously, highlighting incumbents' inadequacies may enable challengers to decrease voters' overall evaluations of their performance and ability. More indirectly, but perhaps more importantly, such efforts may constitute what Riker (1986) called "heresthetical maneuvers," aimed at adjusting the agenda to create a more favorable decision environment. Jacobson (2001) argues that "a challenger cannot hope to win without reordering the campaign agenda" (87), and, by focusing their campaign appeals on themes on which their opponents are weak, challengers may be able to accomplish this, increasing the salience of these issues in voters' minds and leading them to weigh them more heavily in their decisions.

Challengers' campaigns should therefore serve to focus legislators' attention on their weaknesses. If incumbent legislators are unaware that they have neglected salient issues, their challengers will certainly inform them about this in their campaigns. If they suspect that these issues may be important, the campaign will confirm this for them. Of course, there may be other sources of these signals, like newspaper editorials, interactions with constituents and potential donors, opposition research funded by a candidate's own campaign organization, and so on, but the challenger's signals should be particularly effective in attracting the attention of a

---

[1] Arnold's later empirical work on newspaper coverage of House members confirmed this, showing that challengers were "the leading critics of representatives' performance as policymakers" (2004, 180).

legislator. As Marcus and MacKuen (1993) note, emotion plays an important role in the processing of political information. In particular, anxiety and threat serve to stimulate learning and the search for new information. Although their focus is on how citizens process campaign information, these insights certainly apply to candidates as well. Campaigning is an anxious time for legislators – their records, their style, and even their character are being scrutinized, and their reelection prospects may seem threatened. In such a situation, it is likely that rapid "serial shifts" in attention and priorities will occur (Jones 1994, 2001). Marcus and MacKuen put it more colorfully: "Hit it over the head with a two-by-four and you can get the attention of even a mule. Nothing focuses the mind so well as the prospect of one's own hanging" (1993, 672). In short, in the presence of a threat, legislators should become acutely aware of their weaknesses and the need to remedy them. A challenge from an opposing candidate provides just such a threat, and so should motivate legislators to engage in uptake.

Moreover, all winning candidates, even those who do not appear particularly vulnerable in the current election, have the incentive to pick up and act on these signals. This is because legislators are concerned not just with the present, but also with the future (Arnold 1990). In particular, they worry about their district's or state's "potential preferences" – those latent interests that might not currently be of primary concern but, with time and diligent attention from the legislators' critics, could become highly salient. Indeed, in a situation in which constituents are not particularly attentive to their representatives' records, challengers may even be able to create the perception of weakness on issues simply by highlighting them in their campaigns. Even if a legislator wins an election fairly easily, in a future campaign a stronger challenger could pick up on a past challenger's issues and exploit them more successfully, beating the incumbent. Most legislators have faced at least one close election in their careers and are understandably eager to avoid another one (Arnold 1990; Jacobson 2001; Mann 1978). For instance, in the 100th Congress, over half of the members of the House of Representatives and approximately three-quarters of those in the Senate had won at least one election with a vote share of less than 55 percent (Arnold 1990, 61). This bad experience no doubt lingers in their minds, informing their behavior in office well into the future, even when they may no longer be objectively vulnerable.

From this perspective, it would be a mistake to assume that because a given challenger lost, his or her campaign themes were inherently "losing issues." Challengers lose most of the time for a variety of reasons beyond their choices of campaign themes.[2] A weak candidate may still raise important issues, and voters may wish to see the winner address those issues in the next Congress. And, even if a set of issues does not resonate particularly strongly in a district or state at the present time, continued attention to these themes by challengers and other opponents of the incumbent may lead them to become more salient in the future (Arnold 1990). Kingdon (1984) offers a similar argument in his discussion of policy agenda-setting – that many times issues aren't viewed as particularly salient when they are first raised but, after a period of "softening up," come to be seen as priorities. The incentive, then, is for winners to be sensitive to early signals about their potential issue weaknesses and to act on them to take these issues off the table for future challengers looking for openings for their critiques.

Senator Daniel Patrick Moynihan's (D-NY) experiences in the 1988 election provide a good illustration of such behavior. His challenger, Robert McMillan, attacked him on environmental issues, running campaign ads accusing him of a lack of attention and action on coastal pollution (Benenson 1988, 2926). Although Moynihan had a good record on the environment, coastal pollution was an issue of increasing salience to his constituents and an area in which he had not been particularly active, introducing only two bills in the term preceding McMillan's challenge. Moynihan went on to beat McMillan by a comfortable margin but, rather than ignoring his critiques, appeared to respond to them, introducing nine more bills on the environment in his next term than he had in the previous term (from 14 to 25 introductions). More to the point, six of these introductions dealt explicitly with coastal pollution, a record of attentiveness that undoubtedly made it difficult for his next challenger to echo McMillan's criticism.

The idea that incumbents' behavior in office can deter strong challenges is not a new one and is, in fact, one of the general expectations underlying electoral connection theories of legislative behavior (see Fenno 1978; Fiorina 1974; Mayhew 1974). It has been addressed most directly by scholars interested in incumbent–challenger dynamics in congressional races. For example, a number of studies have concluded that quality challengers are more likely to enter a race when they perceive that the incumbent has weaknesses that they can exploit (Canon 1993; Jacobson and Dimock 1994; Jacobson and Kernell 1983), and, as Jacobson (2001) finds,

---

[2] In recent years, incumbent reelection rates for both chambers of Congress have hovered in the 85–95% range.

in races where the incumbent was defeated, voters were more likely to report that the challenger was better suited to handling pressing problems. In addition, political pundits' analyses of campaign strategies are replete with examples of legislators using uptake-like strategies to ward off challenges. Consider, for example, the campaign descriptions provided by the *Congressional Quarterly Weekly Report* (*CQ Weekly*). In commenting on Tim Johnson's (D-SD) prospects against his 1988 challenger, David Volk, reporter Dave Kaplan noted:

> Just as Volk was preparing to attack Johnson for what he deemed the incumbent's failure to protect Social Security recipients, Johnson immunized himself by announcing his cosponsorship of a bill designed to remove the Social Security trust fund from budget-deficit calculations.   (Kaplan 1988, 2942)

Similarly, in describing Jim Jontz's (D-IN) reelection bid against Patricia Williams, *CQ Weekly* editor Phil Duncan claimed:

> On a range of issues that Williams might want to use during the campaign, Jontz can head her off at the pass. He was given a seat on the Agriculture Committee when he got to Washington in 1987 and has used it to good advantage [focusing in particular on drought-relief legislation].   (Duncan 1988, 3102)

As such, there is considerable evidence that legislators' activity in office can have important consequences for their electoral prospects or, at the very least, that they believe it can. Ragsdale and Cook's (1987) research on the linkages between incumbents' and challengers' behavior was one of the first to explicitly tie legislators' attempts to avoid challenges to the process of representation and responsiveness. They studied the impact of the volume of incumbents' activities (trips to the district, number of bill introductions and cosponsorships) and their personal characteristics (seniority, ethical problems, news visibility) on their challengers' campaign expenditures and political action committee (PAC) contributions, arguing that, if incumbents can thwart strong challenges through their activity, then challengers may serve as enforcement mechanisms for representation. In such a situation, responsiveness occurs "less through voters and the election itself than by members avoiding behavior that would precipitate a viable challenger and by their actively pursuing endeavors that would block competition" (Ragsdale and Cook 1987, 46; see also Krasno and Green 1988). Although they approach representation and responsiveness differently than I do, focusing on constituency service and the volume of activity undertaken by legislators, the idea is applicable to uptake as well. In short, elections can promote responsiveness not just by serving as a mechanism through which constituents can replace poorly performing legislators, but also by providing an incentive for all legislators to adapt their behavior in office to avoid a challenge. As legislators exhibit this responsiveness to the issue priorities of their challengers, they also bring about institutional responsiveness, as information from campaigns is carried over into legislative behavior and public policy.

Opportunities for Demonstrating Responsiveness

The desire to be reelected thus provides the incentive for winning legislators to take up their challengers' issues. Once they decide to pursue this strategy, they have a number of options available for putting it into practice. Mayhew (1974) pointed to three general categories of activities that legislators use to express their interests and promote reelection – advertising, credit-claiming, and position-taking. Of the three activities, advertising and position-taking have received the most attention. Advertising, the art and science of making oneself known to the constituency, is the subject of the large literature on congressional "home styles" and constituency service (e.g., Fenno 1978; Johannes 1984). Position-taking has been the focus of a number of studies of legislative decision making and, as discussed at length in Chapter 1, is at the core of most empirical studies of legislative representation, which have investigated how constituents' opinions influence legislators' roll call voting patterns.

Considerably less attention has been paid to credit-claiming, an activity to which Mayhew ascribes equal importance and that allows for a broader view of legislative activity than just looking at the dichotomous choices that legislators make when faced with roll call votes.[3] He explains that congresspersons wish to encourage the belief that they are responsible for obtaining desirable outcomes, and so "it becomes necessary for each congressman to try to peel off pieces of governmental accomplishment for which he can believably generate a sense of responsibility" (1974, 53). Perhaps the best way to do this is to build a record and reputation for action on a given issue. Legislators who believe that attention to environmental issues will help their electoral fortunes have an incentive to associate themselves with bills or resolutions that address the environment and to participate in the legislative process by offering amendments, speaking on

---

[3] Mayhew argued that much credit-claiming activity falls under the category of particularized benefits and casework for the constituency, but that it also occurs on broader policy activity.

the floor, and the like. If they can trace their activity to identifiable positive effects on the issue – for instance, bringing money to the district to finance the cleanup of a polluted river – so much the better, but even barring this, they have much to gain in terms of constituency support merely by making apparent their interest in the issue (Arnold 1990; Mayhew 1974).

That they need not bring about actual results to claim credit on an issue does not mean that they can effectively do so without really acting on it. As Hall (1996) puts it, a record of activity on a given issue is "what makes the claim to credit credible" (61), an intuition that is supported by evidence from interviews with legislative staffers and by large-scale quantitative analyses of campaign discourse and voters' evaluations of the candidates (Schiller 2000; Sellers 1998; Simon 2002). Sellers (1998), in fact, finds that incumbents are helped when they focus on their records in their campaigns, but are hurt when they stray from them and make unsubstantiated claims about their interests or activities. Attempts at credit-claiming are therefore not risk-free; they can backfire, and legislators can expect them to be effective only if they can point to concrete evidence of their activity.

Credit-claiming is so important to legislators, Mayhew argued, that "much of congressional life is a relentless search for opportunities to engage in it" (1974, 53). Fortunately for legislators, this search is not too taxing because there are a variety of activities at their disposal that can be used to demonstrate interest in important issues, including introducing and cosponsoring bills and resolutions, offering amendments to legislation, speaking on the floor, participating in committees, and the like. Recent evidence suggests that legislators do indeed use their activity in this way, introducing legislation and participating more actively in committee deliberations on issues that they perceive as important to their districts (Ainsworth and Hall 2001; Hall 1996; King 1997).

Hall's (1996) study of congressional participation is particularly innovative in this regard. He is interested in how legislators decide to allocate attention among the various measures that come before them in their roles as committee and subcommittee members. Focusing his analysis on the behavior of members of three committees (Agriculture, Education and Labor, and Energy and Commerce), he argues that three factors explain relative levels of participation – the constituency's interest in a bill, the representative's own policy preferences, and the desire (or lack thereof) to promote the president's agenda. To investigate constituency influence, he measures legislators' participation on different bills and then evaluates the constituency's interest in each of these bills by asking legislative staffers to assess their importance to the district. He finds a positive relationship between participation and perceived importance, concluding that, although constituents' interests certainly do not dominate legislators' allocation of attention, they are clearly taken into account when legislators decide how much time and how many resources should be devoted to a given piece of legislation (236–7).

Hall's work shifts our analytical focus away from roll call voting to other forms of legislative activity and points to a different and largely unexplored way in which legislators can be responsive – by using their time in office to act on those issues that are salient to their districts or states. The model of uptake I propose builds on these insights but differs from Hall's model in several ways. Most importantly, my approach, which focuses more explicitly on responsiveness than on participation in the legislative process, begins with an assumption about which issues should be addressed in legislative activity (the challenger's campaign themes) and then investigates the factors that influence the extent to which these issues receive attention.[4] As such, it highlights the broader question of how representatives go about building and balancing their legislative portfolios, which consist of issues that extend beyond their committee assignments. This requires that we step back and investigate how legislators determine the content of their agendas, rather than beginning downstream to focus, as Hall does, on their attention to the issues that come before their committees.

Predicting Variation in Uptake

To summarize, the theory of uptake I develop here is, at its roots, a strategic motivation theory. Legislators' desire to be reelected leads them to demonstrate attention to salient issues they may have previously ignored. Challengers' campaigns serve as a source of information to legislators about these issues because challengers purposefully focus their campaigns on their opponents' weaknesses. To the extent that winning legislators subsequently act on these signals, taking up their challengers' issues in their legislative activity, they are both responsive to their constituencies and attentive to their own electoral interests. Being a faithful representative can thus pay off for legislators in ways both tangible and intangible.

---

[4] This avoids one potential problem of relying on staffers' perceptions to assess the importance of bills: Do the bills receive attention because they are important to the constituency? Or do staffers observe the legislator's level of activity surrounding a bill and then infer its importance?

The motivations behind legislators' uptake decisions have important consequences for the quality of legislative responsiveness and for the content of public policy outputs. If we assumed that uptake had no impact on reelection, then we might expect that few legislators would engage in it, since it requires that attention and resources be diverted away from other issues with potentially higher payoffs. If, on the other hand, we assume that the strategic motivation theory is accurate and that legislators take up their challengers' issues to promote their reelection goals, then we should expect that uptake would be fairly widespread. The theory also points to a number of important predictions about variation in uptake, including who should engage in it the most, where in the process it should be most prevalent, its dynamics over time, and the influence of differing institutional settings. Each of these areas is explored in depth in the coming chapters, but in the interest of mapping the direction of the analysis and providing further theoretical development of the uptake model, it is useful to briefly outline the hypotheses that guide the investigation. They are as follows:

H1: INDIVIDUAL VARIATION – Legislators' uptake levels will vary with their electoral vulnerability.

H2: LOCATION OF UPTAKE – Uptake will occur across all types of legislative activities, though levels of uptake should vary in relation to the difficulty and potential payoff of different activities.

H3: TIMING OF UPTAKE – For senators, uptake levels will increase as the next election grows nearer. For members of the House of Representatives, with shorter terms, there will be no variation in uptake levels within their terms.

H4: VARIATION ACROSS INSTITUTIONS – Uptake levels will be higher in the Senate than in the House of Representatives. Institutional differences between the chambers will also result in differences in patterns of responsiveness.

H5: ELECTORAL IMPACT OF UPTAKE – Engaging in uptake will, all other things equal, increase legislators' vote shares in the next election.

Electoral Vulnerability and Legislative Behavior

As indicated previously, electoral vulnerability is expected to play an important role in explaining why some legislators are highly responsive, while others exhibit lower levels of uptake. Models that posit a linkage between vulnerability and legislative behavior are common in the literature, a legacy of the work of Mayhew (1974) and others on the electoral connection. The basic argument is that legislators' need to be reelected leads them to engage in activities that promote this goal. Scholars recognize that legislators' vote shares are not entirely within their control. The partisan inclinations of their constituents, the diversity of interests in their district or state, the quality of their copartisans running for other offices, and national political and economic conditions can all influence their prospects. Nonetheless, the depiction of legislators as reelection-driven suggests that they do exert some control over their own electoral fortunes. Exploring these linkages between legislators' behavior in office and their success in elections is thus central to the study of representation and responsiveness.

Most empirical studies of these linkages hypothesize that vulnerable legislators should be more likely to engage in activities that promote reelection because, as Arnold (1990) puts it, "legislators will do nothing to advance their other goals if such activities threaten their principal goal" (5). The expectation, then, is that compared to their safer colleagues, more vulnerable legislators will be more active in constituency-oriented legislative activity in Washington, D.C., and more involved in casework in their home districts or states. Kessler and Krehbiel's (1996) study of cosponsorship behavior offers a good example of the standard argument about vulnerability and legislative work. They note that cosponsorship avails legislators of a low-cost way to demonstrate to their constituents their interest in (or position on) a specific issue. More vulnerable legislators should therefore cosponsor at greater rates (563). However, their results fail to provide much support for this hypothesis, a finding that is corroborated by other studies on bill introduction and cosponsorship activity (Campbell 1982; Ragsdale and Cook 1987; Schiller 1995, 2000; Wilson and Young 1997) and by related studies on the influence of vulnerability on the ideological and partisan character of legislators' roll call voting records (Deckard 1976; Fiorina 1973; Kuklinski 1977; Sullivan and Uslaner 1978); on their "home styles" and propensity to do casework (Bond 1985; Cain, Ferejohn, and Fiorina 1987; Fenno 1978; Johannes 1984; Parker 1980); and on the nature of their committee requests (Bullock 1973; Fowler, Douglass, and Clark 1980). Thus, the evidence that vulnerability influences legislative behavior is mixed at best; some find the predicted positive effect and some find an unexpected negative effect, but many find no effect at all.

Given these results, why do I propose that vulnerability should be important in explaining uptake levels? First, the content of legislative activity has a more direct theoretical connection to reelection prospects than the sheer volume of activity, so we should expect that any effect of vulnerability would be stronger for levels of uptake than for overall levels of activity. Second, a review of the literature on vulnerability and legislative behavior suggests that there may be more of a relationship than is commonly assumed, but that our ability to recognize these effects has been limited by our unidirectional focus. Many scholars assume that only a positive relationship between vulnerability and activity supports the predictions of the electoral connection theory when, in fact, there are other possibilities that are equally consistent with this theory.

Most studies of vulnerability and legislative activity have focused on the volume of this activity undertaken by legislators, with the expectation that legislative activities provide representatives with the opportunity to engage in position-taking, advertising, or credit-claiming, and so promote reelection (Mayhew 1974). However, very few detail how the connection between activity levels and reelection might occur, a point that is crucial for establishing a theoretical justification for the vulnerability hypothesis. How, then, might this linkage happen? Perhaps, one might argue, legislative productivity itself is rewarded, either directly or indirectly, by increasing constituents' evaluations of the incumbent or by forestalling strong challengers. It might not particularly matter what issues legislators are position-taking or credit-claiming on, as long as they are doing so on something. Fenno (1978) suggests that this could be the case – that constituents may value having an active, effective, and influential representative and so may reward this behavior. However, there is little empirical evidence to support this hypothesis. Ragsdale and Cook (1987) and Johannes and McAdams (1981) find that introducing or cosponsoring bills has no impact on vote share or on the ability of future challengers to run strong campaigns, and Wawro's (2000) investigation of legislative entrepreneurship finds that this type of intense activity does not help reelection and may, in some cases, actually hurt incumbents' chances.

If, as these results indicate, no direct relationship exists among vulnerability, legislative activity levels, and reelection, this does not necessarily preclude an indirect linkage among the three. This sort of connection might exist if it is actually the content of behavior that is rewarded (as my theory of uptake suggests), but volume of activity serves as a valid proxy for the level of "good" (i.e., responsive, reelection-promoting) behavior. Of course, this argument depends on the quantity of behavior being a strong indicator of its quality. Is this plausible? It is if we make the heroic assumption that legislators act only when it helps their reelection chances, so that any behavior is reelection-oriented. Conversely, it could also be true if we assume that legislators behave somewhat randomly. If certain issues have a higher payoff than others, but legislators are unaware of this or ignore it when deciding whether to introduce or cosponsor a bill, then we might expect that legislators who are more active would, quite by accident, end up associating themselves with more high-payoff measures. These assumptions are admittedly overstated, but even if they are relaxed to accord with what we know about how legislators actually behave, it appears that volume of activity will be, at best, a noisy measure of its quality.

In short, it is not surprising that our findings about the relationship between volume of activity and vulnerability have been mixed. There is very little evidence that quantity of activity is rewarded, and, while it may be correlated with the "quality" of behavior (i.e., whether it indicates responsiveness to salient issues), this correlation is far from perfect. I argue that any relationship that exists between vulnerability and legislative behavior will be made clearer if we focus more directly on the content of legislative activity rather than on its volume, since the theoretical connection to reelection prospects is much more direct for the former.

Reassessing Vulnerability

To fully assess the linkage between vulnerability and uptake, we also need to reevaluate our expectations about the direction the effect should take. As mentioned previously, the standard prediction derived from electoral connection theories is that vulnerable legislators, who have the greatest fear of losing the next election, should be the most motivated to increase their safety and so should display the highest rates of reelection-promoting behavior. In the case of uptake, this hypothesis, which I term the "inoculation hypothesis," predicts that vulnerability will be positively related to responsiveness, with the most vulnerable legislators engaging in the most uptake in the hope that this behavior will ensure their return to Congress after the next election. Safer legislators will be less concerned with reelection and will therefore exhibit lower levels of responsiveness.

While this hypothesis is certainly reasonable, it is important to ask whether it is the *only* reasonable prediction. If we find that safer legislators are more active or more responsive than their vulnerable colleagues, does this necessarily contradict the electoral connection theory? Some have argued that it does – that a negative relationship between vulnerability and whatever behavior they are studying means that activity must not be undertaken with reelection considerations in mind. For example, in their study of bill cosponsorship, Kessler and Krehbiel (1996) find that safer legislators cosponsor more bills than their more vulnerable peers, and hence conclude that cosponsorship must be used more often for intralegislative signaling than for constituency-oriented position-taking (565).

However, such conclusions are potentially shortsighted because they take only a static view of vulnerability and behavior. If we take a more dynamic approach to understanding the linkages between the two, asking what it is that makes legislators safe or vulnerable in the first place, the finding of a negative relationship between vulnerability and a reelection-promoting activity like uptake appears perfectly consistent with electoral connection theories. To assume otherwise oversimplifies the original arguments made about the nature of these connections. Consider, for example, Mayhew's (1974) statements about vulnerability and legislative behavior:

When we say "Congressman Smith is 'unbeatable,'" we do not mean that there is nothing he could do that would lose him his seat. Rather we mean "Congressman Smith is unbeatable as long as he continues to do the things he is doing." ... What characterizes "safe" congressmen is not that they are beyond electoral reach, but that their efforts are very likely to bring them uninterrupted electoral success. (37)

Kingdon (1989) makes a similar observation in his analysis of the factors influencing congressional voting behavior, claiming:

It is not enough to observe that because congressmen win in general elections by large margins and because they rarely face primary opposition, they therefore need not be concerned about constituency reaction to their behavior. Such an argument neglects the possibility that they may be so seemingly secure partly because they were careful about catering to their constituencies. ... I asked a staffer why a politician from a safe district should be worried about how constituents react. His answer was as simple as it was profound: "They're safe *because* they vote that way." (62)

This reasoning suggests that legislators' relative levels of electoral safety can be interpreted as reflections of the quality of their past behavior. Safe legislators are safe because they were responsive, while vulnerable legislators are vulnerable because they were not. If these legislators continue to engage in similar patterns of behavior in the current term, we should expect to see a *negative* cross-sectional relationship between vulnerability and uptake, with the safest legislators engaging in the most. I call this prediction the "electoral selection" hypothesis. The terminology is drawn from Zaller's (1998) work on congressional election outcomes, where he argues that the incumbency advantage that we observe in congressional elections may not be due to voter attachment to the incumbent or to greater resources, but to the fact that incumbents who win time and again are simply stronger candidates. From his perspective, elections select skilled candidates. From the point of view of uptake, elections select skilled legislators.[5]

The inoculation and electoral selection hypotheses share a number of assumptions, most importantly that engaging in uptake will promote reelection, so that legislators who exhibit a high level of responsiveness in one Congress will do better in the next election. Where they differ is in their predictions about what should happen next. The theory underlying the inoculation hypothesis suggests that, having successfully achieved their goal of making themselves safer, legislators will then choose to decrease their uptake and turn their attention to matters of more interest. As such, only the most vulnerable legislators will actively work to promote their electoral prospects. The electoral selection hypothesis tells a very different story: that, having hit upon a useful strategy for making themselves secure, legislators will continue to pursue this activity to maintain their newly acquired safety.

This claim may seem somewhat counterintuitive. The conventional wisdom is that vulnerability leads to accountability and that a safe legislator is one who no longer needs to be worried about prioritizing reelection-oriented activities. However, it is important to remember that, because of the priority legislators place on reelection, they tend to be risk-averse in their behavior. "Safety" is partly a subjective phenomenon and, as Mayhew notes, is potentially fleeting if the behavior that brought it about is abandoned. Thus, if legislators believe that engaging in uptake in past congresses has been useful in achieving their electoral goals, it is likely that they will continue to participate in it.[6] Bendor and Moe (1985) claim that this pragmatism is "the fundamental attribute of an adaptive decision-maker...if an action worked once, try it again"(764). Legislators' beliefs about the success or failure of their past activity in promoting their goals should therefore be important predictors of their current behavior.

---

[5] This is a conclusion shared by recent work on roll call voting patterns. Canes-Wrone, Brady, and Cogan's (2002) work on the subject concludes that "safety itself is a function of members' voting. That is, safe members are 'safe' partially as a consequence of their roll call decisions" (137).

[6] It is important to note too that uptake is only one of a number of reelection-oriented strategies legislators might decide to pursue. Choosing to devote some of their agenda space to their challengers' issues does not preclude being active on other issues as well.

A similar insight informs the literature on how legislators approach campaigning. Kingdon (1968), Hershey (1984), and Fenno (1996) all argue that politicians use election outcomes as a source of information about the utility of their campaign strategies. If they do well, they attribute this to their skill as campaigners and will use the same strategies in future campaigns.[7] Thus, as Fenno notes, "the interpretation placed by successful candidates on their campaigns will have important effects on their subsequent political behavior" (1996, 163). Although these scholars focus on legislators' behavior in the electoral arena, the underlying reasoning applies equally well to the legislative arena. In short, legislators are "superstitious learners " – if they believe that a specific past behavior yielded electoral rewards, they are likely to persist in it, expecting that these rewards will continue.

Therefore, despite the intuitive appeal of the inoculation hypothesis, the predictions of the more dynamic electoral selection hypothesis accord equally well with our knowledge of how legislators actually behave. As should be clear, these alternative hypotheses about the relationship between vulnerability and responsiveness have very different normative implications for how we assess the role of elections in encouraging responsiveness. If the inoculation hypothesis is accurate and the most vulnerable engage in the most uptake, then maintaining competition in congressional elections is of utmost importance because the safer legislators are, the less responsive they will be to their constituents' interests. If, however, the results support the electoral selection hypothesis, then we might conclude that our concerns about incumbency advantage and the "vanishing marginals" in these elections are misplaced. Instead, the electoral security we observe for incumbents should be seen as a manifestation of past responsiveness, and the prospect of future elections provides the incentive to continue to be attentive to important issues. Of course, it is also possible that there is no relationship between vulnerability and uptake, a finding that would necessitate further reassessment of the relationship between elections and legislative responsiveness.

Location of Uptake

Regardless of these results, explaining variation across legislators provides only part of the uptake story. The strategic motivation theory also

---

[7] Of course, legislators fall prey to the same attributional biases as others – they tend to view successes as the result of their own efforts and failures as the result of factors beyond their control. Kingdon (1968) termed this the "congratulation-rationalization" effect.

points to other important predictions – for instance, about the location of uptake in the political process. Investigating location is important for two reasons. First, it presents another opportunity to evaluate the validity of the theory. Second, the location of uptake has important implications for its impact on public policy. If uptake occurs at high levels on policy-relevant activities like bill and resolution introductions, this suggests that it can have a substantial downstream influence on the content of policy. If, on the other hand, evidence of uptake is most prevalent on an activity like floor statements which may be useful for credit-claiming but has few direct policy implications, then we might conclude that its impact on policy is negligible.

For which types of activities should we expect the highest levels of uptake? The answer is not immediately obvious, as there is a trade-off between the relative ease of the activity and its amenability to credit-claiming. All activities require some effort, a point that is made clear when we examine patterns of activity for the typical legislator. In the 105th Congress, for example, a total of 5,982 bills and resolutions were introduced in the House and 3,159 were introduced in the Senate. The average representative introduced about fourteen measures and the average senator introduced about thirty. Legislators in both chambers cosponsored 200–300 of these measures (~5–10 percent of the total) and spoke on the floor about 1–2 percent of them.

It is clearly the case that legislators are selective in their choice of activities, taking formal action on only a small proportion of the total number of measures. However, differences in the frequency with which various types of activities are undertaken do allow us to infer their relative difficulty. The patterns suggest that introductions are the most difficult activity and cosponsorships the easiest, with floor statements falling in between but closer to introductions. This claim accords with intuitions about the amount of effort required for each activity. While introducing a measure involves devoting staff resources to writing it up and possibly shepherding it through the chamber (Wawro 2000) and making a floor statement requires learning enough about the issue to speak about it, cosponsorship entails only officially signing on to an existing piece of legislation.

This might lead us to conclude that uptake rates would be relatively low on introductions. However, while they are clearly the most difficult of the three activities, they also provide legislators with the strongest opportunity to claim credit. Introducing a bill or resolution sends a clear signal that a given issue is important enough to the legislator that he or she is willing to devote a relatively high amount of attention to it and attach his or her name to it. This is important in a setting like Congress, where most outcomes are the result of collective action and it can be difficult to carve out an individual reputation. Schiller's (1995, 2000) analysis of representation in Senate delegations focuses in particular on this point. She explains that legislators rely on introductions to build their reputation in the chamber and to demonstrate attentiveness to issues of interest to the constituency. As one of the Senate staffers in her study remarked, "[Introduced] legislation defines the senator" (1995, 187). Senators (and representatives too) therefore use introductions as a way of expressing their agenda priorities.

Furthermore, legislators' introductions of bills and resolutions are relatively well advertised in the district or state, by the local media, and by the legislator him- or herself in newsletters or campaign literature (Arnold 2004). This activity can be very visible to interested observers, including both constituents and, perhaps more importantly, potential challengers and other political elites. It is not necessary to introduce a lot of bills on a given issue to receive attention – a single bill introduced on an important issue can provide a great deal of leverage in credit-claiming efforts, even more so if the sponsor's name becomes attached to the legislation. (Think, for instance, of the McCain–Feingold campaign finance reform proposals.) Nor is it necessary for the introduced legislation to get very far in the legislative process in order to claim credit. Only about 10 percent of introduced bills ever become law, and while a larger percentage get hearings or are reported out of committee, legislators cannot and do not expect that most of their introductions will make considerable progress. However, introducing the legislation is enough to claim credit, and its lack of passage may be able to be attributed to the obstructionist behavior of other legislators. Since running against Congress has become an increasingly frequent and effective reelection tactic for incumbents, in some cases they may even benefit more if their introduced bills fail to progress very far in the legislative process.

Thus, there is potentially much to be gained by using introductions to demonstrate uptake. However, since legislators are juggling multiple goals and interests, they may not be able or willing to devote all of their relatively scarce introductions to their challengers' issues. Other activities like cosponsorships and floor statements should serve as important complements, allowing legislators to enjoy some of the credit-claiming benefits of introductions without all of the costs. From the point of view of legislators, the primary benefit of cosponsorships is that there are numerous opportunities to engage in them that require almost no time or effort, so they serve as an "inexpensive signal" to constituents (Mayhew 1974,

63). Their corresponding weakness, however, particularly in the case of uptake, is that they do not provide a very strong basis for claiming credit. Cosponsorship reflects participation in a collective effort, rather than an individual one, and so should have a smaller payoff. Multiple cosponsorships in a single area may signal considerable interest in and attention to that area, but a single cosponsorship is not likely to do a legislator much good in claiming credit. Schiller (2000) notes that "Senators do not rest the foundation of their legislative record on cosponsored legislation, but they do use it as a means of extending their legislative portfolio without expending a lot of resources on an issue" (55). Thus, while we should not expect that legislators will concentrate all of their uptake on cosponsorships, given their low cost and the possibility of a credit-claiming benefit, we should still expect to see evidence of relatively high levels of uptake for them.

Of the three types of activities, floor statements are the most difficult to make predictions about because they have received the least scholarly attention, and so our understanding of their relative utility to legislators is weaker. It seems, though, that compared to introductions and even cosponsorships, floor statements are very hard to build a claim of credit on. Merely talking about an issue is unlikely to demonstrate much attentiveness to it. However, these statements do have the potential to be visible to audiences at home in the district or state. They provide easy material for hometown newspapers or television stations looking for a short quote or sound bite and can be used by legislators in their advertising. Moreover, combined with a record of introductions and/or cosponsorships on an issue, impassioned speeches on the floor may enhance the effort to credit-claim, and while they require some effort, they are not very taxing. To the extent, then, that floor statements are used as a supplement to introductions and cosponsorships, uptake rates for them should not be substantially lower.

Each type of activity thus offers distinct advantages and disadvantages in the quest to claim credit. Cosponsorships and floor statements are easier and are undertaken more frequently, so we might expect a higher raw number of these activities to be "challenger-themed." Introductions, while more difficult, offer a clearer claim to credit, so, compared to the other activities, we might expect that a relatively higher proportion of them would be devoted to uptake. Of course, differences in circumstances (e.g., vulnerability or seniority) may lead different legislators to devote different levels of these activities to uptake. Investigating these patterns is therefore interesting from both an empirical and a normative perspective.

Timing of Uptake

The choice of legislative activities is not the only decision that legislators face when planning their uptake strategies. They also must address the issue of timing. Should they concentrate on it the most at the beginning of the term, when the issues of the last election are freshest in the minds of legislators, constituents, and other interested observers? Or should they increase their levels of uptake as the term progresses and the next election grows nearer? The answer depends, at least in part, on what chamber of Congress one is considering. Up to this point, I have generally referred to "legislators" in general, but there are important differences between the House of Representatives and the Senate that should be taken into account. In terms of the timing of uptake, the biggest factor is the length of terms. Given their two-year terms, House members do not have the luxury of putting off electoral considerations. In the first year they are planning their reelection bids, and in the second they are actively campaigning. Jacobson and Kernell (1983) note that most potential challengers decide whether or not to run in the year before the election, so early uptake should be crucial for representatives. As such, there is no reason to expect that uptake levels should differ across the first and second years of representatives' terms.

The situation in the Senate is very different. A six-year term gives legislators much more time to attend to their various interests. While uptake should be relatively high immediately following the election, it seems likely that it would wane in the middle of the term, as it gets trumped by other, more pressing concerns. However, as senators enter their third congress and the next election grows nearer, they should become more focused on their reelection prospects and so should increase their uptake. This hypothesis is in line with other work on Senate behavior, which finds that senators tend to become more visibly reelection-oriented as their terms progress – for example, moderating the ideological extremity of their roll call voting (Ahuja 1994; Shapiro et al. 1990; Wright and Berkman 1986).[8] Of course, for a solely reelection-driven senator, this may not be the best strategy – high uptake levels across all congresses in a term would seem to be more optimal. However, given senators' multiple goals and their limited ability to attend to all of these goals simultaneously, the expected pattern is that uptake should reach its highest levels in the third and final congress of their terms.

---

[8] But see Bernstein (1988) for counterarguments.

Institutional Comparisons

The presence of such institutional distinctions between the chambers opens up the possibility of more fundamental differences in uptake between the House and Senate, both in levels of responsiveness and in the factors explaining individual variation in that responsiveness. In thinking about how this might occur, we should consider differences in representatives' and senators' ability to engage in uptake and in their incentive to do so. This requires that we take into account variations in the nature of legislative work in the two chambers and in the competitiveness of the elections that send representatives and senators to Washington.

The conventional wisdom is that the House should be more responsive than the Senate. This, of course, was the plan of the framers of the Constitution, who designed the Senate to be more insulated from popular control. While House members were to face direct election every two years, senators were appointed by state legislatures for six-year terms. Even after the ratification of the Seventeenth Amendment, implementing direct election of senators, the greater frequency of elections in the House and the smaller constituencies that members there represent have often led scholars to conclude that members of that chamber should be more responsive.

Recently, this assumption has been called into question. Erikson, MacKuen, and Stimson's (2002) work suggests that the two chambers may be equally responsive, but that this responsiveness occurs by different mechanisms. For the Senate, they argue that "the most important channel for governmental representation is electoral replacement." The House of Representatives is responsive because "its members employ rational anticipation to produce a similarly effective public-policy response" (321). Thus, they claim that the House of Representatives responds through adaptations in behavior, while the Senate remains responsive because unrepresentative senators lose their reelection bids, bringing in new members whose positions more closely approximate those of the public. Disaggregating from institutions to individuals, these findings suggest that individual House members are fairly responsive, while individual senators are less so.

However, these conclusions are based on a definition of responsiveness that relies on positions or preferences – in short, on the level of collective policy congruence. Specifically, Erikson et al. (2002) investigate the relationship between the ideological direction of public opinion (referred to as "public mood") and the ideological tenor of congressional decision making, finding more evidence of responsiveness in House members' roll call voting than in senators'. I argue that, when we move away from voting patterns toward an agenda-based measure of responsiveness like uptake, the prediction should be the opposite – senators should rate more highly than representatives.

First and foremost, uptake requires that legislators have the ability and willingness to be entrepreneurial, extending beyond their areas of current expertise or interest to address new issues. Of the two chambers, the Senate is simply more amenable to this. As Sinclair (1989) notes, the Senate is less tightly organized than the House, enabling senators much greater leeway in their behavior. Her depiction of the modern Senate (as compared to the Senate of the 1950s) gives the image of a body in which members can easily set their own agendas:

> In the Senate of the 1980s, influence is much more equally distributed and members are accorded very wide latitude; the Senate has become an open, staff-dependent, outward-looking institution in which significant decision making takes place in multiple arenas. The typical senator no longer specializes; he becomes involved in a broad range of issues, including ones that do not fall within the jurisdiction of his committees. Even though he serves on more committees than his predecessor of the 1950's did, he does not confine his activities to the committee room. He is also active on the Senate floor and often makes use of public arenas as well. He is less deferential to anyone and much less restrained in using the powers granted to him by the rules of the Senate. (2)

Consequently, the structure of the Senate allows members to be generalists, and, perhaps equally importantly, the norms of the chamber encourage this. The House and the Senate are expected to address the same issues, but with only 100 members, it is much more difficult for the Senate to cover them than it is for the House, with 435 members. Institutional imperatives simply don't allow senators to focus their activity in a single area, and, as such, they are less able to develop as much specialized knowledge of policy as their counterparts in the House (Baker 1989). With this comparatively heavier workload comes greater freedom to choose issues and design their agendas. This feature of Senate life is, in fact, one of its attractions, and one that is frequently singled out by former House members who have become senators (Sinclair 1989). This has potential advantages for senators both in terms of satisfying their personal policy interests and in having greater flexibility to engage in uptake.

Senators should also have more incentive to engage in uptake because they typically have more reason to be concerned about reelection. Compared to their House colleagues, they are more likely to face opposition, are challenged by more experienced opponents, are more likely to win by small margins, run more often in intense or hard-fought races, and are ultimately more likely to lose their reelection bids (Burden and Kimball 2002; Krasno 1994; Westlye 1991).[9] In their study of ticket-splitting in congressional elections, Burden and Kimball (2002) summarize this literature by noting that the Senate, though "designed to be more insulated from public influence than is the House – has paradoxically been more influenced by elections than has the House" (127). From the perspective of uptake, we should expect that the memory of highly competitive elections in the past and the potential for more in the future should lead senators to display more uptake than representatives.

Finally, as discussed in the next chapter, uptake may be easier for senators than for representatives because of differences in the nature of their campaigns. Senate challengers tend to highlight more issues in their campaigns, and these races tend to be more issue-oriented overall. These differences should provide more targets for responsiveness for winning legislators and so should increase the amount of uptake we observe.

All of these factors lead to the prediction that senators will be more responsive than representatives. They also point to another, more complicated, yet equally important, expectation – that the dynamics of the uptake decision may differ across the chambers. For example, it is possible that electoral vulnerability may influence representatives' and senators' behavior differently, or that senators and representatives may make different choices about when and where to engage in uptake. As such, in the chapters to come, I will pay particular attention to the similarities and differences in the measurement, analysis, and interpretation of uptake in the House and Senate.

Impact of Uptake

Exploring variation in uptake levels across individuals, across legislative activities, within a term, and across chambers can all provide indirect evidence for or against the strategic motivation theory. To the extent that vulnerability is related to uptake, that legislators engage in it at relatively high levels across activities, that individual levels vary with the proximity

---

[9] As Gronke's (2000) work shows, these differences reflect variation in central tendency rather than fundamental institutional distinctions. Thus, there exist both highly competitive House races and fairly uncompetitive Senate races. Nonetheless, in comparing across the chambers, these aggregate differences in vulnerability should lead to aggregate differences in uptake levels.

of the next election, and that senators exhibit more of it than representatives, the strategic motivation theory receives support. However, a more direct test is in order as well. Specifically, does engaging in uptake actually work to promote electoral security? If it does, high uptake levels in one term should, all other things being equal, increase vote shares in the next election. It could do so via a variety of mechanisms, perhaps increasing legislators' vote shares directly, reducing opposition at the primary or general election levels, or warding off potentially strong challengers. All of these possibilities are explored in considerable detail in Chapter 7. In that chapter, I also examine the influence of choices about the location and timing of uptake. For example, does late-term uptake help reelection or is sustained responsiveness necessary to obtain electoral benefits? Relatedly, does uptake on introductions pay off more or less than uptake on cosponsorships and floor statements? These effects would be particularly important if I find that, in addition to leading to differences in levels of uptake, vulnerability also leads to differences in patterns of responsiveness. The electoral selection hypothesis assumes that safer legislators will be better at responsiveness. If this is the case, we should expect them to make higher-payoff choices in the location and timing of their uptake.

These claims all highlight the broader point that uptake must be assessed in comparative settings. While we can make normative assessments of what a "good" uptake level should be, we can only evaluate whether a given legislator's level is high or low in relation to others. Approaching variation in uptake from many different perspectives is thus crucial for understanding the dynamics of responsiveness. However, before these comparisons can be made, it is necessary to develop a method for measuring uptake, a task that is begun in Chapter 3.

3

The Nature of Campaign and Legislative Agendas

Issue agendas, both in campaigns and in Congress, lie at the core of the theory of uptake. Most fundamentally, these agendas serve as the focal point for assessing issue linkages between campaigns and legislative activity. The extent to which legislators' agendas as policy makers in Washington, D.C., reflect those of their past challengers' campaign priorities provides both the measure of uptake and an indicator of individual and institutional responsiveness. To explore the dynamics of uptake requires that we first understand these agendas, including their size, scope, and variation in content across candidates and legislators. Up to this point, my discussion of agendas and their relation to uptake has been quite general, relying mostly on anecdotal evidence. Although stories about instances of uptake can be instructive, to draw any firm conclusions requires that we go beyond them. For example, the anecdote that opened the book suggested that Senator Bob Graham's subsequent attentiveness to health and the balanced budget was a response to his previous challenger's campaign priorities. Similarly, as described in Chapter 2, Representatives Tim Johnson and Jim Jontz appeared to take up their challengers' issues into their agendas in office in attempts to promote their reelection efforts. However, since we know little about the entirety of these legislators' agendas or those of their electoral opponents, we can only speculate about the nature and extent of their uptake behavior, leaving many important questions unanswered.

To address these questions requires a two-stage approach. The first is to demonstrate, for a large sample of representatives and senators, that their challengers discussed a given set of issues in the past campaign, that they performed a certain number of activities related to those issues in the next term, and that this behavior was indeed a response to their challengers' campaigns. The second is to place individual legislators' behavior in context, explaining why they engaged in a particular level of responsiveness, why they made choices to exhibit uptake on certain types of activities but not others or at some times within their terms but not others, whether there was an electoral payoff for their responsiveness, and, finally, whether their uptake behavior left a trace on the content of public policy outputs. Much of the book is focused on this second goal. Over the next two chapters, however, I lay the foundations by addressing the first. In Chapter 4, I establish the presence of uptake and describe the amount of variation in responsiveness that exists across individual legislators. In this chapter, I focus on the component parts of uptake, exploring the dynamics of campaign and legislative agendas and estimating the impact of uptake on the aggregate congressional agenda.

Defining Agendas

In the discussion and analyses that follow, I use the term "agenda" to refer to the set of issues to which an individual political actor devotes attention. In the campaign setting, this includes those issues that candidates highlight in their literature and advertisements, discuss in speeches, or prioritize in interviews. In the legislative arena, it includes those issues on which representatives and senators engage in some formal activity – introducing a piece of legislation, cosponsoring it, or speaking on the floor about it. Within these broader agendas, I designate a smaller group of issues, those receiving the most attention, as agenda priorities. Thus, I draw a distinction between a candidate who mentions an issue like education in passing and one who centers his or her campaign on it, and between a legislator who cosponsors a single bill on defense policy and one who introduces, cosponsors, and speaks about multiple measures on that issue.

These simple definitions closely parallel those most commonly used by public policy scholars, who define the agenda as that group of issues at the forefront of attention at any one time. While these scholars have traditionally focused their analyses on the aggregate congressional agenda, their insights apply equally well to the study of individual agendas. Kingdon (1984), for example, conceives of the agenda as "the list of subjects or problems to which governmental officials, and people outside of government closely associated with those officials, are paying some serious attention" (3). He and others also distinguish between two levels of the policy agenda: the larger set of issues that is being discussed by governmental officials and the smaller set that is up for serious consideration for action (Baumgartner and Jones 1993; Cobb and Elder 1983; Kingdon 1984).

This discussion of agendas raises an additional important question: if agendas are comprised of issues, what constitutes an "issue"? In common parlance, we might refer to a candidate's or legislator's character or background as an issue, but the focus here is on a particular subset of themes, those that are related to policy. These policy issues are best thought of as general themes that transcend a particular incident, structuring the content of political discourse and policymaking over a relatively long period of time. Subjects like environmental regulation, crime, and the economy clearly meet this criterion. Issues also generally involve conflict or contention between competing groups about what, if anything, should be done to address them (Cobb and Elder 1983, 82). In the case of crime, for instance, some may argue for tougher sentences for those convicted of crimes, while others may advocate for funds for community development as a preventive measure. Nonetheless, both sides are discussing crime. Finally, issues are theoretically distinct from events, though this distinction is not always made explicit in the literature. Compared to issues, events are much more specific "discrete happenings that are limited by space and time" (Shaw 1977, 7), including incidents like the *Exxon Valdez* disaster, a high-profile crime, or the discovery of a particular instance of corporate malfeasance. Although these events do not by themselves qualify as issues, they may play an important role in the larger agenda-setting process, serving to focus attention on a broader issue (see, for example, Birkland 1997; Kingdon 1984).

In reality, the discussion of issues in campaigns or in legislative activity often takes the form of advocating for or against a particular alternative to solving a problem or reacting to a specific contemporary event. Candidates or legislators highlighting an issue like education as an agenda priority could favor or oppose voucher programs or funding for charter schools, could propose more or less government regulation of primary and secondary education, or could focus on the perceived failures or successes of a particular school district or a particular education policy. To compare across agendas, however, we must target the underlying issue concerns rather than the specifics of the campaign appeal or legislative proposal. From the perspective of uptake, this means that winning legislators can address their challengers' issue priorities without necessarily adopting their preferred solution to those problems.

Assessing Agendas

To study uptake requires an approach for identifying and measuring the content of agendas that captures these nuances, identifying broader issues of the type that structure campaign discourse and legislative politics. More specifically, we must have two types of data – information about the themes prioritized by candidates in a number of congressional campaigns and, for the winners of these races, information about the content of their subsequent activities in office. These data must then be coded in a way that allows for straightforward comparisons across campaign and legislative agendas and across individuals and time. In the past, challenges in collecting and analyzing such data would have made an investigation like this prohibitively difficult. Fortunately, recent technological advances in the storage and retrieval of data on individual legislators' congressional activity (e.g., the Library of Congress's THOMAS web site) and on news coverage of campaigns (through electronic archives like Lexis-Nexis) have made studies of agendas and the linkages between them possible.

As the source of data about candidates' agendas, I use news coverage of a sample of 422 House campaigns between 1988 and 1996 and 51 Senate campaigns between 1988 and 1992. The legislative activity of the winners of these campaigns is then followed across their subsequent terms, which fall between the 101st and 105th Congresses. This time period was chosen because it allows for variation in partisan control of the chambers and because it provides sufficient depth and scope to undertake cross-sectional and longitudinal analyses of behavior. For both theoretical and practical reasons, the strategy and procedures for collecting data differ slightly for the Senate and the House and are described in more detail below. Nonetheless, the general approach was the same. I first used my coding scheme to content analyze coverage of campaigns to identify the priority themes for the candidates in each race. Then, to assess the content of winners' subsequent legislative agendas, I used the same scheme to code their bill, resolution, and amendment introductions and cosponsorships, as well as their statements on the floor about pending legislation. Individual legislators' uptake levels can then be measured as the extent to which this activity is related to their challengers' themes.

A complete listing of the winning legislators and their challengers included in the analyses is provided in the Appendix.[1] The sample is

---

[1] Throughout this discussion, I use the term "challenger" to refer to the loser in the election, regardless of his or her status going into the race.

TABLE 3.1   *Characteristics of the House and Senate Samples*

Variable	House	Senate
No. of campaigns	422	51
Years	1988–96	1988–92
States represented	50	31
Mean seniority of winners		
Sample	5 years	10 years
All legislators	11 years	11 years
Percent of Democratic winners		
Sample	49%	55%
All legislators	55%	52%
Mean vote share for winners		
Sample	56%	60%
All legislators	67%	60%

Sources: Summary statistics for the sample were calculated from data collected from *Politics in America* (1990–8 editions). Statistics for all legislators were obtained from *Vital Statistics on Congress* (Ornstein, Mann, and Malbin 1990–8).

not, nor can it be, completely random. Most obviously, studying uptake requires that all of the legislators in the sample be opposed in the previous campaign. Otherwise, there is no source of themes to take up. For this reason, legislators who were unopposed are omitted from the sample. In addition, since I focus on news coverage of campaigns as the source of information about the themes highlighted by the candidates, only those races for which coverage was available at the time of data collection were included.

Table 3.1 presents some comparisons between the samples and their respective populations. As shown, all fifty states are represented in the House sample, as are thirty-one states in the Senate sample. The Senate sample does not differ from the population (i.e., senators who ran for election or reelection in 1988, 1990, and 1992) in any important way. Compared to its population, the House sample does overrepresent more vulnerable and more junior members. However, this difference is largely due to the requirement that a race be contested to be included. Across this time period, approximately 200 House races were uncontested (almost 10 percent of the total), but, of course, none of these appear in the sample. As expected, when unopposed legislators and those with only token opposition (i.e., vote shares of more than 90 percent) are omitted from the calculations, the differences between the sample and the population shrink considerably. For example, the difference in mean winning vote shares drops from 11 percent to 5 percent. Concerns about generalizability should therefore be minimal.

To analyze the issue content of the campaign and legislative agendas for these samples, it is not necessary to reinvent the wheel, as a reliable, unified, and adaptable coding scheme already exists, thanks to the work of the Policy Agendas Project (see Baumgartner and Jones 1993, 2002; Jones and Baumgartner 2005).[2] The basic idea underlying the Project is that a wide variety of policy-related activities (e.g., bill introductions, congressional hearings, budget decisions, news stories, statutes, executive orders) can be systematically coded in a way that enables researchers to compare across sources and to track changes in the agenda across time. A coding scheme consisting of 19 major topic codes and 225 subtopic codes has been developed, and a large number of policy events and activities in the post–World War II period have been collected, coded, and organized into a series of data sets. The scheme is both exhaustive and mutually exclusive, so every policy event receives one and only one code. This provides clear analytic advantages over previous approaches to identifying the content of these events (e.g., the Library of Congress's "key terms," where a single bill or hearing may receive multiple codes).

To accommodate the particular needs of this project, which focuses on both electoral and legislative politics, I merged the Policy Agendas Project coding scheme with one developed by Simon (2002) for his content analysis of campaign discourse in Senate races. Although developed independently, the two schemes are remarkably similar, which provides further confidence in their validity in categorizing issues. I made some slight adjustments to the schemes, occasionally combining categories or promoting one of the Policy Agendas Project's subtopic codes to major topic status, ending up with a set of seventeen issue categories that I use to classify both campaign themes and legislative activity. These categories include agriculture, balanced budget, civil rights and civil liberties, crime, defense, economic issues (other than the budget and taxes), education, environment, family issues (parental leave, child care, domestic violence, etc.), foreign policy, health, immigration, labor and trade, regulation (of technology, transportation, and energy), Social Security, taxes, and welfare. An eighteenth category is used to code legislation that relates to governmental operations – an area that constitutes a good deal of legislative activity but is not "uptakeable," since it is generally

---

[2] Details of the Policy Agendas Project are available at http://www.policyagendas.org.

TABLE 3.2 *Issue Priorities in Campaigns and Activity in Congress*

Issue	No. of Campaigns	No. of Bills and Resolutions
Agriculture	64	1,268
Balanced budget	185	813
Civil rights and civil liberties	137	1,061
Crime	166	2,473
Defense	148	2,995
Economy	163	2,301
Education	98	1,613
Environment	154	4,368
Family issues	26	695
Foreign policy	31	2,843
Health	117	4,490
Immigration	4	700
Labor and trade	86	5,007
Regulation	97	5,090
Social Security	32	639
Taxes	185	1,325
Welfare	38	1,526
Governmental operations		11,207

administrative rather than policy-oriented and so is not a topic of campaigns.[3] Table 3.2 presents each of these categories, including measures of the relative attention paid to each in campaigns and legislative activity across the time period I study. The campaign attention measure is the number of campaigns in the sample for which the issue was a "priority theme,"[4] and the legislative attention measure is the total number of bills and resolutions introduced on each issue in the 101st through 105th Congresses.

The most important point to be taken from this table is that there is considerable diversity and variation in the issue content of congressional

[3] Bills and resolutions that fall into this category refer to subjects like congressional structure and organization, use of the Capitol for ceremonial events, nominations and appointments, and the like. While matters of daily business like these comprise a substantial portion of the legislative activity undertaken by representatives and senators (about 20% of the total number of bills and resolutions introduced in the 101st–105th Congresses), they are seldom, if ever, discussed in campaigns and so are not included as potential targets of uptake.

[4] The total number of campaigns is 825 (422 House challenger campaigns + 301 House winner campaigns + 51 Senate challenger campaigns + 51 Senate winner campaigns), but most campaigns had more than one priority-level theme.

campaigns and in the legislative activity of winning representatives and senators. These patterns are crucial for establishing the validity of the theoretical underpinnings of uptake, so I explore them in more detail later in this chapter. However, I first address the data collection procedures to establish what I mean by priority themes in campaigns and to describe how the issue content of campaign and legislative agendas was identified and coded.

Identifying Priority Issues in Senate Campaigns

For the Senate sample, I rely on the results of a large-scale content analysis of newspaper coverage of these campaigns.[5] Newspaper coverage is the preferred source of data about statewide campaigns because, compared to other sources like local television coverage, campaign advertising, or voter information guides, it most closely approximates the volume and content of information provided by the candidates (Hale 1987; Kahn 1991; Kahn and Kenney 1999; Simon 2002; Westlye 1991). Moreover, it is available in a similar format for a large number of campaigns, and so is amenable to systematic content analysis of the kind necessary to study uptake.

The first step of the analysis was to search electronic news archives (Lexis-Nexis, Datatimes, and Westlaw) for full-text coverage of a major statewide newspaper for each state for which there was a Senate race in 1988, 1990, or 1992.[6] For the fifty-one races for which coverage was available, all articles published between Labor Day and Election Day that mentioned one or both candidates were downloaded and organized into a database. Each article was then skimmed, and duplicates and articles that were, on closer investigation, not actually about the state's Senate campaign (i.e., those that referred to a person with the same name as one of the candidates) were eliminated. Articles that passed these tests were then subjected to closer analysis. Coders who had received extensive training in the coding scheme read each article carefully and noted the percentage of content that was devoted to a series of categories, including the policy issues discussed earlier (health, defense, crime, etc.), broad themes like

---

[5] Much of this data was originally collected and coded by Simon (2002). For a full discussion of his procedures, see Simon (2002, 95–100). I have added data for several races for which coverage was not available at the time of the original data collection and recoded his categories using my scheme.

[6] If two or more newspapers for a given state were available, the one with the largest circulation was selected.

performance or ideology, character themes like personality or integrity, and strategic themes (i.e., relating to the horse race). For the analysis of uptake undertaken here, I focus solely on policy issues.

The software that was used to construct the database of articles (Microsoft FoxPro) standardized the text into lines of coverage, which approximate the length of a line in a newspaper column. Multiplying the percentage of an article devoted to an issue by the total number of lines for the article thus yields a count of the number of lines devoted to that theme. These counts can then be aggregated across all articles for a given race to assess the amount of attention devoted to each of the issues. Of course, different campaigns have different volumes of coverage – the total number of articles per race varies from a low of 55 in Donald Riegle's (D-MI) 1988 campaign against challenger Jim Dunn to a high of 368 in Jesse Helms's (R-NC) 1990 campaign against Harvey Gantt. The Helms–Gantt race also scores the highest in terms of lines of coverage (28,619), with the lowest count belonging to Nancy Kassebaum's (R-KS) 1990 race against Dick Williams (1,687 lines). However, these differences are of little importance to the analysis here because the relevant comparisons are relative, occurring within rather than between races. The goal in every case is to identify those issues highlighted the most, regardless of the total amount of coverage the campaign received.

To study uptake, though, it is not enough to know just that a given issue received a relatively large amount of coverage in a campaign. We also need to know the source of discussion of that issue. Was it a candidate or some other source (e.g., the reporter or newspaper editorial staff), and, if it was a candidate, which one? To ensure that any issue attributed to a candidate actually originated with him or her, a conservative standard was adopted – only statements from candidates or those affiliated with their campaign organizations were included. Thus, a statement that read "Agricultural issues are important in the campaign this year" would not be attributed to either candidate, while one that read "In his campaign appearance at the Chamber of Commerce luncheon yesterday, Candidate X proclaimed his support for new subsidies for soybean growers" would. Combined with the measures of relative content of various themes, this procedure allows me to identify the top issues for each candidate's campaign. To pinpoint the number of issues that should be considered priority themes, I examined the patterns of coverage across all campaigns. These results demonstrate that, while virtually all candidates (95 out of 102) received coverage on three issues, considerably fewer received a substantial amount of coverage (i.e., more than twenty-five lines) on four or more. Thus, for the Senate, three themes is a natural cutoff point.

Interestingly, there is also anecdotal evidence that candidates themselves view three themes as a sort of magic number. As Wyche Fowler (D-GA) explained to Fenno (1996):

One of the things I am working on now is to take the twelve things I could talk about and reduce them to the three things I will talk about. (175)...I know the most successful politicians are those who boil everything down to three things and repeat them over and over again.... (177)

Fowler and his advisors described to Fenno his struggles with narrowing his focus in this manner. Indeed, these difficulties may have contributed to his loss in 1992 to Paul Coverdell (who is one of the senators in the sample studied here).

Identifying Priority Issues in House Campaigns

House races differ from Senate races in several important ways. They tend to be less visible, they generally attract challengers of lower quality, and, with the exception of states with only one representative, they focus on a smaller geographic constituency. All of these factors contribute to the unreliability of newspaper coverage as an indicator of the content of House campaigns. This problem is exacerbated by the mismatch that often occurs between newspapers' circulation areas and congressional district boundaries. For metropolitan areas, the circulation boundaries of the major newspaper may cover a number of congressional districts. Descriptions of House campaigns in these newspapers often refer to multiple races, making it difficult to disentangle one campaign from another. House districts that are located in rural areas present a different, but equally important, problem: If there is no daily newspaper that adequately corresponds to district boundaries, these races may get no detailed coverage at all. More practically, even if there is a daily newspaper that regularly covers the campaign, this content is generally very difficult to retrieve. Electronic services like Lexis-Nexis only archive newspapers with significant circulations, and although many smaller newspapers are in the process of developing their own archives accessible via their web sites, these often go back only a few months.

To study the content of these races, it is therefore necessary to rely on sources other than newspaper coverage. For this reason, I use the campaign summaries provided by *CQ Weekly* in its "Special Election

Issue," published in late October of each election year. These summaries typically consist of three to five paragraphs about a race, describing the candidates, their backgrounds, and any important issues that have defined the campaign. In recent years, about 150 races have been selected for this treatment. These races are not chosen randomly (neglecting, for instance, most races in which the incumbent is running unopposed by a major party challenger or in which there are no compelling issues), but they do attempt a broadly representative sample in terms of geography, party, issues, and so on. As described earlier, this selection procedure does introduce some biases, but it is less of a problem for my investigation than it might be for others because contested campaigns with at least some issue content are actually the population of interest here.

The content analysis procedure for the House began by reading each campaign summary in the 1988, 1990, 1992, 1994, and 1996 editions of the *CQ Weekly* special issue and identifying all of the campaigns for which at least one issue was attributed to the challenger's campaign. A total of 422 races met this criterion. I adopted the same conservative coding standard that was used in the Senate analysis. Specifically, in order for an issue to be identified as a priority issue, it had to be described as originating with a particular candidate or campaign. Once again, candidates generally focused on only a handful of issues, with the number of challengers' themes ranging from one to four. Where information on winning legislators' themes was provided, it was recorded as well. However, unlike in the Senate study, data on both candidates' themes was not available for every race.[7] Regardless, information on both winner and challenger themes is available for enough of the campaigns (over 70 percent) to allow assessment of their impact.

To evaluate the reliability of this approach, I examined newspaper coverage for a group of House races for which this coverage was available, and found few differences between the conclusions reached by the *CQ Weekly* method and the conclusions reached by the newspaper method. A comparable analysis of voter information guides (which, for the states that print them, include a statement from each candidate) yielded similar results.

---

[7] Some campaign summaries indicated the challenger's themes but not the winning candidate's themes or vice versa. Since the discussion of challenger themes was the criterion by which a race was selected for study, the former were included in the sample and the latter excluded.

TABLE 3.3 *Summary of Legislative Activity for the House and Senate Samples*

Activity	Total	Mean	Median	Std. Dev.
Introductions				
House of Representatives	5,673	13	10	11
Senate	11,493	225	192	134
Cosponsorships				
House of Representatives	114,844	272	236	148
Senate	37,087	727	688	364
Floor statements				
House of Representatives	16,257	39	31	26
Senate	14,887	292	273	115
Total	200,242			

Coding Legislative Activities

After identifying the issue foci of campaigns, I collected data on the legislative activity undertaken by the winners in the term immediately following their election or reelection. A list of all of the bills, resolutions, and amendments introduced or cosponsored by each was obtained from the Library of Congress's THOMAS web site.[8] Lists of floor statements made by each legislator were gathered by searching the Congressional Record Index (available via the Government Printing Office's ACCESS Web site), downloading the summary of each legislator's activities, and noting every bill, resolution, or amendment on which remarks were made. Summary results, presented in Table 3.3, indicate that legislators' activity levels were considerable, with over 200,000 activities undertaken by the members of the sample. The average representative performed about 325 activities per term, and the average senator performed about 1,250.[9]

To determine the proportion of this activity devoted to uptake, each of these introductions, cosponsorships, and floor statements was then individually categorized by issue. At the heart of the coding effort lies introduced legislation because all of the legislative activities examined here are linked, either directly or indirectly, to a particular bill or resolution.

---

[8] Amendment cosponsorships are available for the Senate but not for the House, and so are included only for the former.

[9] Senators' terms are, of course, three times as long as representatives', so we should expect a higher count for them. Nonetheless, even after taking this difference into account, senators are still more active than representatives, engaging in about 100 more activities per two-year Congress.

As such, the first step in the process was to code all public bill and resolution introductions (not just those introduced by the sample) for the House and Senate in the 101st through 105th Congresses. This totals 50,760 bills (with H.R. and S. designations), simple resolutions (H.Res. and S.Res.), joint resolutions (H.J.Res. and S.J.Res.), and concurrent resolutions (S.Con.Res. and H.Con.Res.). Coders first read a brief description of each bill or resolution and assigned it one of the Policy Agendas Project codes.[10] Each of the measures was then given a second code that corresponded to one of the eighteen categories discussed previously, and coding of the activities undertaken by the legislators in the sample began. For their bill and resolution introductions and cosponsorships, this process was straightforward. I simply referenced the full dataset (i.e., that contained the codes for all bills and resolutions introduced) to locate the appropriate category code for each measure. For amendments and floor statements, an additional step was required – before they could be categorized, the "parent" bill or resolution had to be identified (e.g., H.Amdt.43 amends H.R.122). The issue category for this parent measure was then recorded as the category for the given amendment or statement. This procedure of tying all activities to introduced bills or resolutions (instead of coding the content of amendments and floor statements directly) ensures reliability and speeds up the process, making it feasible to investigate the activities of a larger sample of legislators.

Once all of the legislative activities were categorized by issue, identifying those that were "challenger-themed" was straightforward. Every introduction, cosponsorship, or floor statement that received the same issue code as a challenger priority issue was denoted as challenger-themed, while all others were identified as non-challenger-themed. Thus, if a legislator's challenger highlighted foreign policy, health, and taxes, all introductions, cosponsorships, and floor statements made by the legislator on those three issues were coded as challenger-themed. For another legislator, whose challenger prioritized agriculture, welfare, and crime, activity on those issues was identified as challenger-themed.

With this task completed, the component parts for studying uptake are all in place. For each of the 422 representatives and 51 senators in the sample, I know what their past challengers' priority themes were

---

[10] Coding of bill introductions was completed under the auspices of the Policy Agendas Bill Introductions Project, funded by NSF# 0080066 to John Wilkerson and Scott Adler. Coding of resolution introductions was performed by the author and a team of research assistants. Intercoder reliability levels for the coding of introductions are between 80 and 90%.

and how many activities they subsequently performed on these issues. For example, in the 1996 elections, Representatives Diana DeGette's (D-CO) and Todd Tiahrt's (R-KS) challengers both prioritized crime and education. In the next term, DeGette made twenty-five introductions, cosponsorships, and floor statements on these issues and Forbes made thirty-one. During that same election, Mark Neuman's (R-WI) and Michael Forbes's (R-NY) challengers highlighted the budget and health. Neuman performed twenty uptake activities and Forbes made forty-five. That these differences in uptake activity can tell us something about individual variation in responsiveness should be obvious, and I devote the next chapter to developing a framework to compare across legislators.[11]

However, before proceeding to this, it is useful to use these data to explore what aggregate campaign and legislative agendas look like across this time period. An understanding of aggregate agenda patterns is crucial both for placing uptake in context (i.e., How much might we expect to see? Should it occur on some issues more than others?) and for assessing the validity of the strategic motivation theory. Uptake relies upon a few basic but critical assumptions about the nature of agendas, some of which contrast with the conventional wisdom on the subject. I assume, for example, that candidates actually discuss issues in their campaigns, that opposing candidates raise different issues, that there is diversity in campaign themes across races and across time, and that legislators have the ability to act on whichever issues they choose. Examining campaign and legislative agendas directly allows me to assess the extent to which these assumptions are true and, in the process, to dispel some common misconceptions about agendas that have important implications for the study of uptake.

Campaign and Legislative Agendas, 101st through 105th Congresses

What, then, do agendas look like across the time period I study? Table 3.4 presents aggregate data on the issue content of the sampled campaign and legislative agendas, including the percentage of challenger and winner

---

[11] Because factors like total activity levels and the amount of overlap between winners and challengers vary across legislators, simply comparing raw levels of uptake does not enable one to draw valid conclusions about relative responsiveness.

TABLE 3.4 *Sampled Candidates' and Legislators' Attention to Issues*

Issue	% of Challenger Campaigns	% of Winner Campaigns	% of Legislators
Agriculture	6	10	21
Balanced budget	21	25	14
Civil rights and civil liberties	19	13	22
Crime	19	22	37
Defense	16	21	37
Economy	22	17	33
Education	13	11	28
Environment	17	21	52
Family issues	4	3	13
Foreign policy	4	4	30
Health	14	14	43
Immigration	.2	.8	12
Labor and trade	10	11	42
Regulation	10	15	46
Social Security	5	3	9
Taxes	24	20	26
Welfare	4	6	24
Governmental operations	—	—	76

campaigns for which each issue received priority-level attention[12] and the percentage of legislators who introduced at least one bill or resolution dealing with that issue.[13]

A few important points stand out from these results. First, a wide variety of issues were highlighted in agendas. Each of the issue categories was a priority theme in at least a handful of campaigns and was acted on in office by multiple legislators. Second, some issues were simply more popular than others. Among those that received the most attention were the economy, crime, and the environment, while categories like family issues, immigration, and Social Security were much less popular. However, overall agendas were fairly diffuse, with no single issue or small group of issues completely dominating attention. Even the most popular issues reached priority-level status in less than one-quarter of campaigns and

---

[12] As discussed earlier, candidates could (and did) highlight multiple priorities, so these do not sum to 100.

[13] This is a conservative approach to determining whether or not an issue was on a legislator's agenda, as it is also possible to cosponsor or make floor statements about issues.

were acted on in office by less than half of the legislators in the sample. Finally, in campaign agendas, there do not appear to be any substantively important differences in the issue choices of challengers and the issue choices of winners, with roughly equal percentages of the two groups raising each theme.

Importantly, this last finding does *not* mean that challengers and winners running against one another in the same race highlighted the same issues. The existence of such overlap in priority themes is one of a number of common misconceptions about agendas that, if true, could undermine the validity of uptake. These misconceptions fall under two basic myths. The first is that most congressional campaigns are without substantive content, so candidates do not discuss issues. The second is that, for those campaigns where issues are discussed, there is a great deal of conformity in agendas, both within and across races. The first myth is the most obviously damaging to uptake because, taken to the extreme, it would render it meaningless. Put simply, there would be no issues for winners to subsequently take up. The second myth, though more subtle, is potentially equally problematic because it raises questions about whether or not legislators' subsequent activity on their challengers' issues can appropriately be interpreted as a response to the challenger. Because of their implications for the validity of uptake, I address both of these myths in some detail.

Myth 1: Candidates in Congressional Campaigns Don't Discuss Substantive Issues

The content analysis procedures discussed earlier and the results presented in Table 3.4 would appear to dispel this myth fairly easily. It is indeed possible to extract the issue content of candidates' campaigns, and winners and challengers in congressional elections highlight a variety of themes. As such, uptake has the potential to be widespread, occurring across many different issues, although it should be most prevalent on those issues that are raised most frequently in campaigns. However, this claim that campaigns have clear and diverse issue foci is in contrast to the picture of campaigns that comes out of many scholarly and most journalistic accounts. The discussion of issues and agendas in the larger elections literature has typically focused much less on explaining their content and variation and much more on noting their relatively infrequent appearances in campaign discourse (see, for example, Jacobson 2001; Mann and Wolfinger 1980; Patterson 1993).

How can this difference be reconciled? I attribute it primarily to differences in perspective between the broader literature on elections and my approach, which focuses specifically on candidates' agendas. If the goal is to describe the nature of congressional campaigns and elections, it is certainly true that the amount of attention paid to policy issues often pales in comparison to attention to other sorts of themes. Indeed, campaign appeals may more often take the form of general indictments of ideology or partisanship ("He's too liberal" or "She's too conservative"), symbolic statements, or attacks on candidates' characters and personal lives. Perceptions of the nonsubstantive nature of these campaigns may be further exacerbated by reporters' propensity for horse race coverage of campaigns, focusing on who's ahead and who's behind in the polls, in fund-raising, and so on at the expense of more in-depth coverage of issues.[14]

The problem occurs if we take these findings about the relative paucity of issue coverage in campaigns to mean that candidates do not discuss issues at all. If, rather than offering a general characterization of the role of issues in elections, the goal is to identify those issues that are discussed in campaigns, we uncover considerable attention to substantive themes. In my Senate sample, I find that 98 percent of the challengers and 100 percent of the winners had at least two identifiable issue priorities. For the House sample, these numbers are slightly lower, but, nonetheless, over two-thirds of challengers and winners had at least two priority issues.[15] Moreover, these results are echoed in other literature on campaigns. Simon found that nearly 30 percent of news coverage of Senate races was devoted to the types of specific issues discussed here (2002, 105; see also Kahn and Kenney 1999). Similarly, Herrnson noted that approximately 47 percent of House candidates prioritized issues in their advertising (1998, 172), and Spiliotes and Vavreck's (2002) study of campaign ads in the 1998 midterm elections found that nearly all (92 percent) of candidates discussed issues in at least one of their ads.

My conclusion, then, is that the two perspectives do not contradict one another. In most campaigns, the discussion of issues does not predominate,

---

[14] Importantly, horse race coverage is generally less prevalent for House and Senate races than for presidential races (Arnold 2004; Kahn and Kenney 1999). Perceptions about the predominance of such coverage may be a result of the fact that studies of campaign coverage have traditionally focused more on presidential campaigns than on congressional campaigns.

[15] For the House sample, these figures are likely to be inflated relative to the population because the availability of information about issues was the primary selection criterion for the sample. Nonetheless, as discussed earlier, the sample does not differ from the population on many other variables of interest.

but that should not obscure the fact that it does indeed occur. It therefore seems safe to conclude that enough issue content exists to reliably identify candidates' agendas and to give winning representatives and senators a target for responsiveness. Before assessing this responsiveness, it is necessary to first examine my assumptions about the nature of the issue content in campaigns. As mentioned earlier, these assumptions are equally important for establishing the viability of uptake. I view challengers' campaigns as sending signals to winning legislators about issues they may have previously ignored. By acting on these issues in the next term, winners respond to their challengers' critiques. This assumes that candidates choose their issues independently based on their own backgrounds and expertise and the particular strengths and weaknesses of their opponents. The end result should be considerable diversity in campaign themes across candidates and across races.

What if this is not the case? What if campaign agendas in a given year are very concentrated, so that many candidates highlight the same small set of issues? What if opposing candidates in races routinely prioritize the same themes? Or what if the same set of issues is raised in a district or state in election after election? To the extent that any of these scenarios are true, we should be concerned that winning legislators' uptake behavior might be better interpreted as a response to exogenous cues rather than to the campaigns of their challengers. Dispelling the myth that campaign agendas are quite concentrated is thus crucial for establishing uptake as a useful concept.

Myth 2: Campaign Agendas Exhibit Considerable Conformity Both within and across Races and over Time

In contrast to the literature on individual candidates' issue selection strategies, which supports the assumption that aggregate agendas are diffuse (see, for example, Carsey 2000; Sellers 1998; Simon 2002), the view of agendas coming out of the larger congressional elections literature is one of greater conformity. Once again, this literature does not focus specifically on campaign themes and so does not yield explicit predictions about the content of agendas. In describing the factors influencing election outcomes, however, many scholars offer general characterizations of issues in campaigns that highlight the similarities between them. This often takes the form of a discussion of the relative impact of national and local conditions (Jacobson and Kernell 1983), both of which suggest that we should see large numbers of candidates focusing on the same issues.

If issue selection is driven by national trends, we should expect the most conformity. For example, in the aftermath of the September 11, 2001, terrorist attacks, we might see hundreds of candidates across the country prioritizing homeland security in their campaigns. However, despite the appeal of this "political folk wisdom" regarding the role of national-level factors, most elections scholars have concluded that truly nationalized campaigns are relatively rare events and that congressional elections are more often driven by local issues and conditions (Jacobson and Kernell 1983, 2; see also Herrnson 1998; Jacobson 2001). If this is true and candidates look to these conditions when choosing their agendas, the prediction would be for less conformity at the aggregate level but significant overlap in the priority themes of competing candidates. For instance, if a large factory in a district closes and if the impact of that closure is severe, then we might expect to see both candidates in that district picking up on it and discussing economic issues in their campaigns. The problem for uptake in both of these situations (i.e., high conformity in themes at the national level or at the local level) is that it makes it difficult to determine whether a legislator who is subsequently active on his or her challengers' themes is responding to the specific challenger or to outside signals about the salience of those issues on the local or national agendas.

Diversity in Campaign Themes

To explore these possibilities, it is necessary to examine agenda patterns in more detail. The findings in Table 3.4 demonstrated that the overall campaign agenda between 1988 and 1996 was quite diverse, but this aggregate approach may have obscured more subtle patterns. It is possible that all of the mentions of a particular issue could have occurred in the same year rather than being spread evenly across the elections, so that campaign agendas in a single year would be quite concentrated. In Table 3.5, I present the results of a simple analysis designed to address this question. To construct this table, I first broke out the samples by election year and then calculated the percentage of campaigns in each year that highlighted each of the seventeen substantive issue categories. The analysis is limited to the 1988, 1990, and 1992 elections since those are the years for which I have data on both House and Senate races. As shown, although many issues received relatively stable levels of attention across this time period, attention to other issues changed considerably.

TABLE 3.5 *Relative Attention to Issues across Election Years*

Issue	% of 1988 Campaigns	% of 1990 Campaigns	% of 1992 Campaigns
Agriculture	12	8	6
Balanced budget	12	24	17
Civil rights and civil liberties	7	23	23
Crime	27	9	11
Defense	30	24	19
Economy	28	26	31
Education	9	9	7
Environment	27	28	14
Family issues	1	1	9
Foreign policy	9	5	3
Health	13	4	15
Immigration	0	1	0
Labor and trade	16	7	10
Regulation	22	12	13
Social Security	9	2	1
Taxes	13	22	21
Welfare	6	2	1

For example, taxes and civil rights and liberties became more prominent in campaigns, while attention to crime and the environment waned.[16]

One effect of these patterns is that campaign agendas in a single election year do indeed display more concentration than the aggregate agenda across all years. Importantly, though, we still observe considerable diversity in campaign themes within election years, with the most popular issues reaching priority-level attention in less than one-third of all campaigns. This finding holds even after I further break out the election year samples by party and by chamber. Thus, it is simply not the case that all Democrats in 1992 were discussing health or all Republicans in 1996 were discussing the economy. At the national level at least, congressional campaigns look very diverse.

Overlap in Campaign Themes

Even if campaign agendas display diversity at the national level, conformity in the guise of overlapping priorities between competing candidates

---

[16] However, attention to crime did increase again in the 1994 House campaigns, when it was a major plank in the platform of the Republican "Contract with America."

may still be a possibility. This overlap might be good from a normative perspective, as many scholars argue that encouraging dialogue in campaigns would increase voters' understanding of the candidates' differences and make campaigns more substantive (Hart 2000; Simon 2002). In a more practical sense, however, it would make it impossible to discern whether or not uptake had occurred because we could not distinguish between "challenger issues" and "winner issues." If both the challenger and the winner in a given race talked at length about tax policy, we would be on shaky ground if we suggested that all of the legislator's subsequent attention to this topic was uptake of his or her challenger's priorities.

Overlap between competing candidates' themes could arise in a number of ways. As discussed previously, it could occur if candidates look to the same national or local conditions or events when choosing their campaign agendas. It could also occur if challengers consciously choose to focus their campaigns on issues on which the incumbent has been very active, perhaps in the hope of criticizing his or her positions on those issues. Since incumbent candidates tend to focus their own campaigns on issues for which they have built a reputation (Sellers 1998), the end result would be many races in which candidates discuss the same issues. In either situation, the ability to interpret uptake as a response to the challenger would be compromised.

Fortunately, overlap rates are fairly low. Of the winners in the Senate sample, 28 percent had no overlap at all with their challengers' themes and only 7.8 percent had complete overlap. In the House sample, complete overlap is more common (18.6 percent), but so is no overlap (45.8 percent).[17] These patterns caution against the argument that challengers focus their campaigns on their opponents' preexisting priorities. Instead, they suggest that challengers generally raise unique issues, a finding that corresponds with the conclusions reached by recent work on candidate strategy in congressional campaigns (Sellers 1998; Simon 2002; Spiliotes and Vavreck 2002). As such, the issues raised by challengers are distinct and provide a clear target for subsequent responsiveness on the part of legislators. And in instances where overlap in themes does occur, it is easily controlled for when assessing relative responsiveness.

These patterns in overlap also caution against another alternative interpretation of uptake – that challengers raise issues in response to exogenous cues and that winners' subsequent activity on those issues is a response

[17] This difference between the House and Senate is not unexpected given that fewer issues are discussed in the former.

to the same cues (rather than their challengers' campaigns). To return to the example given previously, if the closure of a factory in a district is important enough for a challenger to raise the economy as a theme in his or her campaign and for the winner to become active on this issue in the subsequent term, then it is reasonable to assume that the winner would also see it as important enough to highlight in his or her campaign. In short, it is unlikely that these exogenous cues would affect challengers' campaigns and winners' post-election conduct but not winners' campaign agendas. Thus, we can be confident that, after controlling for any overlap in themes between candidates, winners' subsequent activity on their challengers' issues is, in fact, a response to these campaigns.[18]

Election-to-Election Change in Campaign Themes

One final issue relating to conformity in campaign themes remains to be addressed. In this case, the potential conformity of concern is not across candidates or races but across time. If most districts or states have perennial issues, themes that come up again and again in successive races, one might rightly question the role of campaigns in bringing these issues to the attention of incumbent candidates. Issues that are highlighted in every campaign will come as no surprise at all to the winners. As discussed in Chapter 2, the theory of uptake relies upon campaigns sending signals to winners about issues they have previously neglected. Winners then act on these issues in an effort to remedy these weaknesses. If these issues are never new, or if acting on them never takes them off the table for future challengers, the hypothesized motivations for uptake become suspect.

To study this question rigorously would require data on the issue priorities in successive Senate and House campaigns over a long period of time. Unfortunately, data availability issues prohibit this possibility. However, I can get some leverage on this question by examining the issue content of the campaigns of eighty-two representatives in the House sample who appear in consecutive cross sections. Using the same approach to assessing challenger-to-challenger overlap across time that I used to measure challenger-to-winner overlap within races, I find that, for 56 percent of the representatives, the issue priorities highlighted by their challenger in

---

[18] In the analyses in the chapters to come, I also control for the collective attention paid to each challenger's themes in Congress as a whole. Taking into account the aggregate popularity of issues provides further assurance that uptake isolates a winner's response to his or her challenger's campaign.

the second race were completely different from those highlighted in the first race. Only 8 percent of legislators ran in races where the same set of issues was highlighted both times. Consequently, there appears to be considerable change in campaign themes across time, so that each new election cycle raises new issues.

In sum, these findings about aggregate campaign agendas provide considerable support for the assumptions underlying uptake. At the same time, they underscore the need to control for factors like overlap and issue popularity when analyzing uptake and comparing levels across individuals, a point I return to in the next chapter. First, though, I address the second component of the uptake puzzle – the legislative agendas of winning representatives and senators.

Legislative Agendas, 101st–105th Congresses

In earlier analyses, we saw that the average legislator undertakes hundreds of activities in a single term, which should provide many opportunities to engage in uptake and demonstrate responsiveness to the challenger's themes.[19] However, the opportunity to be active, while necessary, is not a sufficient condition for uptake to occur. Legislators must also have the ability to exercise some choice about the issue content of their activities. In other words, their agendas can't be so constrained, either formally or informally, that they are unable to be active on their challengers' issues.

The aggregate data presented in Table 3.2 demonstrated that all of the issue categories were the subject of significant numbers of introductions (and even more cosponsorships and floor statements) across the time period studied. Even the least addressed issue, Social Security, received 639 introductions and was acted on by nearly 10 percent of the samples. From the perspective of uptake, the real question of interest is how much dispersion exists in individual legislators' agendas (rather than in the aggregate agenda). Is the typical legislator active on only one or two issues or is there evidence of more widespread activity? If we found that legislators introduced in only a single area, we might infer that there are some limits to being more broadly active, which would have important implications for their ability to address their challengers' priority themes.

---

[19] Importantly, though, they do not engage in so many activities that their choices of where and when to participate are meaningless. For example, the average legislator cosponsors only 5–10 percent of the measures introduced.

To explore the scope of individual agendas, I focus on introduction activity, calculating for each legislator the number of issue categories on which he or she introduced at least one bill or resolution. Legislators generally undertake more cosponsorships and floor statements than introductions, so this provides a conservative standard for assessing the scope of agendas (i.e., I would expect the scope to be larger if I investigated all activities). For the Senate, I find that the average legislator introduces in thirteen of the seventeen issue categories (standard deviation = 2.4). The typical representative makes introductions in approximately five categories (standard deviation = 2.5), a difference that is to be expected given the lower introduction output per member in the House of Representatives.

Overall, these results suggest that legislators have considerable discretion to pursue their activities across issues as they see fit, a finding that is in contrast to much of the conventional wisdom on legislative behavior. The general assumption in this literature is that the content of activity is shaped primarily by the committee assignments of legislators, and that these structures limit legislators' ability to be entrepreneurial about issues that lie outside the parameters of their committees. Schiller (2000) claims, for example, that bill introductions are "very strongly determined by committee assignment" (53). However, while committee assignments definitely influence the content of legislators' activity, there is considerable theoretical and empirical support for the proposition that they do not solely determine it. As Salisbury and Shepsle (1981) note, all legislators head an enterprise consisting of a number of staff members who "expand the scope and range of [their] policy-relevant activity" well beyond what they might individually be capable of (565), enabling legislators to address almost any issue they wish. Along these lines, Ainsworth and Hall (2001) find that, in the House of Representatives, about three-quarters of the bills are introduced by sponsors who do not sit on the committee of referral. They conclude that legislators' independent resources (those not tied to their party or committee memberships) allow them to be active on issues outside of their committee assignments (2).[20] The same is true for senators, for whom "committees are important but by no means their only arenas for participation" (Sinclair 1989, 71).

---

[20] However, there is evidence that bills introduced by committee members are more likely to receive hearings, be reported out of committee, and eventually pass into law (see Schiller 1995, 2000).

The point, then, is that legislators who want to be active on issues that extend beyond the jurisdictions of their committees are free to do so.[21] The system is flexible in this regard because legislators' interests are not always captured by their committee assignments. While they do have the opportunity to request assignments to committees and subcommittees that focus on issues in which they are particularly interested, they don't always get their first choices. However, because of electoral considerations or personal interests, they may choose to remain active in these areas. Legislators from the state of Washington, for example, are likely to be attentive to policies regarding salmon fisheries, even if they do not sit on a committee dealing with natural resources. They may view their activities on such issues as entirely separate from their role as a member of a certain committee, or they may act in the hope that their entrepreneurship will set a precedent, eventually expanding the turf of their committees to include these issues (King 1997; Talbert, Jones, and Baumgartner 1995). Regardless, introducing, cosponsoring, and speaking about legislation are activities that are available to all legislators, whatever their committee positions.

The same holds true for characteristics like party affiliation and seniority. Of course, not all legislators participate equally; factors like their tenure in office or the size of their staffs, and characteristics of their districts or states (size, diversity, etc.) may lead legislators to differ in their overall activity levels (Hall 1996; Schiller 1995; Wilson and Young 1997). However, this variation is easily controlled for and does not impede investigation of the major issue here – the content of the activities legislators do engage in and their relative attention to different issues in their legislative portfolios.

Agendas and Uptake

These explorations of campaign and legislative agendas have demonstrated that the assumptions underlying the strategic motivation theory are valid and that uptake is indeed a viable mechanism for responsiveness. Most candidates in House and Senate elections have clear and identifiable issue priorities and their agendas are fairly diverse, varying considerably

---

[21] Baumgartner, Jones, and MacLeod (2000) note as well that jurisdictional clarity for committees has declined in recent years, as committees have become increasingly open to addressing new issues. They attribute this change to increased resources to committees and their individual members.

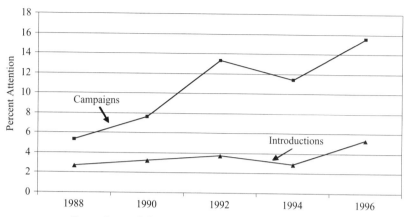

FIGURE 3.1   Campaign and Congressional Attention to Tax Policy, 1988–1998.

across candidates and campaigns. Equally importantly, winning legisla-tors appear to have the ability to act on a variety of issues during their time in office, enabling them to take up their challengers' themes if they wish to do so.

In the chapters to come, I will focus mostly on individual uptake – the impact of challengers' campaigns on winners' agendas in office. Before doing so, however, it is useful to get a sense of the magnitude of the uptake effect by exploring the relationship between campaign agendas and congressional agendas at the aggregate level. More specifically, is it the case that issues get more attention in Congress when more challengers have highlighted them in campaigns? If many legislators are incorporat-ing their challengers' themes into their activities in office, we should see an aggregate relationship between issue attention in campaigns and in Congress.

Figure 3.1 illustrates just such a relationship. It focuses on attention to tax policy in the House of Representatives between 1988 and 1998.[22] Over this time period, taxes were raised as a priority issue by the challenger in 93 of the 422 House campaigns in the sample, and a total of 893 bills and resolutions were introduced on this topic. The top line in the figure represents the percentage of issue mentions made on taxes by challengers in each of the five election years studied. The bottom line represents the

---

[22] Given the overlapping terms in the Senate and the small number of election years included, it becomes impossible to disentangle the effects of campaigns on aggregate legislative attention to issues. For this reason, I limit this illustration to the House sample.

percentage of legislation introduced that focused on taxes in each of the five congresses. As is clear from the picture, the two are indeed associated. In congresses following elections where a high percentage of challengers highlighted the issue, a high percentage of introductions are devoted to it.

The important questions to ask, though, are whether the relationship we see for tax policy reflects a more general pattern and whether it stands up to more rigorous analyses. To address these questions, I use an ordinary least squares (OLS) regression model to test whether campaign attention to an issue is a significant predictor of the level of subsequent activity on that issue in Congress. Each case in the analysis is a campaign-Congress/theme (e.g., 1988–101st Congress/tax policy), and there are a total of eighty-five observations (seventeen issue categories times five campaigns–Congresses). Since the analysis is aggregate in nature, a number of controls are necessary. Most obviously, we need to take into account differences in the issues themselves. Some just get more legislative attention than others, regardless of the amount of campaign attention given to them. To control for this, I include a series of dummy variables for each of the issue categories. I also add dummies for the different campaigns–Congresses to control for differences in the number of campaigns in the sample and for differences in overall activity from congress to congress.[23] Finally, I take into account the number of winning representatives' campaigns that highlighted the issue, which allows me to ascertain the independent effect of challengers' campaigns on the congressional agenda.

Table 3.6 presents the results of this analysis. The dependent variable in each of the two specifications is a measure of legislative attention to issues. In the first model it is a raw count of the number of bills introduced on each issue during each congress, and in the second model it is a percentage measure (i.e., the number of bills on an issue divided by the total number of bills introduced). The primary independent variable in each is a measure of challengers' attention to each issue. The first model uses raw counts of the number of challenger campaigns in each year that highlighted each issue, and the second uses a percentage measure. The models also include the dummy variables described earlier and the control for the number

---

[23] It should be remembered that the data on the number of campaigns that highlighted a certain issue come from the sample. We don't know, therefore, what the topics of the campaigns not in the sample were, so we need to interpret the aggregate results with some caution. Nonetheless, to the extent that the sample is broadly representative of the types of themes prioritized in campaigns and the distributions of these themes, this approach is valid.

TABLE 3.6 *Impact of Campaign Attention on Legislative Attention to Issues*

	Model 1 Raw Counts	Model 2 Percentages
Challenger campaigns	4.87***	.093**
	(1.73)	(.041)
Representative campaigns	−2.32	−.017
	(2.41)	(.022)
Constant	32.30	1.54
	(33.05)	(.45)
N	85	85
Adjusted R^2	.91	.93

Note: Cell entries are unstandardized OLS regression coefficients with standard errors in parentheses.
*** $= p < .01$; ** $= p < .05$; * $= p < .10$.

of representatives' campaigns that highlighted the issue (raw counts in Model 1 and percentages in Model 2).

The coefficients for the issue and year/Congress dummy variables are not particularly interesting from a theoretical perspective and so, in the interest of saving space, are not reported here. Their inclusion, though, allows for a more precise estimation of the impact of challengers' campaigns after all other variation has been taken into account. As the results indicate, this impact is significant and robust. All other things being equal, every House challenger campaign that highlights an issue results in an additional five bills and resolutions introduced on that issue in the following Congress. This translates into about a 1 percent increase in the proportion of overall legislative activity devoted to that issue. This effect may seem small when the unit of change is one campaign, but it becomes substantial when we think about larger (but still reasonable) numbers. For instance, for the average issue, if ten more challengers highlight it, we should see about fifty more bills and resolutions introduced – a difference that has the potential to exert a significant impact on public policy.

In the aggregate, then, uptake decisions can leave an important trace on the content of the congressional agenda. Ultimately, however, uptake is an individual phenomenon. To understand it thus requires that I measure it and model its variation at the individual level. These are the tasks of Chapter 4.

4

Assessing Uptake

The previous chapters have established the general theoretical underpinnings of uptake. I have shown that challengers generally discuss distinct issues in their campaigns, that legislators enjoy considerable discretion in choosing their issue agendas, and that reelection considerations provide winning legislators with clear incentives to take up their challengers' themes and act on them in office. With these pieces of the puzzle in place, it is now possible to assess uptake, exploring its dynamics across individuals, across activities, across chambers, and across time. I begin this process in this chapter by addressing three fundamental questions. First, how should uptake be measured? Second, how much does the average legislator exhibit and how much variation exists across individuals? Finally, what factors need to be taken into account to explain this variation and draw reliable conclusions about relative responsiveness?

As a point of departure, it is useful to focus on the behavior of a single legislator. As such, I once again consider the situation faced by Senator Bob Graham. Graham's 1992 election challenger, Bill Grant, highlighted health care, economic issues, and the need for a balanced budget in his campaign. Graham subsequently responded by performing a number of activities on these issues, many more than he had in his previous term. To illustrate my approach to investigating uptake, I begin by identifying more precisely how much uptake Graham's behavior reflects and determining whether his raw level is high, low, or about average compared to those of his peers. I then develop a systematic framework for making such comparisons and illustrate how the model comes together using legislators' uptake on a single issue – health care.

Measuring Legislators' Uptake

Perhaps the most obvious method for measuring individual legislators' uptake is to count the number of challenger-themed activities undertaken by each representative and senator in the term following the campaign of interest. An examination of Graham's legislative activity after the 1992 election reveals that he made 206 introductions, cosponsorships, and floor statements dealing with Grant's issues. The mean uptake count for the Senate sample was 188 activities, so Graham scores somewhat above average in the volume of his uptake activity. If we use this count measure to rank order senators, the results indicate that the highest uptake count belongs to Dennis DeConcini (D-AZ), who engaged in 499 challenger-themed activities in his term. The lowest belongs to Mitch McConnell (R-KY), with an uptake count of only thirty-one activities. Graham's particular count ranks him thirty-fifth out of fifty-one senators, between John Danforth (R-MO), who performed 204 activities related to his challenger's priorities, and Bill Bradley (D-NJ), who engaged in 209 such activities.

By this measure, Graham, Danforth, and Bradley were about equally responsive to their challengers. However, although they engaged in similar numbers of challenger-themed activities, they differed substantially in their overall volume of activity. While Graham and Danforth both performed about 1,100 activities throughout their terms, Bradley was considerably more active, making a total of 1,340 introductions, cosponsorships, and floor statements. Graham's and Danforth's uptake behavior thus constitutes about 19 percent of their activity during that term, but Bradley's challenger-themed activities comprise only 15–16 percent of his agenda. This difference is slight in magnitude, but it does suggest that Graham and Danforth devoted more of their agendas to uptake than did Bradley, even though their raw uptake scores are similar. Because this taps into how much of their activity legislators are willing (or able) to commit to taking up their challengers' themes, it should be taken into account when assessing relative responsiveness.

In measuring uptake, then, we need to consider two different ways of expressing the responsiveness of individual legislators: as a count of those activities related to their challengers' themes and as a proportion of their total activity counts.[1] Each of these measures is particularly appropriate

---

[1] These measures of uptake do not themselves take into account overlap in themes between the winner and his or her challenger. They simply reflect all of a legislator's activity on his or her challenger's priority themes. In analyses that compare across legislators, overlap is included as a control variable.

TABLE 4.1   *Volume of Uptake in Legislative Activity*

	House of Representatives	Senate
Raw counts		
Mean	35	188
Range	1–221	31–499
Percentage of total activity		
Mean	11%	15%
Range	<1–56%	3–31%
Percentage of policy activity		
Mean	14%	19%
Range	<1–73%	4–42%

for use in answering different types of questions about uptake, so both appear in the analyses in later chapters, and I describe in some detail in this chapter the situations in which each measure will be used. The first step of the analysis is to get a sense of average levels of uptake and the amount of variation that exists in legislators' responsiveness. Table 4.1 presents some descriptive statistics on the uptake levels for the House and Senate samples for both of the uptake measures. The first row in the table presents data on the count measure – an aggregation of all of the activities undertaken by a legislator on his or her challenger's priority themes. The second and third rows present these uptake activity counts as a percentage of the overall activity performed by a legislator, using two different denominators, "total activities" and "policy activities." As its name indicates, total activities is a count of all of the introductions, cosponsorships, and floor statements made by each legislator. The problem with using this denominator to calculate uptake rates is that it dampens the true extent of responsiveness because it includes governmental operations measures, which are not uptakeable.[2] Therefore, a theoretically more appropriate denominator is what I call "policy activities," the value obtained when each legislator's governmental operations activities are subtracted from his or her total number of activities. For example, 267 of Graham's 1,097 activities were related to governmental operations, so the adjusted denominator for his uptake is 830. When this new figure is used, the uptake measure consists of the percentage of a legislator's policy-related activity

---

[2] As discussed in Chapter 3, discussions of daily business in the chamber, the scheduling of ceremonies, and the like constitute a significant portion of legislative activity, but are not raised in campaigns and so cannot be the subject of uptake.

that is devoted to the challenger's campaign themes. These percentages are, of course, higher, and they provide a better assessment of the relative amount of attention legislators pay to their challengers' issue priorities.[3] Because of this, in analyses where I present uptake percentages or control for legislators' activity levels, I will use the policy activities measure.

These results, though simple, point to a number of critical findings about uptake. First, they confirm that it is widespread, with all legislators engaging in at least one challenger-themed activity. Moreover, the average legislator devotes about 15–20 percent of his or her policy-relevant activity to uptake, a level of responsiveness that is impressive when we consider all of the other demands on legislators' time – addressing their own campaign issues, participating in activities relevant to their committee and subcommittee assignments, and so on.[4] Across the 101st–105th Congresses, the typical representative faced 1,100 roll call votes, performed 325 activities, attended dozens of committee meetings, and visited the district numerous times. Senators are similarly active; although they cast fewer roll call votes per two-year Congress (700 on average), they participate in more activities (~415). In general, then, these results indicate that many legislators allocate substantial portions of their discretionary activity to uptake.

Second, and equally importantly, regardless of how we calculate uptake, there is substantial variation in levels of responsiveness across legislators. As is illustrated by the ranges, some devote almost none of their legislative energies to pursuing their challengers' themes, while others appear to place these issues at the top of their agendas. Explaining this variation and exploring the extent to which it accords with the predictions of the strategic motivation theory is the goal of the chapters to come. That uptake is both very widespread and quite varied suggests that such an investigation will yield some interesting implications for the nature and dynamics of responsiveness.

Finally, although it is not illustrated in the table, this uptake behavior reflects a *change* in legislators' agendas. Most representatives and senators pay more attention to their challengers' issues in the term after the campaign than in the term before. In the aggregate analyses that follow, I do not measure uptake itself as a change score, for reasons both theoretical

---

[3] By this measure, McConnell remains the lowest-uptake senator in the sample, with 4% of his policy-relevant activity devoted to his challenger's themes. However, the highest-scoring senator is not DeConcini (whose 499 activities constitute 27% of his policy-relevant activity), but John Warner (R-VA), with an uptake rate of 42%.

[4] As a point of comparison, senators generally devote about 25% of their policy-relevant activity to uptake of their own campaign themes.

and practical. To do so would require excluding newly elected legislators and would fail to take into account a variety of other factors that vary across terms, like individual activity levels and the collective attention paid to each issue in Congress. Perhaps more importantly, such an approach assumes that all activity on the challenger's issues in the previous term is nonuptake. However, it is possible that challengers in successive elections could raise the same issue or set of issues (so that those issues would be the focus of uptake for the winning legislator in both terms) or that legislators could begin taking up challengers' issues as the campaign itself is ongoing and continue into the next term. A change score can thus provide only a conservative estimate of the magnitude of uptake. Nonetheless, keeping these caveats in mind, it is useful to get a sense of the degree of change by exploring differences in legislators' pre- and post-campaign attention to their challengers' issues.

Legislators' Post-Campaign Increases in Attentiveness

For this illustration, I investigate the magnitude of the post-campaign increases in attention to the challengers' issues for a subset of the House and Senate samples. It is not possible to study these changes for the entire sample, since I do not have data on the behavior of all of the legislators across at least two terms. This information does exist, however, for bill introduction activity for thirty-four of the fifty-one senators[5] and for all activities for the eighty-two representatives in the larger House sample who appear in at least two consecutive cross sections.[6] To determine whether these legislators paid more attention to issues after their challengers highlighted them, I first measured their uptake of their challengers' priority themes in the second term for which I have data on them. I then investigated their behavior in the term before their most recent challenge to measure the amount of attention that was paid to these issues at that

---

[5] The sample is necessarily limited to those senators who were in at least their second term following the campaign of interest and who completed that term (so that the two terms are comparable). Due to the length of Senate terms, it was not feasible to collect and code data on senators' pre-campaign amendments, cosponsorships, and floor statements, but I did collect these data for bill introductions. Uptake rates are similar across activities, so there is little reason to believe that a larger post-campaign increase would exist for introductions than for other activities.

[6] These representatives do not differ from the sample as a whole in any important way. Their mean uptake rates, vulnerability levels, volume of activity, seniority, ideological extremity, and the like are not appreciably different from the sample means.

point. Change scores are calculated for raw counts and as a percentage of legislators' activity counts. I opted for a conservative approach, calculating these scores using only issues that were unique to the challenger (i.e., not on overlapping issues).

Beginning with the Senate sample, the results indicate that attention to the challengers' issues does indeed increase after the campaign. The average post-campaign increase in introduction activity is about two to three additional bills ($t = 1.88; p < .10$), or an increase of about 3 percent of the share of their total introductions ($t = 1.53; p = .14$). This difference may seem modest at first glance, but if I were to include introductions of resolutions and amendments, cosponsorships, and floor statements, the pre- and post-campaign difference would be considerably larger (i.e., because the average senator performs a total of about 1,250 activities in a term, the average increase in attention to the challenger's issues would likely be about 35–40 activities). In addition, as is shown in Table 4.1, there is substantial variation in uptake rates across senators, with some engaging in very little uptake of their challengers' issues. For these low-uptake senators, we should not expect to see much post-campaign difference in attentiveness. To get a sense of the magnitude of the difference for more responsive senators, I did a median split of the sample by uptake rate and recalculated average change scores for the seventeen senators who fall in the upper half. The post-campaign difference here is about four to five introductions ($t = 2.51; p < .05$), or a 7 percent increase in the proportion of their agendas devoted to these issues ($t = 2.71; p < .05$). And, of course, some senators engaged in considerably more. The top scorers for each year were John Danforth (R-MO) in 1988, whose challenger, Jay Nixon, prioritized Social Security, labor and trade issues, and defense, and who responded by increasing the proportion of his agenda devoted to these issues by 19 percent (from twenty-eight to forty-four introductions); Nancy Kassebaum (R-KS) in 1990, with an increase of 32 percent of her agenda devoted to health (from one to twenty-four introductions), the sole unique issue prioritized by her challenger, Dick Williams; and Bob Graham (D-FL) in 1992, with an increase of 24 percent of his agenda (from twelve to twenty-two introductions) devoted to Grant's priorities of health and the balanced budget.

It is important to keep in mind that even for these high-uptake senators, change scores may not capture the true extent of uptake because they do not take into account the themes of the previous challenger (i.e., in the campaign preceding the campaign being studied as the source of issues for uptake). The results presented in Chapter 3 indicated that election-to-election overlap in themes is fairly rare but it does exist, and it may influence the differences we observe in legislators' pre- and post-campaign attention to their challengers' themes. Because legislators should already be attentive to these issues after the first campaign in which they are prioritized, we may not see a significant increase in activity on those issues after they are raised again in the second campaign. Without data on the themes highlighted in consecutive Senate campaigns, I cannot test this directly.

Fortunately, for the House sample, with data on challengers' priority issues in multiple campaigns *and* legislative activity in multiple terms, it is possible to conduct a more nuanced analysis. I find that, for the full sample, there is, on average, only a small, statistically insignificant increase in post-campaign attention to the challengers' themes (of about one activity). However, after taking into account election-to-election overlap in these themes (by looking only at those legislators whose challengers raised different issues in the first and second campaigns studied), the increase in winners' post-campaign attention is about 4.5 activities ($t = 2.20$; $p < .05$), or about 1.5 percent of their agendas ($t = 1.39$; $p = .17$).[7] And, again, when I limit the analyses to those representatives who fall in the upper half on uptake, the difference increases considerably. For those in the "no election-to-election overlap" group, for instance, the average difference is about ten activities ($t = 2.73$; $p < .05$), or an increase of 3 percent of their total agenda space ($t = 2.71$; $p < .05$). Among the top scorers in the House for each Congress were Wayne Owens (D-UT), who performed nineteen more activities on his challenger's issues in the 102nd Congress than he did in the 101st; Larry LaRocco (D-ID) in the 103rd Congress, who increased his attention to his challenger's themes by twelve activities; Sherrod Brown (D-OH) in the 104th Congress, who showed an increase of thirteen activities; and J. D. Hayworth (R-AZ) and Charlie Norwood (R-GA) in the 105th Congress, who both increased their attentiveness to their challengers' issues by thirty-six activities.

---

[7] Interestingly, if a particular issue is raised by the challengers in a district in two consecutive elections, it receives less subsequent attention from the winner the second time it is raised. This accords with the theory that uptake is induced by the "shock" sent by the challengers' campaigns. If the issues highlighted in these campaigns are not new or different, the signal may be weaker and the representative may be less likely to act on it. Alternatively, he or she may feel that the uptake engaged in on the issue in the previous term was enough to keep it from being a major threat. In fact, the amount of overlap is negatively correlated with challenger vote share (though weakly: $r = -.15$), suggesting either that weaker candidates choose to repeat issues or that repeat issues do not resonate as well with the constituency.

A final point to consider is that legislators do indeed appear to begin the uptake process while their campaigns are ongoing, engaging in immediate responses to their challengers' campaigns. The result is that representatives' "anticipatory" uptake rates in year two of their first term are statistically indistinguishable from their post-campaign uptake rates, even though their year one attention to these issues is significantly lower than their post-campaign levels ($t = 1.63$, $p < .10$).[8] This reduces the magnitude of the pre- and post-campaign differences we observe, but it does not compromise the validity of uptake. To the contrary, because it reflects the fact that legislators increase their attention to their challengers' issues as a result of the challengers' campaigns, it provides further support for my arguments.

Comparing across Legislators

Exploring patterns in raw uptake counts, in percentages of challenger-themed activities, or in change scores provides some crucial insights into the dynamics of uptake. The results thus far have demonstrated that uptake is widespread, that it varies considerably across representatives and senators, and that it reflects a change in legislators' agendas. However, for most comparisons we might want to make, these raw measures of uptake are of limited utility. It may be tempting to conclude that a senator with an uptake level of 20 percent is more responsive than one with 15 percent; that a representative who introduces seven bills on her challengers' issues is more responsive than one who introduces only three; or that a legislator who increases his attention to the challenger's themes by thirty activities is more responsive than one with an increase of twenty-five activities. However, this temptation should be avoided. Up to this point, I have used the terms "uptake" and "responsiveness" more or less interchangeably, but the two are synonymous only under certain circumstances. All other things equal, higher levels of uptake do indicate higher levels of responsiveness, but simply comparing counts or percentages does *not* hold all other things equal. There are a number of other factors that might increase or decrease the number of challenger-themed activities we observe for legislators, but are unrelated to their decisions about whether or not to be attentive to their challengers' issues. In addition

---

[8] This anticipatory uptake cannot be interpreted as uptake of the previous campaign's issues because, as discussed earlier, challengers' issues change from campaign to campaign and because I control for any election-to-election overlap that might occur.

to theoretically interesting differences between individuals that might be related to their willingness or ability to engage in uptake (like their relative electoral vulnerability or seniority or ideological extremity), there is also variance in more mundane factors like the amount of overlap between the incumbent's and challenger's campaign themes, the number and legislative amenability of these themes, the overall popularity of the challenger's issues, and the volume of activity undertaken. Differences in these structural factors can result in differences in uptake levels that have nothing to do with legislators' actual responsiveness.

For example, consider the challenge presented by overlap in campaign themes between winners and challengers. In Chapter 3, I discussed the general problems concerning the validity of the theory of uptake that could occur if we observed consistently high levels of overlap across legislators. Fortunately, the aggregate results showed that overlap, particularly complete overlap, is fairly rare. My conclusion was that overlap does not pose problems for the analysis of uptake so long as it is controlled for when assessing relative responsiveness.[9] To elaborate further on the reason why this control is so important, imagine two legislators whose challengers both discussed the same set of themes. The first winner's campaign agenda was completely different from his challenger's, but the second overlapped with hers on one issue. For which legislator should we expect to see the higher uptake level? It seems likely that the second legislator will engage in more activities on her challenger's themes because one of those themes was also her own. In comparing the responsiveness of these two legislators, we need to control for this, in effect discounting the second legislator's uptake rate to take into account the influence of overlap.

Bob Graham's uptake activity provides a more concrete illustration of this point. His own campaign priorities in the 1992 election were the environment, governmental regulation, and general economic issues. Because challenger Bill Grant's issues were health care, the balanced budget, and general economic issues, they overlapped on the theme of economic issues. As discussed previously, Graham subsequently performed 206 activities on Grant's set of themes, constituting 19 percent of his policy-relevant activity, the same percentage that John Danforth devoted to his challenger's themes. Importantly, though, Danforth and his challenger

---

[9] One option for dealing with this would be to limit the analyses to nonoverlapping issues, as is done in the change score illustration. However, because overlap is only one of several variables that must be controlled for in comparing across legislators, and because there may be an additive effect of both the winner and challenger highlighting an issue, I choose instead to incorporate overlap as a control in the multivariate analyses.

highlighted completely different sets of themes, so his uptake rate of 19 percent may actually reflect *more* responsiveness than Graham's 19 percent.

A similar challenge becomes clear when we consider that those winning legislators whose challengers highlighted multiple issues are likely to exhibit higher uptake percentages than those whose challengers highlighted fewer. The reason for this is simple – there are just more issues for them to take up. This becomes particularly problematic when we try to compare across senators and representatives because, while virtually all senators have three issues identified as "challenger priorities" that they can address in their agendas, most representatives have fewer (for only about a quarter are there more than two issues). It would thus be premature to conclude, based on the percentages presented in Table 4.1, that senators are more responsive than representatives. A representative who devotes 10 percent of her attention to her past challenger's one issue may be equally or more responsive than a senator who devotes 25 percent to his challenger's three issues, but unless we consider the number of challenger themes, we can't reach any firm conclusions.[10]

Finally, there are differences among the issues themselves that make some easier to take up than others. Two that are particularly important are the varying amenability of issues to legislative action and the varying popularity of issues.[11] A legislator whose challenger made education his major campaign theme will have a more difficult time taking up this issue than one who stressed a broader issue like the economy because there are simply more legislative avenues available for expressing interest in the economy than in education. Hence, when we look at the total number of bills and resolutions introduced on these topics in the 101st through 105th Congresses, we see that there are considerably more measures devoted to economic issues (2,301 measures) than to education (1,613 measures). Those legislators whose challengers highlighted issues that score higher on amenability are likely to exhibit higher uptake levels, not because they are more committed to responsiveness but because their task is easier.

Perhaps more importantly, controlling for the total amount of attention the challengers' issues receive in Congress provides further confidence that uptake isolates the response of a particular legislator to his or her

---

[10] In addition, senators' terms are three times as long as representatives' terms, so this needs to be taken into account when comparing raw uptake counts.

[11] These are, of course, somewhat interrelated. When issues increase in popularity or are redefined, it is likely that a number of committees will claim jurisdiction, providing more venues for action on that issue (see Jones, Baumgartner, and Talbert 1993).

TABLE 4.2   *Factors to Consider in Comparing Uptake Levels*

	Graham	Danforth	Bradley
No. of uptake activities	206	204	209
No. of policy activities	1,097	1,100	1,340
% overlap in winner and challenger themes	33%	0%	0%
No. of challenger themes	3	3	3
Collective attention to challenger themes	1,278	2,140	966

challenger. If an issue is high on the national agenda and is receiving a great deal of legislative attention in a particular Congress or term, individual legislators should have a higher probability of acting on that issue, regardless of whether their challengers highlighted it. Subsequent activity on that issue by winning legislators whose challengers *did* prioritize the issue is likely a combination of two factors: a response to the challenger and a response to the overall salience of the issue. Taking into account the total number of introductions made on each challenger's themes, a measure I call "collective attention," allows me to parse this out.

Table 4.2 summarizes these structural controls for Senators Graham, Danforth, and Bradley. These senators all have very similar raw counts of challenger-themed activities, but they differ on a number of factors that could conceivably influence the number of activities they make on their challengers' themes. Given these differences, who should we conclude is the most responsive? Of the three, Bradley is the most active, so his raw count reflects less attentiveness to his challenger's themes than Graham's and Danforth's. However, his challenger's themes score fairly low on collective attention, which should lower his expected uptake count. Danforth's situation is just the opposite – he has a lower total activity count, but his challenger's issues received a higher collective attention count. Graham falls in the middle in terms of volume of activity and collective attention, but, unlike the others, he overlapped with his challenger on one issue, so his uptake count may not reflect as much responsiveness as those with no overlap.

In short, uptake is a complicated phenomenon, and without a multivariate approach, it becomes impossible to compare reliably across legislators. If we want to judge relative responsiveness or isolate the impact of a more theoretically interesting variable like electoral vulnerability on legislators' uptake levels, we must therefore control for variation in all of these structural differences. This point is admittedly simple, but I highlight it because the structural factors that can influence uptake are not always immediately obvious, making the temptation to jump to conclusions on the basis of aggregate percentages very strong. However, we can draw no conclusions until we test the hypotheses using more rigorous analyses, with uptake as the dependent variable and the hypothesized predictors of uptake and the appropriate structural controls used as independent variables. In the analyses of uptake that follow, I use this general approach to ask and answer three basic types of questions. Each of these categories of questions requires slightly different methods of analysis and measures of uptake, so it is useful to briefly outline my strategy for addressing them.

The first category of questions consists of those where the relevant comparison is *between* legislators. These questions focus on identifying the characteristics that distinguish highly responsive legislators from those who are less so. In the next chapter, I explore whether vulnerable or safer legislators exhibit more uptake. In these analyses, raw counts of challenger-themed activities are used as the dependent variable of interest. These counts are best suited to the analysis for a couple of reasons. First, they have a natural and intuitive scale and so are easily interpretable. For instance, I can make conclusions like "For every 2-point increase in vote share, the number of challenger-themed introductions increases by three," which makes the effect more clear and concrete than concluding that the same increase in vote share increases the uptake level by 5 percent. Second, since policy activity counts for legislators are often low (particularly in the House, where, for instance, the average number of introductions is only about thirteen), percentages can be somewhat misleading. A legislator who introduces two bills, one of which is on one of the challenger's themes, has a 50 percent uptake level, the same as that of a legislator who introduces fifty bills, twenty-five of which are devoted to the challenger's themes, and considerably higher than that of a colleague who introduces three bills, one of which is about the challenger's issues. Common sense would lead to the conclusion that the middle legislator is probably the most responsive, but this is not captured by the percentage measure of uptake. By using raw counts of challenger-themed activities and controlling for total activities and the other factors mentioned earlier, I can draw more reliable conclusions about patterns in uptake behavior.

The second category of questions consists of those where the comparison of interest is *within* individual legislators' behavior. These questions ask whether legislators generally engage in more uptake on one activity than another or at particular times in the term rather than at others. In

Chapter 6, I investigate whether variation in uptake levels exists across activities – more specifically, whether or not legislators generally devote more of their introduction activity than their cosponsorship and floor statement activity to uptake. In this type of analysis, uptake percentages rather than raw counts are the appropriate measure since the activities differ in the frequency with which they are undertaken. In addition, for these questions, I design the analysis to assess the average difference within individual legislators' introduction, cosponsorship, and floor statement uptake rather than the difference between the average uptake levels for the chamber on these activities. This difference is subtle, but extremely important. To illustrate why, consider the uptake percentages for the five hypothetical legislators listed below. For the sake of simplicity, assume that these legislators have identical scores on all of the variables we might want to control for, so there is no problem in directly comparing their uptake percentages.

	Introductions Uptake	Cosponsorships Uptake
Legislator 1	25%	45%
Legislator 2	15%	10%
Legislator 3	20%	15%
Legislator 4	15%	10%
Legislator 5	20%	15%
Mean	19%	19%

If we calculate the mean percentage for their introductions and cosponsorships, we reach the conclusion that legislators engage in the same amount of uptake on both. However, this result is driven entirely by legislator 1's unusual behavior (he or she exhibits much more uptake on cosponsorships than on introductions), and so we miss the fact that the other four legislators all devote more attention to their challengers' themes on their introductions. While this approach can tell us whether there is an aggregate difference in uptake on introductions and cosponsorships for the chamber as a whole, it offers little insight into individual legislators' uptake patterns, which are presumably the issue of interest. Thus, any time I am interested in exploring whether legislators' uptake varies across another variable like activity or time, I compare within legislators' behavior.

The final category of questions consists of those that are a hybrid of the first two categories. These questions ask whether legislators who differ on a particular characteristic of interest also differ in their patterns of uptake behavior. In Chapter 6, I explore whether safer and more vulnerable legislators make different choices about where and when to engage in uptake. For this type of question, I am interested in explaining variation in uptake both between subjects (i.e., as it relates to their relative vulnerability) and within subjects' individual behavior (i.e., in their choices of activity and in their timing of this activity within their terms). Imagine that, of the five legislators discussed previously, legislator 1 is vulnerable and the others are all safe. If their uptake behavior reflects the behavior of other safe and vulnerable legislators, this leads us to a very different conclusion – a significant difference exists for all legislators in their uptake behavior on introductions and cosponsorships, but the direction of this effect depends on their individual vulnerability levels. Specifically, vulnerable legislators engage in more uptake on cosponsorships than on introductions, while safer legislators do just the opposite. Only by considering variation both between and within legislators' behavior can we capture this theoretically interesting interaction effect.

Plan of Analysis

The approach I use in testing my hypotheses about uptake takes all of these considerations into account. As such, the design is mixed – the unit of analysis is always the individual legislator, but the methods vary depending on the particular question at hand. In Chapter 5, which develops and tests a model of individual uptake behavior, I seek to explain variation across individuals, so I use a pooled cross-sectional design (i.e., pooling all of the election year cross sections) and multiple regression analyses to identify the factors that influence responsiveness. My goal in Chapter 6 is to identify those activities for which legislators exhibit the most uptake and to explore the dynamics of uptake behavior within a legislative term, so I take a different approach. I use a series of paired t-tests to compare individual legislators' uptake levels across introductions, cosponsorships, and floor statements and across the first and second years of their terms (for House members) and the first, second, and third congresses of their terms (for senators). In Chapter 7, I explore the impact of uptake on legislators' electoral fortunes, measured in a variety of ways. For this analysis, I once again perform a series of cross-sectional multiple regression analyses of all legislators in the sample. Finally, in Chapter 8, I focus on the policy implications of uptake, using an aggregate approach to determine the legacy of challenger-themed bill and resolution introductions in the content of public policy outputs.

TABLE 4.3 *Activity on Health Policy by the House and Senate Samples*

	House	Senate
Campaign themes		
No. of challengers' campaigns	53	13
No. of legislators' campaigns	35	14
Overlap	8	6
Legislative activity		
Mean no. of health-related activities	39	134
Standard deviation	25	71
Range of health-related activities	3–182	32–353

An Illustration: Uptake on Health Policy in the 101st–105th Congresses

In the analyses of uptake that follow, I aggregate across all issues. If a legislator's challenger focused on agriculture, the economy, and immigration, those issues were coded as challenger-themed. Another legislator, whose challenger highlighted Social Security and family issues, would have those issues coded as challenger-themed. This aggregate approach is necessary to compare across legislators, but before moving on to these broader analyses, it is useful to illustrate the basic logic using uptake on a single issue. The plan is to compare the activity of two groups – those legislators whose challengers highlighted the issue and those legislators for whom it was not a challenger-themed issue.

For this illustration, I chose activity on health care in the House and Senate in the 101st through 105th Congresses. Any of the seventeen issue categories could potentially be used for this analysis, but I selected health care because a number of challengers chose it as one of their priority themes (sixty-six in all), and it received a good deal of legislative attention during the time period studied (4,490 introduced bills and resolutions). Consequently, it has enough campaign and legislative activity to make analyses possible, but it is not an outlier in either of these areas.[12]

Across this time period, the members of the House and Senate samples made 23,436 bill, resolution, and amendment introductions and cosponsorships and floor statements about health. Table 4.3 lists some summary

[12] The difficulty in conducting separate analyses for each of the issues is that most receive too little attention, by themselves, to make systematic statistical comparisons possible. The advantages of aggregation are that it yields the N's necessary to conduct systematic statistical analyses and allows me to examine legislators' uptake of all of their challengers' priority issues together.

TABLE 4.4   *Uptake on Health Policy in the*
101st –105th Congresses

	House	Senate
Challenger theme?	3.50*	27.81*
	(2.08)	(15.97)
Legislator theme?	5.16**	7.88
	(2.13)	(16.03)
Collective attention	.01	.09
	(.01)	(.07)
Democrat?	8.06***	17.43
	(1.44)	(13.02)
Policy activities	.15***	.16***
	(.01)	(.02)
Constant	−9.76	−116.12
	(6.29)	(60.93)
N	301	45
Adjusted R^2	.80	.64

Note: Cell entries are OLS regression coefficients with standard
errors in parentheses.
*** $= p < .01$; ** $= p < .05$; * $= p < .10$.

statistics for these legislators. As shown, there is considerable individual
variation in the amount of activity devoted to health policy, ranging from
a handful of activities to hundreds of them. In addition, as expected, senators' activity levels are higher than representatives', so the two groups
should be analyzed separately.

The question of interest is whether those legislators for whom health
was a challenger priority theme paid more attention to this issue than
those for whom it was not. Table 4.4 presents the results of a series
of OLS regression specifications designed to answer this question. The
dependent variable for each model is a count of the number of introductions, cosponsorships, and floor statements made by each legislator
on health during his or her term. The independent variable of interest is
a dummy called "challenger theme," which was coded 1 if health was
a priority theme for the legislator's challenger and 0 otherwise. To the
extent that the coefficient on this variable is positive and large, it suggests
that having health as a challenger theme increases the amount of attention legislators pay to it in their activity in office. I include a number of
controls, including the legislator's party affiliation (since it is likely that
Democrats paid more attention to health than Republicans), the number
of themes highlighted by the challenger, and, because we are interested

in *relative* responsiveness, the total number of policy-relevant activities undertaken by the legislator. I also include a dummy variable indicating whether health was one of the legislator's own campaign themes (coded 1 if health was one of the winner's priority themes and 0 otherwise). This is important to include for two reasons. First, all other things being equal, those legislators for whom health was a priority theme should be more likely to act on it in office. Second, it serves as a control for those situations in which both the challenger and the legislator had health as a priority theme. Including this variable in the specification thus allows me to identify the independent impact of challengers' campaigns on winners' attentiveness to health policy. Finally, because congressional attention to health varied across the time period studied here, I include a "collective attention" measure – the total number of bills and resolutions introduced on health during each legislator's term.

The model for the House includes the 301 legislators for whom I have information on both their own campaign themes and their challengers' themes.[13] The Senate sample is limited to those senators who completed the term of interest, yielding an N of forty-five. The results indicate that the specifications do a good job of explaining individual variation in the volume of health activity, with between 64 and 80 percent of the variation explained by the variables included in the analysis. I also find that the control variables are all generally in the expected direction. The total number of policy-relevant activities engaged in by legislators is a significant predictor of their attention to health, with legislators who were more active in general also more active on health care in particular. The results also confirm that Democratic representatives were more active on health policy than Republicans, and that representatives who highlighted health in their own campaigns were more active on that issue than those who did not.

Of course, the variable of particular interest is the challenger theme dummy. As shown, the coefficient on this variable for both the House and Senate is positive and (marginally) significant. As such, legislators for whom health was a challenger priority theme engaged in more health-related activities than their colleagues for whom this issue was not a challenger priority, even after controlling for legislators' own attention

---

[13] For only 301 of the 422 representatives did the CQ summaries provide information about the legislator's own campaign themes. The 121 for which this information was not available are omitted from the analysis since I control for legislators' own attention to health.

to the issue and its overall popularity in Congress that term. Moreover, this effect can be large in magnitude. House winners whose challengers highlighted health made about 3.5 more introductions, cosponsorships, and floor statements on this issue in their two-year terms, and Senate winners for whom health was an uptakeable issue performed about 28 more health activities across their six-year terms.

In sum, these results provide compelling initial evidence of the uptake effect, particularly when we consider that we have not controlled for any other individual-level factors that might influence uptake levels (e.g., electoral vulnerability, seniority, ideological extremity, district characteristics) and that most of the legislators for whom health was a challenger priority theme also had other challenger priority themes on which they could choose to be active. If similar patterns hold for these other activities and we aggregate their uptake across all of their challengers' themes, the effect should become even more pronounced.

The goal of the chapters to come is to rigorously address these possibilities, going beyond establishing the existence of uptake on a single issue to explore patterns of responsiveness across individuals, across activities, across time, and across institutions. Chapter 5 begins this process by developing and testing a model of individual variation in uptake in both the House and Senate that focuses, in particular, on the role of electoral vulnerability. Determining whether or not vulnerability explains the observed variation in individual responsiveness and, if so, the direction of this effect can both increase our understanding of the dynamics of legislative responsiveness and offer some intriguing normative implications about the ways in which elections do (or do not) promote accountability on the part of legislators.

5

Who Responds?

Explaining Individual Variation in Uptake

The results presented in the previous chapter indicate that uptake is widespread among legislators, with nearly every representative and senator engaging in at least some activity related to their challengers' themes from the last campaign. However, levels of responsiveness vary considerably across individuals. Some legislators devote substantial amounts of their legislative activity to uptake, while others are only rarely attentive to their challengers' issues. Why is this the case? More specifically, how do highly responsive legislators differ from their less responsive colleagues? These questions are central to the theory developed here, and their answers offer insight into normative and practical arguments about improving the quality of legislative responsiveness. As such, the analyses in this chapter are devoted to addressing them.

The basic puzzle is this: if all legislators desire reelection and uptake is a reelection-promoting activity (a hypothesis that is addressed in detail in Chapter 7), then why don't all legislators engage in it at high rates? The competing hypotheses about the relationship between electoral vulnerability and uptake are both motivated by this puzzle, and each provides a very different explanation for variation in responsiveness. These differences are best illustrated by a brief review of each of the hypotheses, focusing in particular on the theoretical arguments underlying their predictions.

The inoculation hypothesis provides the simplest account, which explains much of its appeal. It assumes that, given the choice, legislators would prefer to not engage in uptake and instead to devote their time and resources to other issues of more interest. After all, there is probably a reason they neglected their challengers' issues in the past. However, the more concerned they are about their electoral prospects, the more they will prioritize reelection-enhancing activities like uptake. The prediction, then, is that the most vulnerable legislators will exhibit the highest levels of responsiveness in the hope of securing their reelection. Their safer colleagues will recognize that, with their return to office not in jeopardy, they can afford to abstain from uptake. Overall, we should expect to see a positive relationship between electoral vulnerability and uptake – the more vulnerable the legislator, the more responsive he or she should be.

The electoral selection hypothesis predicts just the opposite: that the safest legislators will engage in the most uptake and the most vulnerable the least, resulting in a negative relationship between vulnerability and responsiveness. The rationale behind this expectation is that legislators' current levels of electoral security are manifestations of their past good (or bad) behavior. Thus, those legislators who are safe are in this situation, at least in part, because they have been responsive in the past. This relative security does not lead them to abandon uptake, though. Instead, because legislators are exceedingly cautious in their assessments of their own safety, once they happen upon a strategy like uptake that contributes to their success, they will stick with it, even after it may no longer be needed.[1] Those who engage in uptake will be rewarded electorally and will become safer over time, while those who, for whatever reason, choose not to be responsive in this way will maintain their vulnerability. From a cross-sectional perspective, we will see high levels of responsiveness corresponding to high levels of safety.

What is not immediately obvious from this account is why vulnerable legislators, those who most need to promote their reelection, would not come to see that uptake could help them and so increase their levels. Undoubtedly, some would reach this conclusion; for example, a newly elected legislator who starts his or her career in a relatively vulnerable situation might decide to adopt an uptake strategy in an effort to increase his or her electoral security. However, there are numerous reasons to expect that others would persist in consistently low levels of responsiveness across time. Perhaps some legislators are just less skilled than others – less able to identify salient issues, less able to understand

---

[1] Hershey (1984) notes that legislators need not understand the exact mechanism by which a particular behavior helps them to be prompted to continue it. They simply must believe that their approach as a whole has paid off for them, and so maintain it in the next campaign or next term in office.

the benefits of focusing their attention on these issues, and less able to act in a way that promotes their goals. These less-skilled legislators may remain vulnerable because they do not recognize the advantages of engaging in uptake. Alternatively, some vulnerable legislators may understand the potential benefits of responsiveness, but their vulnerability may make them too risk-averse to attempt it, particularly if they are concerned about alienating their bases. Uptake is certainly not the only behavior that can be used to promote reelection. Legislators may also benefit from fulfilling their own campaign promises, engaging in casework, and taking action on new issues that hit the agenda (e.g., in the wake of the September 11 attacks, becoming active on issues surrounding terrorism and homeland security). Of these activities, uptake may have a potentially high payoff, but it is also relatively risky. If legislators choose the right pieces of legislation to pursue and can effectively claim credit, then it can help them, but if they fail to make this connection, attempts at uptake may result in a wasted use of time and resources. The more electorally secure the legislator, the more he or she can afford such a mistake, and so the more likely it may be that the amount of risk involved in uptake will be seen as acceptable. Finally, there may exist a small group of legislators who are just not willing to engage in the compromise necessary to address their challengers' issues, and so may knowingly risk their electoral safety in the interest of principle.

The inoculation and electoral selection hypotheses thus have starkly different implications for our understanding of the dynamics between vulnerability and responsiveness. The first supports the conventional wisdom that safety leads to a lack of accountability, while the second suggests that the causal relationships between safety and responsiveness may be more complicated than is generally assumed. As such, it is crucial to determine where the empirical evidence lies, exploring how vulnerability and other factors shape legislators' responsiveness.

Electoral Vulnerability and Uptake

I begin by examining the bivariate relationship between legislators' electoral vulnerability and their levels of uptake, with the goal of determining how strongly and in what direction the two are related. In this and the analyses to follow, legislators' vulnerability is measured as their challengers' percentage of the two-party vote share in the most recent election. It varies substantially across legislators, from 15 percent to 50 percent for representatives and from 17 percent to 50 percent for senators, with higher

TABLE 5.1   *Correlations between Electoral Vulnerability and Uptake*

Uptake Measure	House	Senate
Count of challenger-themed activities	.04	−.08
	(.48)	(.58)
Percentage of policy activities	.12	−.16
	(.01)	(.28)
Percentage of total activities	.12	−.14
	(.01)	(.32)
Change in no. of activities on challenger themes	.02	−.26
	(.87)	(.13)
Change in percentage of activities on challenger themes	.09	−.20
	(.43)	(.25)

Note: Cell entries are Pearson correlation coefficients with *p* values in parentheses.

percentages reflecting greater vulnerability.[2] Table 5.1 presents the results of a series of correlations between vulnerability and uptake, which are assessed using the measures described in Chapter 4 – as a count of legislators' challenger-themed activities, as a percentage of their policy-relevant activities, as a percentage of their total activities, and, for the legislators for whom information on previous activity is available, as both raw and percentage change scores.

These results are admittedly very preliminary, but they suggest several important points for further investigation. First, there is evidence of a relationship between legislators' vulnerability and their responsiveness, but, at the bivariate level at least, this association is fairly weak. Second, and perhaps more interestingly, vulnerability appears to impact representatives' and senators' behavior differently. In the House, there is a consistently positive relationship between vulnerability and uptake (so that the most vulnerable demonstrate the most responsiveness), while, in the Senate, the relationship between the two is consistently negative, with the safest exhibiting the most uptake.

More rigorous analyses are necessary to confirm whether or not these intriguing findings are robust. Is it in fact the case that electoral safety

---

[2] It is important to note that the vulnerability range seen in the samples differs for the House and the Senate. While the entire possible range of vulnerabilities can be observed in the Senate sample (where an unopposed race is exceedingly rare), the House sample is necessarily truncated. In any election year, there are a number of representatives who run unopposed, but they cannot be included in the analysis of uptake because there are no campaign issues for them to take up.

is associated with a lack of responsiveness in the House but increased responsiveness in the Senate? Or are these relationships spurious, the result, perhaps, of other factors that are associated with both responsiveness and vulnerability? The OLS regression analyses that follow are intended to answer this question, asking whether, after the appropriate controls are included, there is a statistically significant and substantively important relationship between legislators' vote shares and their uptake levels.

The dependent variable in every model in this chapter is a measure of individual uptake – a count of the number of activities engaged in by each legislator on his or her challenger's priority issues from the last campaign.[3] All types of activities (introductions, cosponsorships, and floor statements) are weighted equally in these counts so that the effect for the more abundant cosponsorships doesn't swamp the others.[4] The resulting uptake counts range from 1 to 268 activities for representatives and from 30 to 496 activities for senators.

The independent variables in the analyses include vulnerability and a series of "structural control variables," summarized in Table 5.2. These controls are necessary because, as discussed at length in Chapter 4, there are a variety of factors that may influence the number of challenger-themed activities we observe for a given legislator, but are outside his or her control and so need to be taken into account when assessing relative responsiveness. Because legislators' overall uptake levels should be influenced both by these structural conditions and by their decisions to be responsive (or not), we need to control for the former to gain insight into the latter. For example, the more priority issues highlighted by the challenger in the campaign, the more issues there are for the winner to take up. As such, all other things being equal, a winner whose challenger highlighted multiple issues will probably have a higher uptake level than one whose challenger highlighted a single issue. Similarly, the greater the amount of overlap there is between the challenger's and winner's priorities,

---

[3] Given that the dependent variable is a count, it might seem that event count models would be a more appropriate procedure than the OLS models I use. However, the counts are generally high enough that OLS provides an efficient and consistent estimator (Long 1997). The analyses were also performed using negative binomial regression, with no difference in results. Therefore, for ease and consistency of presentation, I report the OLS results.

[4] These weighted uptake counts were constructed by calculating an uptake percentage for each legislator for each category of activity, averaging these three percentages, and multiplying this average uptake percentage by the total number of policy-relevant activities performed.

TABLE 5.2   *Summary of Structural Control Variables*

Variable	Measured As:	Range	Median
No. of issues	No. of priority issues highlighted in the challenger's campaign	1–4 (H) 1–3 (S)	2 (H) 3 (S)
Overlap	% challenger's themes that were also a priority theme for the winning legislator	0–100% (H) 0–100% (S)	33% (H) 33% (S)
Policy activities	No. of all introductions, cosponsorships, and floor statements made by each legislator on nongovernmental operations matters	63–920 (H) 218–1818 (S)	229 (H) 878 (S)
Collective attention	No. of bills and resolutions introduced by all legislators on a particular challenger's priority themes	53–2310 (H) 416–2441 (S)	555 (H) 1238 (S)

the more uptake we should expect to see. I also take into account the total volume of policy-relevant activities undertaken by legislators, since those who are more active should perform a greater number of challenger-themed activities, even if their rates of uptake do not differ from those of their less active peers.

Finally, I include the amount of collective attention paid to each legislator's challenger's themes. As described previously, this control performs two important functions. First, since some issues are more amenable to legislative action than others, variation in the amenability of challengers' issues should be related to variation in legislators' uptake rates. Perhaps more importantly, though, controlling for the overall popularity of the challenger's issues allows me to account for the fact that legislators are more likely to act on issues that are high on the national agenda, even without their challengers highlighting them. By including this measure, I can isolate the impact of the challengers' campaigns themselves on the winners' agendas in office.

The results presented in Table 5.3 thus reflect the impact of legislators' vulnerability and their structural situations on their uptake levels.[5] Several important points can be taken from these findings. First, and most simply, they validate the inclusion of the control variables discussed previously. Any condition that makes uptake easier for a legislator increases

[5] Because the design is a pooled cross section, I also include a series of dummy variables representing each of the five cross sections for the House sample and each of the three for the Senate sample to account for any across-time differences that may exist.

TABLE 5.3 *Impact of Electoral Vulnerability on Uptake*

	House	Senate
Vulnerability	.87**	−2.43**
	(.36)	(1.01)
No. of issues	2.95	44.35**
	(2.81)	(20.77)
Collective attention	.038***	.067***
	(.006)	(.018)
Overlap	.025	.92***
	(.044)	(.28)
Policy activities	.19***	.20***
	(.013)	(.024)
1988 election	−2.19	−.12
	(5.93)	(21.85)
1990 election	1.69	2.40
	(5.22)	(18.80)
1992 election	−3.62	—
	(5.09)	
1994 election	6.17	—
	(4.85)	
Constant	−80.03	−148.43
	(16.69)	(65.93)
N	301	51
Adjusted R^2	.62	.75

Note: Cell entries are unstandardized OLS regression coefficients with standard errors in parentheses. The dependent variable is a weighted count of individual senators' and representatives' uptake activities.
*** = $p < .01$; ** = $p < .05$; * = $p < .10$.

the amount we observe. For both representatives and senators, the collective attention devoted to their challengers' issues and their own activity levels are important predictors of the amount of uptake they exhibit. In addition, senators' levels of responsiveness are influenced by the number of priority themes highlighted by their challengers and by the amount of overlap between their themes and their challengers' themes. Once these structural factors are taken into account, the models do a good job of explaining variation in responsiveness (as is evidenced by the adjusted R^2 values) and enable us to obtain a more accurate assessment of the impact of more theoretically interesting variables like vulnerability.

By far the most important finding from this analysis is that vulnerability exerts a significant impact on legislators' uptake levels. Uncovering a relationship between vulnerability and legislative behavior is itself a contribution, as many other empirical studies of the electoral connection have failed to find supporting evidence for this often hypothesized linkage. These results support my prediction that vulnerability will exert a stronger influence on the *content* of legislators' behavior than on the sheer volume of this activity, as well as Arnold's (1990) intuition that "The power of the electoral connection may actually be greater at earlier stages of decision-making, when legislators are deciding what problems to pursue or which alternatives to consider, rather than at the final stages, when legislators are voting on particular amendments or on a bill's final passage" (269).

Even more interesting is the confirmation of the difference in the direction of the relationship for representatives and senators, supporting the predictions of the inoculation hypothesis in the House, where vulnerability is positively associated with responsiveness, and those of the electoral selection hypothesis in the Senate, where it is negatively related. Moreover, as indicated by the size of the coefficients on vulnerability, this effect is more than just a statistical regularity – it also has a substantively important impact on legislative behavior. A 1-point increase in vulnerability (i.e., the difference between the challenger receiving 44 percent and 45 percent of the vote) is associated with an increase of about 1 challenger-themed activity for House members and a decrease of about 2.5 activities for senators.

A sense of the overall magnitude of the vulnerability effect (how much the uptake activity of the most vulnerable legislators differs from that of their safest peers) can be obtained by using the coefficients from the regression analyses to estimate "predicted uptake counts" for representatives and senators across the vulnerability spectrum, from 15 percent to 50 percent challenger vote share. These counts are calculated by holding all of the structural control variables at their means, multiplying them by their coefficients, summing them, and then adding to this sum the constant from the specification and the product of challenger vote share times the coefficient on vote share for different levels of vulnerability.

Figure 5.1 illustrates these relationships, plotting the predicted counts against vulnerability. As shown, the impact is substantial. All other things being equal, the safest House members are expected to engage in about fifteen uptake activities in a two-year term, while their most vulnerable colleagues should participate in about forty-six activities, over three times as many. For the Senate, the safest members are expected to introduce, cosponsor, and speak about close to 250 challenger-themed

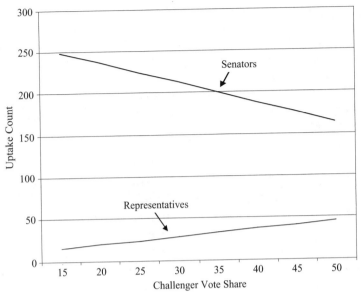

FIGURE 5.1   Predicted Uptake Counts by Vulnerability.

measures across their six-year terms, while their most vulnerable colleagues undertake only about two-thirds as many (approximately 165 activities). These differences in individual uptake activity can have a large influence on the content of overall legislative activity and, hence, on the extent of institutional responsiveness to campaigns.[6]

The Impact of Individual and Constituency Characteristics on Uptake

Electoral vulnerability therefore appears to have a considerable impact on levels of responsiveness and, intriguingly, seems to influence representatives and senators differently. Before investigating why this difference occurs, it is necessary to confirm once again that the vulnerability effect is real and not an artifact of other explanatory variables that are not included in the model. After all, legislators differ in a myriad of ways that have yet to be examined. To name just a few, they have different party affiliations, different ideological leanings, different histories in office, and different sorts of constituencies to represent. If these characteristics are

---

[6] The magnitude of this effect is explored in more detail in Chapter 8.

also associated with variation in vulnerability, then their inclusion in the model may lessen or even erase the vulnerability effect. In addition, apart from any impact they may have on vulnerability, these variables are themselves potentially interesting in understanding the dynamics of uptake.

The characteristics of individual legislators that are most important to consider are those that relate to their ability or willingness to engage in uptake. For instance, Fenno argues that responsiveness is something that is learned (or not) over time (1996, 10–11). If this is the case, we may see senior legislators exhibiting more uptake than their junior colleagues. Similarly, legislators' ideology may matter if those with more extreme ideological leanings are less willing to engage in the compromise necessary to take up their challengers' issues, and so choose to risk their electoral security in the interest of remaining true to their ideological principles. The party affiliation of legislators could also influence uptake levels if one party's members are more able or willing to respond.

Characteristics of the legislators' home districts or states may also impact responsiveness. We might expect that relatively heterogeneous constituencies would be more difficult to represent than those that are more homogeneous, so legislators from these areas would have, on average, lower uptake levels. Thus, characteristics like the racial diversity of the constituency and, in the case of the Senate, the size of the population itself may be related to uptake rates. In addition, some legislators may face more demanding constituencies or a larger pool of potentially strong challengers, which may increase their attention to uptake. This could occur, for instance, for those from relatively wealthy districts or states.

To investigate these potential influences on uptake, I replicated the regression specifications presented in Table 5.3, including vulnerability and the series of structural control variables,[7] and added indicators of members' seniority (as measured by their number of years in office), their ideological extremity (measured as the absolute value of their Poole-Rosenthal common-space NOMINATE scores, so that higher scores equal more extreme ideological leanings, both liberal and conservative), the racial diversity of their constituencies (as measured by the district's or state's majority ethnic group's percentage of the population), the relative wealth of the district or state (its median income in dollars), and, for the Senate, the size of the population in thousands. The results for the new specifications are presented in Table 5.4.

---

[7] The dummy variables for the different cross sections were included in these specifications but, in the interest of saving space, I do not report these coefficients.

TABLE 5.4 *Impact of Individual and Constituency Characteristics on Uptake*

	House	Senate
Challenger vote share	.91**	−2.04**
	(.37)	(.98)
No. of issues	3.14	59.49***
	(2.86)	(20.63)
Collective attention	.037***	.061***
	(.006)	(.019)
Overlap	.026	1.07***
	(.045)	(.27)
Policy activities	.19***	.20***
	(.014)	(.026)
Democrat?	−3.32	−16.83
	(3.90)	(16.60)
Seniority	−.015	1.10
	(.26)	(1.09)
Ideological extremity	−1.90	−108.39**
	(12.81)	(49.34)
Racial diversity	−.15	−1.76
	(.18)	(1.27)
Median income	−.0001	.007*
	(.000)	(.004)
Population	—	−.040
		(.18)
Constant	−64.07	−160.06
	(22.77)	(125.36)
N	301	51
Adjusted R^2	.62	.78

Note: Cell entries are unstandardized OLS regression coefficients with standard errors in parentheses. The dependent variable is a weighted count of individual senators' and representatives' uptake activities.
*** = $p < .01$; ** = $p < .05$; * = $p < .10$.

These findings demonstrate that including personal and constituency-level variables in the analysis has very little impact on the vulnerability effect. For the House, it increases by a small amount, and for the Senate, it decreases a bit, but in both cases it remains basically unchanged. It is not the case, then, that vulnerability is serving as a proxy for other characteristics of legislators or their constituencies in these models. The results also indicate that few of the contextual variables exert significant independent effects on uptake. For senators, ideological extremity and state median income both have the expected influence. All other things being equal, the more ideologically extreme a senator, the less likely he or she is to engage in uptake, and the richer the state, the more responsive the senator. However, other factors like seniority and party have no discernible impact on their uptake behavior. The same is true for representatives, for whom, in fact, none of the added contextual variables influences responsiveness. Importantly, this does not mean that these factors have no impact on legislative activity as it is more broadly conceived. In fact, seniority, party, and district/state wealth have a clear relationship with the overall *volume* of activity undertaken by legislators, with Democrats engaging in more activities than Republicans, senior members exhibiting higher activity levels than their more junior colleagues, and representatives from wealthier constituencies demonstrating more activity than their peers from less well-to-do districts. In investigating uptake, however, I purposely control for any individual differences in the volume of activity undertaken since it is the relative content of this activity that is of interest, not the total amount.

Exploring House–Senate Differences

The general conclusion to be drawn from these analyses is that vulnerability clearly matters in explaining why some legislators are more responsive than others. However, it seems that the "competing" hypotheses about the direction of this effect may not actually be competing. Instead, the patterns in the House of Representatives are consistent with the predictions of the inoculation hypothesis, and those in the Senate support the expectations of the electoral selection hypothesis. While this result certainly presents somewhat of a puzzle, addressing it, as I will demonstrate, yields considerable insight into the dynamics of responsiveness in the two chambers.

There are at least two different paths one could take in attempting to reconcile, or at least explain, this difference. The first is substantive – to think more theoretically about vulnerability and what it means to legislators in the two chambers. Vulnerability is, in part, a subjective phenomenon. If representatives with a given vote share *feel* more or less vulnerable than senators with the same election margins, then we might expect to see the two groups behave differently when it comes to reelection-promoting activities like uptake. Most studies of legislative behavior focus on only one chamber, for reasons theoretical, methodological, and practical. It may be that differences of the type identified previously are not uncommon and instead reflect variation in the particulars of the electoral connection in the House and Senate that are missed when analyses are limited to one chamber or the other.

The second path to exploring this difference is more methodological in nature but is related to the first. The approach I've used thus far to explaining individual variation in uptake has assumed that the relationship between vulnerability and responsiveness is linear, that is, as one rises or falls, the other follows in a proportional fashion. It is possible, however, that the relationship between the two is more complicated and may even differ between the House and Senate, driven, perhaps, by differences in what it means to be safe or vulnerable. If this is the case, it could provide an explanation for the differences we observe in the direction of the regression coefficients on vulnerability in the two chambers.

My strategy for disentangling this puzzle will be to explore both paths, beginning with the substantive question raised previously. Specifically, is there reason to believe that representatives and senators perceive their electoral situations differently? Because we can't get into legislators' minds, it is not possible to answer this question directly. Nonetheless, prior research on congressional elections points to a number of factors that should lead us to conclude that senators, as a group, probably feel more vulnerable than representatives. Compared to their colleagues in the House, they are much more likely to face opposition in their reelection bids (in both the primary and general elections), tend to attract higher-quality challengers in those races, and more frequently have won at least one election by only a very slim margin. For these reasons, Burden and Kimball (2002) argue that, compared to representatives, "members of the Senate have less reason to feel safe" (129). Their feelings of insecurity may be further exacerbated by the lesser frequency of elections in the Senate, which give them fewer points of reference to determine whether or not their vote shares are stable. A representative who has been in office for twelve years and has earned about 65 percent of the vote in each reelection attempt has seen his or her vote share hold for that particular constituency across five elections. A senator in office for a similar amount of time has seen this happen only once and may therefore worry more about its stability. The end result may be that even those senators who are objectively safe view their positions as more tenuous than do House members with similar vote shares. As such, while some representatives may feel very safe – those, for example, who have been in office a long time, who represent a homogeneous district, and who only rarely face serious opposition – it is unlikely that any senators view their situation this way.

If we imagine breaking legislators into groups based on their feelings of vulnerability, we might therefore envision two categories of senators: those who are relatively vulnerable and those who are relatively safe. In the House, there might be *three* categories – the relatively vulnerables, the relatively safes, and an additional group who feel very safe, perhaps to the point where they are no longer concerned about their reelection prospects. The possible existence of three categories of legislators in the House complicates the predictions about vulnerability and uptake, since both the inoculation and electoral selection hypotheses assume two basic groups. The inoculation hypothesis is built upon the assumption that legislators are either vulnerable or safe and that vulnerable legislators engage in reelection-promoting activities because they need to and safe ones do not because they don't. The electoral selection hypothesis assumes that all legislators feel somewhat vulnerable, so that none fall into the third very safe category. The negative vulnerability effect for the Senate sample thus accords well with this account.

However, the positive coefficient on vulnerability we observe in the House is consistent with two different accounts. If a positive relationship between vulnerability and uptake holds for all three groups, this would suggest support for the inoculation hypothesis. It is also possible that the relationship is nonmonotonic, and that the difference in the direction of the vulnerability effect in the House and Senate is driven by the behavior of the very safe group of representatives. Relatively vulnerable and relatively safe representatives may behave like their Senate counterparts, with responsiveness decreasing as vulnerability increases. However, once a certain level of safety is reached, we may see a drop-off in responsiveness, so that the real relationship between vulnerability and uptake is not linear, but instead looks something like an inverted U. This pattern would be consistent with a merging of the insights of the inoculation and electoral selection hypotheses. The conclusion would be that some feeling of vulnerability is necessary to motivate uptake (explaining the lower levels for the very safest representatives) but that, as in the Senate, those who are relatively safe demonstrate more responsiveness than their most vulnerable peers.

Rather than adopting complicated statistical procedures to explore these possibilities, it is best to begin more simply with a graphical depiction of the relationship between vulnerability and uptake for representatives and senators. Figures 5.2 and 5.3 are scatterplots that illustrate the findings from the regression analyses discussed earlier. Each legislator's vulnerability (i.e., the challenger's vote share) was plotted against his or

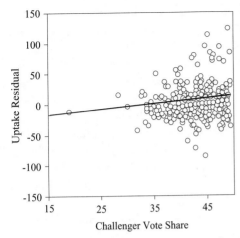

FIGURE 5.2 Vulnerability and Uptake in the U.S. House.

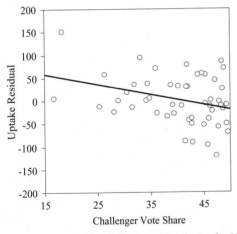

FIGURE 5.3 Vulnerability and Uptake in the U.S. Senate.

her uptake score, resulting in an overall positive relationship between vulnerability and uptake in the House and an overall negative relationship between the two in the Senate.

The measure of uptake in these figures is an "uptake residual score," which is simply another way of indicating relative uptake after controlling for structural factors. To calculate these scores, I first reran the OLS specifications from Table 5.3, omitting the vulnerability variable. By including only the structural variables, I can estimate the predicted uptake rates for each legislator based on his or her activity level, the number of challenger themes available to take up, the collective attention to these themes, the amount of overlap between his or her own themes and the challenger's themes, and the election year in which he or she ran. The residuals from this specification thus reflect the differences between legislators' actual uptake and their predicted uptake based on their structural situations. For example, a senator who scored at the median on all of the structural variables would have a predicted uptake count of 175 activities. If, in reality, this senator engaged in more than 175 challenger-themed activities, his or her residual score would be positive and, if fewer were undertaken, the residual score would be negative. By examining the relationship between legislators' residual scores and their challengers' vote shares, I can thus assess the extent to which their vulnerability is associated with deviations from their predicted uptake counts.

As expected, approaching the data in this way lends insight into the overall patterns of uptake in the House and Senate that a simple comparison of regression coefficients can lead us to miss. First, there appears to be more variation in the uptake residuals for the Senate than for the House, which may help to explain why the Senate models account for variation in uptake better than the House models (as reflected by the higher R^2 values for the Senate in Tables 5.3 and 5.4). Second, for both chambers, but particularly for the House, there is considerable heteroscedasticity, with much more variation in responsiveness for vulnerable members than for safer ones. This latter point is particularly important for putting into context the differences in patterns we observe for senators and representatives. As such, rather than treating it as a statistical problem to be controlled away, it is useful to think about it more theoretically, asking what might cause this pattern and what implications it has for our conclusions about the relationship between vulnerability and responsiveness.

Causes of Heteroscedasticity

The insights about vulnerability underlying the electoral selection hypothesis provide one possible explanation for the greater variation in the uptake levels of vulnerable legislators. To restate the general argument, we can explain legislators' current electoral vulnerability by their behavior in previous terms. Those who were highly responsive should be fairly safe and those who were less so should be more vulnerable. What, though, of the most junior legislators, those with little or no history in office? Many of these newly elected legislators, who have yet to enjoy any incumbency advantage that may exist, win their races by slim margins and so fall into the vulnerable group. Over time, some of them will choose to actively engage in strategies like uptake to make themselves safer, while others will, for one reason or another, demonstrate low levels of responsiveness and maintain their initial vulnerability. Because of the existence of these two types in the group of legislators who are both vulnerable and junior, we should expect to see considerable variation in their uptake levels.

We can explore this possibility by comparing uptake patterns when the samples are broken out by seniority and vulnerability.[8] The result is four groups of legislators – those who are vulnerable and junior, those who are vulnerable and senior, those who are relatively safe and junior, and those who are relatively safe and senior. If the previous account is valid, the mean uptake levels for each group (as a percentage of policy-relevant activity) and the standard deviations associated with these means should display two patterns. First, there should be more variation around the mean for vulnerable junior legislators than for vulnerable senior legislators, as well as for safer legislators, both junior and senior. Second, compared to their more senior colleagues, vulnerable junior members should demonstrate higher levels of uptake.[9] Table 5.5 presents the results of such an analysis and, as shown, they conform to these predictions. Of the four groups, vulnerable junior members have the highest standard deviations and, compared to those who are senior and vulnerable, demonstrate more uptake. Thus, there is some evidence that an interaction between seniority and vulnerability leads to the considerable variation we observe in the uptake behavior of vulnerable members.

Impact of Heteroscedasticity

Regardless of the cause of this variation, its effect is the same: to make the relationship between vulnerability and uptake nonlinear. Uptake appears to increase with vulnerability for safer representatives and decrease with

---

[8] For this analysis, junior legislators are those senators who are starting their first or second terms (i.e., six or fewer years in office) and those representatives who are beginning their first, second, or third terms (i.e., four or fewer years in office). The most vulnerable legislators are those who fall into the top quartile of challenger vote share in the House (~47 percent). The basic patterns hold when other coding rules are applied.

[9] This difference is likely to be modest because the vulnerable junior group should, as indicated earlier, include both high- and low-uptake individuals.

TABLE 5.5   *Uptake Patterns by Seniority and Vulnerability*

	House	Senate
Vulnerable members		
Junior	16%	19%
	(14%)	(11%)
Senior	12%	17%
	(8%)	(6%)
Safer members		
Junior	14%	18%
	(11%)	(7%)
Senior	14%	22%
	(12%)	(7%)

Note: Cell entries are the mean uptake levels for each group with standard deviations in parentheses.

vulnerability for safer senators but level off for more vulnerable legislators, a pattern that is illustrated in Figures 5.4a and 5.4b. These figures show, for the House and Senate samples, the relationship between uptake residuals and challenger vote share for those legislators who fall in the broader vulnerable range (i.e., 40–50 percent challenger vote share). When compared to the patterns for all legislators presented in Figures 5.2 and 5.3, it becomes clear that across this range, the slope of the regression line flattens significantly, nearly approaching zero.[10] This means that, for vulnerable legislators, there is no systematic association between vote shares and responsiveness. Those with challenger vote shares of 40 percent are, on average, no more or less responsive than those whose challengers received 45 percent or 50 percent of the vote.

The broader impact of this pattern (or lack thereof) is that the coefficients for the vulnerability effect in the regression analyses are driven largely by the behavior of the nonvulnerables – those legislators with challenger vote shares of less than 40 percent. In the Senate sample, these legislators are generally more responsive than their more vulnerable colleagues, while in the House sample, they are less so. The important question to investigate is what the shape of the relationship between vulnerability and uptake looks like for these safer legislators, particularly in the House of Representatives. If there is a linear association between

---

[10] For the House, the correlation between challenger vote share and uptake for vulnerable members is .05 ($p = .40$). For the Senate, it is $-.10$ ($p = .59$).

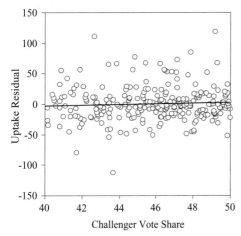

FIGURE 5.4a Relationship between Vulnerability and Uptake for Vulnerable Representatives.

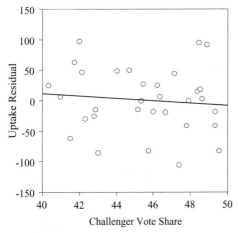

FIGURE 5.4b Relationship between Vulnerability and Uptake for Vulnerable Senators.

vulnerability and uptake for both relatively safe and very safe legislators, the relationship would look something like that pictured in Figure 5.5. This figure reflects both the zero slope of the regression line across the vulnerable range in both chambers and the overall negative relationship between vulnerability and uptake for relatively safe senators and

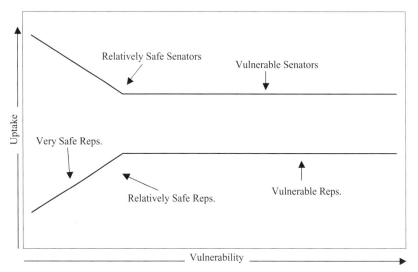

FIGURE 5.5   Relationship between Vulnerability and Uptake – Hypothesis 1.

the positive relationship for relatively safe and very safe representatives. If the actual pattern in the data approximates this picture, it suggests that the dynamics of the electoral connection are, in fact, different in the two chambers, with a revised version of the electoral selection hypothesis explaining Senate behavior and a revised version of the inoculation hypothesis explaining House behavior.

However, as discussed previously, it may be that relatively safe and very safe representatives are qualitatively different when it comes to uptake. Perceptions of their own vulnerability may lead relatively safe representatives to behave more like their relatively safe colleagues in the Senate and less like their very safe peers in the House. If this is the case, then the real relationship between vulnerability and uptake may more closely approximate the shape pictured in Figure 5.6, a pattern that is consistent with the electoral selection hypothesis in the Senate and with a merging of the insights of the electoral selection and inoculation hypotheses in the House. The conclusion to be reached if the actual relationship looks more like this one is that the dynamics of uptake in the House and Senate are very similar, and that the reason for the difference in coefficients is the presence of a group of very safe legislators in the former but not the latter.

Determining whether the real relationship between vulnerability and uptake more closely approximates the stylized versions presented in

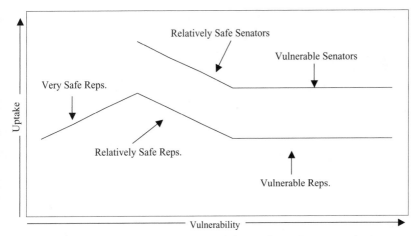

FIGURE 5.6 Relationship between Vulnerability and Uptake – Hypothesis 2.

Figure 5.5 or 5.6 is thus crucial for understanding the motivations underlying responsiveness, as well as for explaining the observed differences between the chambers. To investigate this issue, I first split the samples by vulnerability. As before, in both chambers, relatively vulnerable members are those with challenger vote shares greater than 40 percent. In the Senate, those with challenger vote shares less than 40 percent are considered relatively safe. In the House, this group is split once again, into relatively safe (challenger vote shares between 35 and 40 percent) and very safe (challenger vote shares less than 35 percent). I then reran the OLS specifications from Table 5.3 (minus vulnerability) for each of the groups and plotted the uptake residuals against vulnerability. Figures 5.7a and 5.7b present the patterns for the Senate, which accord with expectations.[11] We see a clear negative relationship between vulnerability and uptake across the relatively safe group ($r = -.36$) and, as described earlier, almost no relationship across the vulnerable group ($r = -.10$).

Figures 5.8a, 5.8b, and 5.8c present the patterns for the House of Representatives, and the conclusion to be drawn should be clear – the actual relationship between vulnerability and uptake looks very similar to that pictured in Figure 5.6. As such, the association between the two is decidedly nonlinear. As in the Senate, we see no relationship between vulnerability and uptake for vulnerable legislators ($r = .05$) and a negative

[11] I also investigated the possibility of nonlinearity in the Senate but found no evidence of it.

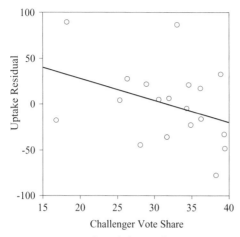

FIGURE 5.7a   Vulnerability and Uptake for Relatively Safe Senators.

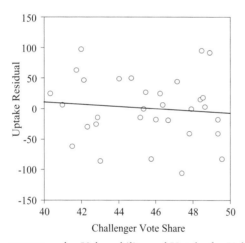

FIGURE 5.7b   Vulnerability and Uptake for Vulnerable Senators.

relationship between the two for relatively safe legislators ($r = -.20$). However, for the small group of the very safest legislators, there is a positive relationship between the two ($r = .57$), with increasing safety leading to decreasing uptake.

This finding thus helps to reconcile the aggregate differences in the direction of the vulnerability effect in the House and Senate and provides further insight into the relationship between electoral considerations and

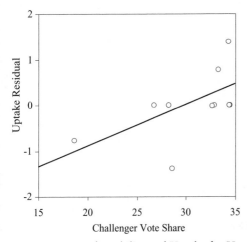

FIGURE 5.8a Vulnerability and Uptake for Very Safe Representatives.

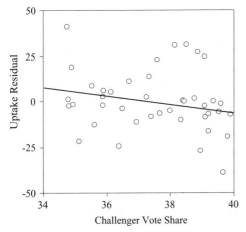

FIGURE 5.8b Vulnerability and Uptake for Relatively Safe Representatives.

responsiveness. In one sense, the conventional wisdom that safety leads to a lack of accountability is correct – legislators who feel very safe engage in relatively little uptake. However, the evidence presented here suggests that this characterization applies to only a handful of members of the House of Representatives. For all senators and the vast majority of representatives, more vulnerability does *not* mean more responsiveness. Instead, the most

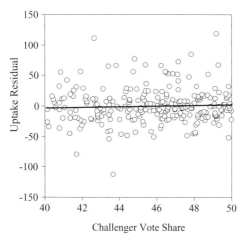

FIGURE 5.8c   Vulnerability and Uptake for Vulnerable Representatives.

responsive legislators are those who fall in the middle of the vulnerability spectrum; they are neither exceedingly vulnerable nor so safe that they are immune from electoral pressures.

Conclusions

It may seem that the point of this chapter has been to take some very simple hypotheses about the impact of vulnerability on uptake and complicate them considerably. While the results presented here should certainly lead to the conclusion that neither the inoculation nor the electoral selection hypothesis alone is sufficient to fully explain how reelection concerns influence responsiveness, this should not be the only conclusion drawn. There are also some more basic, but equally important, findings that should not be obscured in the process.

Most fundamentally, the analyses demonstrate that uptake is indeed a measurable and predictable phenomenon, and that it varies systematically across individuals in a manner consistent with the expectations of the theory I develop. Specifically, electoral vulnerability clearly matters in explaining why some legislators are highly responsive and others are less so. This relationship between the two holds even after controlling for differences in structural situations and in characteristics of individual legislators and their constituencies. Such an electoral connection is often hypothesized in the literature on legislative behavior, but these results actually establish this effect. They are also among the first to show that legislators' experiences in campaigns shape the content of their subsequent activity in office, so that challengers' campaigns have an institutional legacy in legislative activity and, perhaps, in public policy outcomes.

Another major finding to come from these analyses is that there are important differences between the chambers in the relationship between electoral vulnerability and uptake. In the Senate, the safest legislators are the most responsive, while in the House they are the least. This is a difference that should not be understated, even though the results presented in this chapter provide a good explanation for it and indicate that the underlying dynamics of responsiveness are quite similar across the chambers. The fact that relatively safe legislators are the most responsive but that complete safety leads to a drop-off in uptake has important implications, both empirical and normative. It suggests, for example, that vulnerability is best approached as a phenomenon with both objective and subjective components. Two legislators with identical vote shares may not feel equally vulnerable, and this difference may impact their behavior. As such, theories about legislative behavior and practical proposals for reform need to take into account institutional differences that may shape how characteristics like vulnerability influence such behavior.

In general, the finding of a significant and robust vulnerability effect provides initial evidence that elections do work to reward responsiveness, and that many legislators seem to understand the incentives and constraints this imposes and respond in a way that helps them to promote their reelection goals without neglecting other goals they may have. Engaging in uptake is thus a choice that legislators make – one that has, as I will demonstrate in the chapters to come, a considerable impact on their own careers and on the content of the legislative agenda. However, understanding the causes and effects of individual variation in responsiveness is only the first step in the uptake puzzle. Uptake has the potential to greatly influence congressional politics and policy, but the extent to which this influence is realized depends on the decisions that legislators make about where and when to engage in it. Exploring these dynamics is the task of Chapter 6.

6

Patterns of Responsiveness in Congress

Having investigated the reasons for individual variation in uptake, the next step is to explore the broader contours of responsiveness across chambers, across legislative activities, and across time. These aggregate patterns run the risk of being obscured by the detail of the individual approach, but understanding their variation is crucial for assessing the potential contributions of an agenda-based model of responsiveness like uptake and for estimating its impact on legislative politics and public policy. As such, two questions lie at the heart of the analyses in this chapter. First, does uptake vary systematically in the manner predicted by the strategic motivation theory (i.e., Do representatives or senators exhibit more? Is uptake more prevalent on some activities than others? Do legislators spread their uptake behavior evenly across their terms, or is it concentrated at the beginning or end?). Second, do these patterns hold across all legislators or do choices about when and where to engage in uptake vary with factors like vulnerability?

Comparing Uptake Rates in the House and Senate

Beginning with variation across chambers, the prediction of the strategic motivation theory is that senators will exhibit higher levels of uptake than representatives. This expectation is, of course, at odds with the conventional wisdom on the subject, which assumes that members of the House of Representatives, having smaller constituencies and more frequent elections, will be more responsive. However, I have argued that there are a number of reasons why we should expect to observe higher levels of uptake in the Senate. The most important are the differences

TABLE 6.1   *Uptake Patterns across Chambers and across Activities*

	All Activities	Introductions	Cosponsorships	Floor Statements
% who engage in uptake				
House	100%	56%	99%	79%
Senate	100%	100%	100%	100%
Mean uptake activities				
House	35.36	1.63	29.73	4.05
Senate	188.11	32.75	113.18	42.18
Mean uptake % (policy acts)				
House	15%	16%	13%	15%
Senate	19%	20%	20%	19%

in institutional structures and norms between the chambers that support generalist and entrepreneurial behavior in the Senate much more than in the House, and the differences in their electoral circumstances, which lead senators, as a group, to feel more vulnerable than representatives.

From both a theoretical and a methodological perspective, the first issue to be addressed is deciding what the appropriate unit of comparison should be. The average rates of uptake across the chambers presented previously have suggested that Senate levels are higher than those in the House. For this analysis, though, it is important to be more systematic. To say that one chamber demonstrates "more" uptake than the other can mean several things, each with different implications. It could be that a larger percentage of legislators in one chamber engage in any uptake at all, or that, on average, the legislators in that chamber devote a higher proportion of their activity to uptake, or that the raw count of uptake activities undertaken in that chamber is higher. Table 6.1 presents House–Senate comparisons on all of these measures for all activities and broken down by activity type. All of the indicators point to the same conclusion – senators are, as predicted, more responsive than their House counterparts. However, there are some subtle differences between them that are worth noting.

If, for instance, we compare the proportions of legislators who engage in uptake, we see that all legislators in each chamber participate in at least one challenger-themed activity. Compared to House members, though, individual senators engage in substantially more challenger-themed activities in a term, even after we account for the fact that their terms are three times the length of House terms. This effect is most evident for introductions, where the average senator introduces about eleven challenger-themed measures in a two-year congress, while the average representative introduces only one or two. The aggregate impact of this difference is that there should be about 400 more challenger-themed bills, resolutions, and amendments introduced in the Senate every congress than in the House.[1] When we examine individual legislators' uptake activities as a percentage of their policy-relevant activity (i.e., omitting from their total count those activities that relate to governmental operations), the difference between the two chambers, though still significant, is considerably smaller. On average, senators devote about 5 percent more of their activity to uptake than do House members.

The conclusion about the magnitude of the House–Senate difference in responsiveness is thus dependent upon the measure chosen. Nonetheless, the difference itself is robust, a finding that is interesting and important for a number of reasons. First, it adds to the mounting empirical evidence that the House and Senate differ significantly in terms of representation and responsiveness, but not necessarily in the way that conventional wisdom predicts (see also Erikson et al. 2002). In short, smaller constituencies and more frequent elections do not make the House more responsive than the Senate. Second, this difference in responsiveness levels is in the direction predicted by the strategic motivation theory. Compared to the House, the structure of the Senate makes its members more able (and, due to their greater vulnerability, perhaps more willing) to engage in the kind of entrepreneurship that uptake requires, so they exhibit higher levels than their colleagues in the House. This finding increases confidence in the value of uptake in identifying a qualitatively different kind of legislative responsiveness than that identified by previous preference or position-based approaches.

Comparing Uptake across Legislative Activities

The next issue to be addressed is how uptake varies across legislative activities. In the analyses of variation in individual responsiveness in the previous chapter, an overall count of uptake activities was used, combining introductions, cosponsorships, and floor statements into a single measure. It is also quite important to determine whether uptake rates vary across activities because the location of uptake can offer insight into the

---

[1] (435 House members * 1.63 challenger-themed introductions) = 709. (100 Senators * 32.75 challenger-themed introductions)/3 = 1,091.

longevity of the legacy of campaigns in later stages of the political process. If legislators' uptake is concentrated on activities like cosponsorships and floor statements that have few direct policy implications, we might conclude that uptake has little lasting impact on the content of public policy. On the other hand, if there is evidence that it also exists at relatively high levels for the introduction of legislation, then its relevance to policymaking is clearer.

The strategic motivation theory predicts that, because different activities offer different advantages in the quest to claim credit, uptake should be evident across all of them. More precise predictions about individuals' relative levels of uptake across introductions, cosponsorships, and floor statements are difficult to make because a tension exists between those activities that are relatively resource-intensive, but offer a clear claim to credit (e.g., introductions), and those for which the link to credit-claiming is weaker but are easier to undertake (e.g., cosponsorships). Disentangling these relationships is therefore interesting from both an empirical and a theoretical perspective. The first question to be addressed is whether aggregate differences in uptake rates exist across activities. The second is whether whatever overall pattern is uncovered holds across all types of legislators or whether individual differences shape legislators' choices about how to demonstrate their uptake. In addition to influencing overall levels of responsiveness, vulnerability may be associated with differences in the patterns this behavior takes across activities. We might then see safer legislators concentrating their uptake on one activity, while their more vulnerable colleagues focus theirs on another activity.

In investigating aggregate differences across activities, the appropriate units of comparison are legislators' uptake percentages. Because nearly all legislators engage in many more cosponsorships than introductions or floor statements, raw counts of activities are of little use in understanding relative responsiveness among them. The results presented in Table 6.1 suggest that allocation of uptake is quite similar across activities, an intuition that is largely confirmed by more rigorous analyses. For the Senate, a comparison of the aggregate mean percentages for each activity yields no significant differences, so, on average, senators devote the same proportion of their introduction, cosponsorship, and floor statement activity to uptake. In the House, however, the uptake rates for introductions (16 percent) and floor statements (15 percent) are significantly higher than the 13 percent rate for cosponsorships ($t = 2.24, p < .05; t = 2.18, p < .05$), though, of course, the substantive difference is small. Regardless, these results indicate that uptake has the potential to leave an important mark on the content of legislative and policy agendas. It is just as prevalent on introductions, the most policy-relevant activity, as it is on cosponsorships and floor statements, which might be considered more symbolic.

Before drawing any conclusions based on these findings, we need to consider whether or not they hold when the comparison is *within* individual legislators' behavior. It is possible that some devote significantly more attention to one activity or the other, but that these effects are canceled out in the aggregation process. As was illustrated in Chapter 4, a few particularly high- or low-uptake individuals can unduly influence the mean uptake levels for the sample. To gain a more complete understanding of uptake patterns, it is necessary to move from aggregate comparisons across legislators to comparisons within individual legislators' behavior. For this type of analysis, paired t-tests are particularly appropriate because they can be used to assess the significance of any differences that exist within individual legislators' uptake percentages on introductions, cosponsorships, and floor statements. As a starting point, a series of these tests was performed comparing uptake rates for all legislators across the different activities. These results do not differ significantly from those of the aggregate means comparison. Once again, in the Senate, none of the observed differences are statistically significant, and in the House, uptake is higher on introductions than on cosponsorships ($t = 2.57$; $p < .05$) and is higher for floor statements than for cosponsorships ($t = 2.75$; $p < .05$).

To understand more fully the dynamics of the uptake decision, a final question about variation across activities must be addressed. Specifically, are the overall patterns identified here invariant across all groups of legislators or do they themselves vary? Previous analyses demonstrated that safer and more vulnerable legislators differ from one another in their levels of uptake, and there is reason to believe that they may also differ in their choices about where to demonstrate this responsiveness. As discussed in Chapter 5, the very safest legislators in the House exhibit relatively low levels of uptake, most likely because they are not concerned about devoting their time and attention to such responsiveness in order to secure their reelection. When faced with the choice of where to engage in the little uptake that they do undertake, the same reasoning should apply. Instead of pursuing uptake on relatively time- and resource-intensive introductions, we might expect that they would instead focus their meager uptake efforts on the easier task of cosponsorship. Their responsiveness on cosponsored legislation may not have a large payoff for them, but because they are not particularly concerned about their vote shares, they have little incentive to allocate their scarce introductions to their challengers' issues. In contrast,

TABLE 6.2 *Impact of Vulnerability on Representatives' Uptake on Introductions, Cosponsorships, and Floor Statements*

	Introductions	Cosponsorships	Floor Statements
Challenger vote share	.044*	.002	.073*
	(.024)	(.22)	(.041)
No. of issues	.18	3.02*	1.07***
	(.19)	(1.72)	(.32)
Collective attention	.002***	.032***	.002***
	(.000)	(.004)	(.001)
Overlap	.004	.024	.008
	(.003)	(.027)	(.005)
Policy activities	.11***	.13***	.16***
	(.011)	(.009)	(.01)
Constant	−3.45	−25.65	−6.90
	(1.11)	(10.23)	(1.91)
N	301	301	301
Adjusted R^2	.44	.69	.55

Note: Cell entries are unstandardized OLS regression coefficients with standard errors in parentheses.
*** = $p < .01$; ** = $p < .05$; * = $p < .10$.

those who do not feel completely secure may feel the need to demonstrate responsiveness on those activities that allow them to make a stronger claim to credit. They should therefore be more willing to accept the costs of engaging in uptake on activities like introductions.

The end result of these individual calculations should be an interaction between legislators' electoral vulnerability and their relative rates of uptake across activity types. The first step in testing this hypothesis is to determine how vulnerability is (or is not) related to uptake rates for each of the activities. The models presented in Tables 6.2 and 6.3 investigate this issue. They reflect a replication of the individual variation analyses undertaken in Chapter 5, but instead of using overall uptake counts as the dependent variable, the dependent variables here are counts of the number of challenger-themed introductions, cosponsorships, or floor statements undertaken by each legislator (i.e., uptake on each activity is analyzed separately). "Introductions" include public bills, resolutions, and amendments for which the legislator was the primary sponsor.[2]

---

[2] Amendment introductions are arguably qualitatively different from bill or resolution introductions in that they entail a legislator responding to a bill or resolution already introduced. However, when bill/resolution and amendment introductions are analyzed separately, no differences are evident. For this reason, they are aggregated in this analysis.

TABLE 6.3 *Impact of Vulnerability on Senators' Uptake on Introductions, Cosponsorships, and Floor Statements*

	Introductions	Cosponsorships	Floor Statements
Challenger vote share	−.69**	−.55	−.41*
	(.33)	(.55)	(.21)
No. of issues	5.48	40.14***	7.20*
	(6.72)	(11.07)	(4.32)
Collective attention	.012**	.040***	.013***
	(.006)	(.010)	(.004)
Overlap	.22**	.45***	.16***
	(.09)	(.15)	(.059)
Policy activities	.12***	.18***	.14***
	(.019)	(.021)	(.015)
Ideological extremity	−5.57	−96.57***	−17.28*
	(15.63)	(25.83)	(9.90)
Median income	.003**	−.002	.002***
	(.001)	(.002)	(.001)
Constant	−58.45	−95.80	−61.73
	(30.82)	(51.31)	(19.83)
N	51	51	51
Adjusted R^2	.58	.79	.78

Note: Cell entries are unstandardized OLS regression coefficients with standard errors in parentheses.
*** = $p < .01$; ** = $p < .05$; * = $p < .10$.

"Cosponsorships" include all of a legislator's cosponsored legislation. "Floor Statements" include all statements legislators made in reference to a specific bill or resolution. The independent variables include the standard measure of electoral vulnerability (challenger vote share in the previous election), all of the structural control variables included in the previous individual variation analyses, and, for senators, those individual and constituency-level characteristics found to be significant predictors of overall uptake.[3]

Two points from these results are of particular interest. First, the direction of the vulnerability effects identified in Chapter 5 is robust across activities. In the House, the coefficients on vulnerability for uptake

[3] Recall that, for the House, none of these characteristics was systematically related to uptake. For the Senate, ideological extremity was negatively related to overall uptake and state median income was positively related. I also included dummy variables for each of the election cross sections in the specifications in Tables 6.2 and 6.3 but, in the interest of saving space, do not report their coefficients.

on introductions, cosponsorships, and floor statements are all positively signed, while in the Senate they are negatively signed. Second, as suggested previously, the influence of vulnerability does indeed vary by activity. In both chambers, it is significantly associated with uptake for introductions and floor statements but not for cosponsorships. As such, knowing legislators' relative vulnerability offers us little insight into their uptake behavior on cosponsorships. This result is most likely due to the relative ease of cosponsorship as an avenue for uptake. Because it is so easy, all legislators should use it as a low-cost way of credit-claiming on important issues, and so all should show similar levels. Only those legislators who are more committed to the task of uptake (because of its potentially positive impact on their reelection prospects) should engage in it on more resource-intensive activities.

If such an interaction exists, we should observe differences in the aggregate uptake patterns of different groups of legislators across the vulnerability spectrum. Compared to the high-uptake group in each chamber, the low-uptake group should differ in the relative priority it gives to introduction uptake versus uptake on other activities. To explore this possibility, I split the samples according to the vulnerability divisions used in the previous chapter. For the House, those legislators with challenger vote shares of less than 35 percent are considered very safe, those with challenger vote shares between 35 and 40 percent are considered relatively safe, and those with vote shares greater than 40 percent are considered vulnerable. For the Senate, those with less than a 40 percent challenger vote share are considered relatively safe, and those with greater than 40 percent are considered vulnerable. The uptake percentages by activity can then be recalculated for each group and separate series of paired *t*-tests run. Figure 6.1 presents these results. The relevant comparison is how the cosponsorship uptake rate for each group (represented by the solid black column) compares to the rates for introductions and for floor statements.

These results largely conform to predictions. For the low-uptake groups in each chamber (i.e., very safe representatives and vulnerable senators), the uptake rate for cosponsorships exceeds that of introductions and floor statements.[4] For the higher-uptake groups, the patterns are different. Vulnerable representatives engage in proportionately higher levels of uptake for their introductions and floor statements than for their

---

[4] For very safe representatives, this difference is significant at $p < .10$ for the cosponsorship–introduction comparison. For vulnerable senators, the difference is significant at $p < .05$ for the cosponsorship–floor statement comparison.

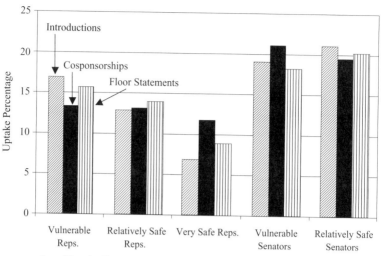

FIGURE 6.1   Uptake Patterns across Activities by Vulnerability Group.

cosponsorships ($t = 3.08$; $p < .01$; $t = 3.07$; $p < .01$), while relatively safe senators exhibit similarly high levels of uptake across all of their activities.

These findings indicate that legislators' decisions about where to engage in uptake are connected to their decisions about how much to perform, and so may be part of a larger reelection strategy. Determining whether this strategy pays off is, of course, a crucial issue and, as such, is the goal of the next chapter. For present purposes, what is most important are the implications of this linkage between levels of responsiveness and location of responsiveness. To the extent that there is a large group of low-uptake legislators, it may also be the case that the uptake that does occur will have less of a legacy in legislative activity and public policy. On the other hand, high-uptake legislators engage in equally high if not higher rates for introductions, so their uptake activity may carry over more clearly into policy.[5] Over-time variation in the relative vulnerability status of legislators (i.e., the proportion who are vulnerable) may therefore influence the extent of institutional responsiveness from one congress to another.

[5] Of course, very few introduced measures ever become law. The extent to which uptake introductions are more or less successful in this process than other introductions is explored in Chapter 8.

Timing of Uptake in the Political Process

An additional pattern of interest, both in assessing the impact of uptake and in testing the strategic motivation theory, is the timing of legislators' uptake activities within their terms. Uptake might be an activity that is undertaken at fairly steady levels throughout a term, or it might ebb and flow with proximity to an election. Furthermore, any aggregate pattern could be constant across legislators, or it too could vary with legislators' vulnerability.

If uptake promotes reelection, then the optimal strategy for legislators might be to engage in high levels throughout the term. However, given their multiple and sometimes competing goals, it is possible that uptake will be a higher priority at some times than at others. If so, we should expect to see legislators concentrating their responsiveness where it can do them the most good. When in the term should this be? Given the difference in term length for representatives and senators, the precise prediction is different for the two chambers, though the reasoning is the same. It seems most logical that uptake would be relatively high immediately following the election, when the campaign is fresh in the minds of winning candidates, and just preceding the next election, when the desire to ward off strong challengers and win the ongoing race is the most proximate goal of incumbents.

The natural division in the House is between the first and second years of representatives' terms. As with the across-activities comparison, the appropriate measures here are uptake percentages because the volume of activity itself varies within a term. Introductions, for example, occur at greater rates in the first year of a congress. Based on the previous argument, the predicted finding for the House is a null one – there should be no difference in uptake between the first and second years of legislators' terms. In the first year, with the past campaign so recent, they should be attentive to the lessons learned from it, and should be actively attempting to ward off potential challengers, who at this time are typically making the final decision on whether or not to run in the next election (Jacobson and Kernell 1983; Ragsdale and Cook 1987). For almost all of the second year, the reelection campaign is in progress, so it would make little sense to cease uptake at this point. As Arnold (2004) describes it, "With two year terms [representatives] have no time to spare. As a consequence, no sharp line exists between periods when representatives are legislating and periods where they are campaigning" (156). As a result, uptake rates should be constant across their terms.

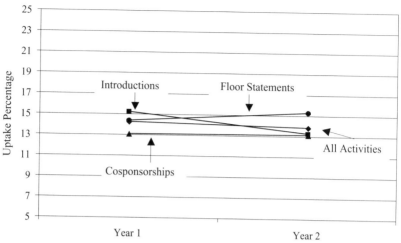

FIGURE 6.2   Uptake Levels across the First and Second Years of House Terms.

The patterns presented in Figure 6.2 confirm these expectations. Each representative's uptake percentages for all activities and for introductions, cosponsorships, and floor statements were calculated separately for year 1 and year 2 and then were compared using a series of paired *t*-tests. There is a slight dropoff in introduction uptake and a slight increase in floor statement uptake, but none of the observed differences is statistically significant, indicating that representatives engage in roughly equal amounts of uptake at the beginning and end of their terms.

For the Senate, the longer terms yield a different prediction. With elections relatively distant from one another, constant uptake should not be as necessary (though, of course, it shouldn't hurt), and so we should expect to see more variation in levels across the term. In the first congress of a term, uptake should be relatively high because of the recentness of the last campaign and the desire to demonstrate the error of the past challenger's critiques. In the second congress, uptake might wane a bit because the memories of the past election are dimming and the next one is still a few years away. It should pick up and reach its highest level in the third congress because, as in the House, this is the time when potential challengers are confirming their decisions to run or sit out and when the next election actually takes place.[6] Once again, the uptake percentages

---

[6] This argument is similar to the one underlying research on whether senators "strategically moderate" their voting behavior as the next election nears (see, for example, Wright and Berkman 1986).

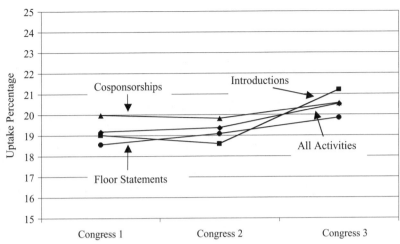

FIGURE 6.3   Uptake Levels across Congresses in Senate Terms.

for each legislator for each activity were calculated and a series of paired *t*-tests run. Figure 6.3 illustrates these patterns. Compared to the House, there appears to be more systematic variation across the congresses in a term, and this variation largely conforms to theoretical expectations, with uptake reaching its highest level in the third congress following the election. Only for introductions, though, is this difference statistically significant ($t = 1.81$; $p < 10$), and the substantive differences are fairly small. In general, then, we once again observe fairly stable levels of responsiveness throughout the term.

Breaking out the samples by vulnerability yields a bit more leverage. If vulnerability does indeed influence legislators' timing of responsiveness, we might expect to see that the hypothesized patterns discussed above would be most evident for those most in need of uptake to promote reelection. The goal, then, is to determine whether the patterns illustrated in Figures 6.2 and 6.3 hold across both vulnerable and safer legislators. To do this, the samples can be split according to the standard vulnerability breakdown and the percentages and paired *t*-tests recalculated. For ease of comparison and presentation, the "all activities" uptake measure is used as the focus of analysis, and the patterns are illustrated in Figure 6.4. The important finding is that vulnerability does seem to influence the timing of uptake behavior. In both chambers, vulnerable legislators differ from their safer colleagues in their uptake timing decisions. In the House, relatively safe legislators decrease their uptake in the second year of their terms ($t = 2.11$; $p < .05$), while very safe and vulnerable members' behavior

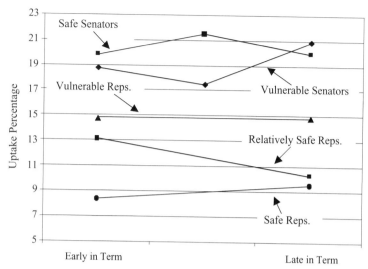

FIGURE 6.4   Within-Term Uptake Patterns for Safe and Vulnerable Legislators.

remains unchanged. In the Senate, vulnerable legislators exhibit significantly more uptake in the third congress following their election ($t = 2.90$, $p < .01$), while their relatively safer colleagues' uptake does not vary significantly across time. In fact, by the third congress, safer and more vulnerable senators' uptake levels are statistically indistinguishable, a result that holds even when more stringent criteria for vulnerability are used.

While it is the relatively safe representatives and the more vulnerable senators who exhibit significant variation in their uptake behavior within the term, the effect itself is actually consistent across chambers. In both chambers, the most vulnerable legislators, those who are most in need of help in their reelection efforts, engage in relatively high levels of uptake in the time period immediately preceding the next election. In the case of senators, this represents a significant increase in uptake, while for representatives, it means that they maintain the level of uptake they exhibited when the past election was a recent memory. This pattern suggests once again that legislators are conscious of the fact that uptake can help them in their reelection efforts.

Conclusions

What general conclusions can we draw from the findings presented in this chapter? Like the results for the individual variation analyses presented in Chapter 5, the across-activities and across-time comparisons conducted here provide evidence that legislators approach their uptake strategically. They exhibit similar levels of responsiveness on all types of activities, supplementing high-visibility but also high-cost activities like introductions with those that are less resource intensive yet still amenable to some level of credit-claiming, and they engage in relatively high levels of uptake at the times when and where it should be most valuable to their reelection efforts.

Moreover, legislators' choices about levels, locations, and timing of uptake appear to be linked, both to each other and to their relative electoral vulnerability, suggesting that they are all part of a larger strategy of responsiveness. Compared to their low-uptake colleagues, high-uptake legislators in both chambers are more likely to devote a relatively high percentage of their introduction activity to uptake and to exhibit less variation in their levels of responsiveness across their terms. Exploring the impact of these decisions on legislators' electoral fortunes, as is done in Chapter 7, is crucial because it completes the theoretical circle of the strategic motivation theory, demonstrating whether or not such decisions actually pay off.

That uptake may be strategic, however, does not mean that it is merely symbolic. The across-activities results presented here indicate that uptake is not concentrated solely on relatively easy activities like cosponsorships, but also occurs frequently for introductions, the most policy-relevant of the activity types. Similarly, the timing findings suggest that uptake is neither a last-minute attempt to win votes nor a quickly forgotten nod to the last race. Instead, uptake has the potential to fill multiple roles, promoting legislators' reelection and resulting in responsive public policy.

7

The Electoral Impacts of Uptake

The analyses presented in the previous two chapters have shown that legislators' uptake behavior conforms to our expectations of uptake as a reelection-oriented activity. In short, legislators behave as though they believe that engaging in it helps them to secure reelection. Vulnerability is related to overall levels of uptake in the manner predicted by the strategic motivation theory, and legislators appear to be conscious of reelection considerations in deciding when and how to demonstrate their responsiveness. These findings provide support for the central proposition of the theory of uptake developed here – that legislators are motivated to take up their challengers' campaign issues because this behavior can pay off for them in the next election. To address this critical issue more directly, this chapter investigates in detail the dynamics of the linkages between legislators' uptake behavior and their future electoral fortunes.

It is a common conclusion of research on legislative behavior that representatives and senators believe that their activities in office impact their electoral prospects (see, for example, Fenno 1978; Kingdon 1989; Mayhew 1974). Consequently, the view of legislators as reelection-driven (or at least reelection-oriented) has become the organizing concept of the literature on congressional roll call voting, constituency service, and committee participation. Furthermore, we generally assume that legislators' beliefs about the importance of their actions are not unfounded and that reelection-oriented behavior does in fact yield a payoff in future elections. Engaging in these activities is therefore a reasonable and strategic choice on the part of legislators, even if it occasionally comes at the expense of pursuing their own policy goals. Thus, when Mayhew (1974) asked "Are, then, congressmen in a position to do anything about getting reelected?" his response was clear:

If an answer is sought in their ability to affect the percentages in their own primary and general elections, the answer is yes . . . it will be argued that [legislators] think they can affect their own percentages, that in fact they can affect their own percentages, and furthermore that there is reason for them to try to do so. (32–3)

Perhaps surprisingly, however, confirming evidence of a strong electoral effect has been elusive. Numerous studies of legislative behavior, particularly roll call voting, have addressed this issue, but the results have been very mixed. There is some evidence that legislators with more ideologically extreme roll call voting records attain lower vote shares than their more moderate peers (Brady, Canes-Wrone, and Cogan 2000; Erikson 1971; Erikson and Wright 1993; Jacobson 1996), but even those studies that uncover an effect find that it is modest at best. Except for perhaps the most vulnerable legislators, roll call voting patterns do not appear to have enough of an impact to influence the probability that an incumbent candidate will be reelected (but see Canes-Wrone et al. 2002). Instead, most legislators are sufficiently secure that the loss of a few percentage points in vote share will not make the difference between winning and losing. Accordingly, a recent study summarized the literature on the subject as "far from conclusive that legislative voting systematically affects House electoral outcomes" (Canes-Wrone et al. 2002, 129).

The potential electoral impact of legislative activities beyond roll call voting has received considerably less attention in the literature, but the evidence for the effect of activities like introductions and cosponsorships is no stronger and, in fact, suggests even less of a linkage. Johannes and McAdams (1981), for example, studied the impact of activity in Washington on incumbents' reelection prospects and found no relationship between legislators' volume of activities and their vote shares. Similarly, Ragsdale and Cook's (1987) work on the linkages between incumbent activities and challenger campaigns found that introducing and cosponsoring many measures had no impact on incumbents' ability to forestall strong challengers.

Does this mean that legislators are unnecessarily cautious about the impact of their activities in office on reelection? If they believe that casting a single "wrong" vote or making one less introduction is likely to cause them to lose, the answer is probably yes. However, there are a number of ways in which legislative behavior might be related to electoral goals, so evidence that the effect of a single category of activities is small in magnitude is not sufficient to reach the general conclusion that representatives' and senators' behavior in office does not matter for reelection. Taken together, the overall impact of voting patterns, volume of activity, and behaviors like uptake could be substantial. Although roll call voting has received the most attention, it is certainly not the only legislative behavior with a potential electoral payoff. And, as I have argued before, the content of legislators' activity in office may matter more than the volume of that activity, so the lack of findings in the legislative activities studies does not rule out an effect of uptake.

It is also possible that the impact of legislative activity on reelection is subtle, and so is not easily identified in cross-sectional analyses that focus on voters' reactions to legislators' decisions. Arnold (1990) argues that legislators work hard at anticipating the reactions of their constituents and take preventive actions to minimize any adverse effects. In his formulation, representation occurs through legislators' avoidance of actions that are likely to elicit negative responses in the future. This theory posits a clear connection between legislative behavior and reelection, as legislators use their activities in office to ward off potential problems in the next campaign and maintain their current levels of security. However, the hallmark of their success at this strategy is a *lack* of constituent reaction to their specific activities, so it is difficult to capture this with traditional methods of measuring electoral impact. Relatedly, because most legislators behave as though reelection matters, we only observe a small range of the entire spectrum of possible behaviors. We simply don't know what would happen if a legislator chose to act in a way that would minimize the probability of reelection because, as Mayhew put it, "there is no congressman willing to make the experiment" (1974, 37). Arnold (1990) concurs, lamenting that "Legislators as a group have been quite uncooperative in providing scholars with the kind of evidence we would need to assess the potential importance of issues in congressional elections" (37).

Combined with the findings from the legislative voting and activities studies, these insights into the subtleties of the electoral connection provide an important backdrop for my investigation of the effects of uptake, informing expectations about the magnitude of any potential effect and suggesting possible methods for uncovering an electoral impact. In particular, because there are many dimensions of electoral success and because the impact of a behavior like uptake may be complicated, it should be useful to investigate a number of ways in which responsiveness may influence legislators' subsequent electoral prospects. Accordingly, although I

TABLE 7.1 *Status of Sample in the Next Election*

	House	Senate
No. who win reelection	328	28
No. who lose in general election	38	2
No. who lose in primary election	3	0
No. who retire	28	18
No. who run for other office and lose	14	0
No. who run for other office and win	9	3
No. who die in office	2	0

will estimate the impact of uptake on the probability of reelection success or failure, I will also explore its relationship to legislators' career decisions, its effect on change in vote shares across elections, and its influence on the presence and quality of the opposition that legislators face in their reelection bids.

In addition, I will take the opportunity to test hypotheses about the impact of responsiveness that are specific to uptake activity and to the predictions of the strategic motivation theory. Previous chapters have demonstrated that vulnerable and safer legislators behave differently when it comes to uptake, both in their levels and in their choices about when and where to engage in this behavior. Do these differences have an influence on electoral prospects? For example, does uptake on highly visible yet more resource-intensive introductions have a greater payoff than uptake on cosponsorships and floor statements? Is consistent responsiveness across the term necessary to reap any benefits that uptake might offer or does late-term uptake work just as well? More generally, do vulnerable legislators benefit more from uptake than their safer peers or is the effect constant across all legislators?

A full accounting of the electoral impacts of uptake must examine all of these possibilities. However, before delving into these analyses, it is useful to get a sense of what becomes of the legislators in the sample in their next election. Although we should expect that many would run for and win reelection, some might lose and others might leave voluntarily, either by retiring from public life or by choosing to leave their current seats to run for other offices.[1] Table 7.1 presents breakdowns for both the House and Senate samples, indicating the number of legislators who

---

[1] Most who ran for other offices or retired did so at the end of their terms, but some left in the middle. For example, Al Gore, who was a member of the 1990 cross section, left in 1992 to become vice president.

returned to Congress after the next election and the number who, for a variety of reasons, did not. As shown, approximately three-quarters of the House sample stood for and won reelection, as did over half of the Senate sample. Only about 10 percent of the nonreturnees lost their reelection bids, with the remainder retiring, running for other office, or dying in office. These results raise two important questions for investigation. First, and most obviously, do uptake levels help us to differentiate successful incumbent candidates from unsuccessful ones? Second, is uptake related to legislators' career decisions, in particular their choice to retire or to stand for reelection?

Most studies of the electoral impacts of a particular legislative behavior focus on election outcomes, but to start at the beginning of the electoral process, we must investigate how uptake might influence legislators' decisions to run again (and vice versa). The results in Table 7.1 indicate that a substantial proportion of the sample chose to retire at the end of their terms, and it is possible that this decision is not independent of their uptake behavior in office. Other scholars have noted that the high reelection rates we observe for incumbents are due in part to the phenomenon of "strategic retirement" – the tendency of those who believe that their chances of reelection are slim to choose to retire rather than face likely defeat (see, for example, Groseclose and Krehbiel 1994; Jacobson and Dimock 1994; Jacobson and Kernell 1983). If this is the case, then we may observe important differences between the uptake behavior of those who choose to run and those who choose to retire, which should offer insight into the place of uptake as a reelection-oriented activity.

Unfortunately, addressing this issue is more complicated than just comparing the uptake levels of retirees and candidates because there are actually two theoretically distinct categories of retirees: what we might call the "strategic" and "sincere" groups. The strategic group consists of those who sense that they face an uphill battle in the next race and so choose to retire rather than run. The uptake prediction for this group is straightforward. The strategic motivation theory leads us to assume that their lack of responsiveness is what encourages potentially strong challengers to decide to run against them in the first place, so we should see these retirees exhibiting lower levels of uptake than their colleagues who stand for reelection. The uptake prediction for the sincere group (i.e, those who retire for reasons like age or health concerns) is different. If they know early on in their terms that they will retire before the next election, then they have little incentive to continue to be responsive and so may decrease their uptake. If, however, uptake has become routine for them or if they

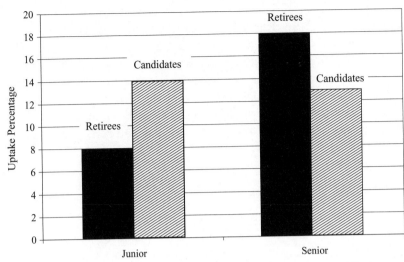

FIGURE 7.1 Comparing the Uptake Levels of House Candidates and Retirees.

decide late in the term to retire, then we should see no difference between their uptake levels and the levels of those who run.

To identify whether legislators' career decisions are related to their uptake activity, the strategic retirees must be separated from the sincere ones. There is no foolproof method for doing this, but dividing them by seniority seems the best option. Sincere retirees should be concentrated among the most senior members, while more junior retirees likely make that choice for strategic reasons. To test the hypothesis raised previously, I break out the samples into senior and junior groups (more than two terms = senior; two terms or less = junior) and compare the mean uptake levels for candidates and retirees in each group. For the Senate sample, I find no significant differences across any of the groupings – junior and senior candidates and retirees all exhibit roughly the same levels of responsiveness (about 20 percent of their overall policy-relevant activity).[2] In the House, however, there are substantial differences, which are reflected in Figure 7.1. This figure presents the uptake levels for four groups of representatives – junior retirees, junior candidates, senior retirees, and senior candidates. I find that junior (i.e., strategic) retirees demonstrate less uptake, on average, than their peers who stand for reelection (8 percent

[2] The lack of significant differences is not unexpected given the smaller sample size and greater variation in uptake in the Senate.

vs. 14 percent, $t = 1.64$; $p < .10$), while senior (sincere) retirees are actually more responsive than their reelection-seeking colleagues (18 percent vs. 13 percent, $t = 2.14$, $p < .05$). For representatives, then, there appears to be a clear relationship between uptake and career decisions – less responsive legislators are more likely to engage in strategic retirement to avoid a probable loss to a strong challenger. The threat of defeat leads the weakest legislators (at least in terms of their responsiveness) to voluntarily pull out of the process and should also serve to encourage uptake among other legislators.

Uptake and Electoral Fortunes

Is this threat grounded in reality? Do legislators' uptake levels actually affect their probability of reelection? Legislators could believe that uptake matters and behave as though it does even if it had no real impact on their electoral fortunes. It is therefore necessary to address this question directly. Although responsiveness could conceivably influence electoral prospects in a variety of ways, its most substantial impact would be to make the difference between winning and losing. In the Senate sample, where only two incumbents lost their next elections (Alfonse D'Amato and Carol Moseley-Braun, both in 1998), there is simply not enough variation to address this question systematically. In the House, however, I can compare the uptake behavior of the 41 representatives who lost their reelection bids to that of their 328 more successful colleagues.

To assess the impact of responsiveness on reelection, I model the probability of winning the next election as a function of individual legislators' uptake levels and a number of other variables that may influence success. The most obvious factor to take into account is prior vote share, since those legislators who performed relatively poorly in the previous election should be more likely to lose the next race. Personal characteristics like party, seniority, and ideological extremity may matter as well, as might the volume of activity undertaken by members (which also serves as an important structural control for uptake). Finally, it is possible that some election years are simply harder on incumbents than others. If a wave of anti-incumbent sentiment sweeps the country, previously safe legislators may find themselves voted out of office.

The results presented in Table 7.2 are from three logistic regression specifications designed to assess the impact of uptake on representatives' reelection prospects after these other factors are taken into account. The dependent variable in each is coded 1 if a representative stood for and

BLE 7.2 *Does Uptake Influence Representatives' Probability of Reelection?*

	Model 1 All Reps.	Model 2 Vulnerable Reps.	Model 3 Vulnerable Reps.
o. of challenger-themed activities	.006 (.008)	.032* (.019)	.035* (.021)
olicy activities	.001 (.002)	.000 (.003)	.000 (.004)
nior?	−.28 (.40)	−.19 (.81)	−.44 (.87)
emocrat?	.30 (.39)	1.45** (.73)	1.50** (.76)
leological extremity	2.61* (1.34)	4.25* (2.35)	3.58 (2.41)
ote share in last election	.12*** (.05)	—	—
hallenger quality	—	—	−1.26* (.66)
onstant	−5.09 (2.63)	−.80 (1.29)	−.09 (1.42)
J	353	90	89
ercent correctly predicted	88.4	83.3	83.1
seudo R^2	.12	.22	.30

Iote: Cell entries are unstandardized logistic regression coefficients with standard errors in arentheses.
** $= p < .01$; ** $= p < .05$; * $= p < .10$.

won reelection and 0 if he or she lost, so a positive coefficient on any of the independent variables means that a high score on that variable increases the probability of winning the next election. The independent variables include uptake (measured as the total number of challenger-themed introductions, cosponsorships, and floor statements undertaken), a count of the policy-relevant activities engaged in by each representative, vote share in the previous election, party affiliation, seniority, ideological extremity, and a series of dummy variables representing each of the years in the sample (which, once again, are not reported in the table).

Model 1 presents the results for all 353 representatives running in contested races.[3] They indicate that, after controlling for other factors that

[3] The analyses are limited to those representatives who faced a major party challenger, as the fates of the sixteen legislators who were unopposed were not in question – they had a 100% probability of winning. The question of whether lack of opposition is related to uptake levels is taken up later.

might influence success, there is no systematic relationship between uptake levels and the probability of winning the next race. This result is not unexpected, given the lessons from the roll call voting literature that the magnitude of any electoral effect of legislative activity should be fairly small. If uptake does indeed influence electoral prospects, the effect is not strong enough to cause the average legislator to lose his or her seat.

What, though, of legislators who are very vulnerable, having won their previous elections by only a slim margin? For these legislators, on the edge of losing, a small impact on vote share can have large consequences. To explore this possibility, I reran the analysis, limiting it to the most vulnerable representatives – those with a winning margin in the past election of 5 percent or less. Model 2 presents these results. For this group, uptake levels *are* significantly related to reelection prospects, albeit marginally so. The more responsive the legislator, the greater the probability of success in the next election. And, as shown in Model 3, these results hold even after controlling for the quality of the challenger (coded 1 if the challenger had any prior elective experience and 0 otherwise).[4] The conclusion to be drawn from these results is that the impact of agenda-based responsiveness on electoral fortunes may be small in magnitude, but it is fairly equivalent to the effect of the position-based measures of responsiveness traditionally studied by legislative voting scholars.

Responsiveness and Vote Shares

In most cases, however, uptake behavior does not make the difference between winning and losing. This finding does not necessarily eliminate legislators' incentives to engage in it because we know that members of Congress are risk-averse about their current and future electoral prospects. As Fenno puts it, they tend to "see electoral uncertainty where outsiders would fail to unearth a single objective indicator of it" (1978, 11). In short, they don't just want to win reelection, they want to do so by a comfortable margin. If demonstrating high levels of responsiveness helps them to accomplish this, then the payoff should be enough to motivate uptake. This point accords with a central tenet of the electoral selection

---

[4] Challenger quality is included in most analyses that focus on predicting electoral success, but in the case of uptake, it may present some endogeneity issues, as the presence or absence of an experienced challenger might itself be a result of legislators' uptake behavior. I address this possibility in some detail later in this chapter, but regardless of the results, its inclusion in this model provides a more conservative test of the impact of uptake itself on electoral success.

TABLE 7.3 *Impact of Uptake Levels on Changes in Electoral Security*

	Model 1 Did Vote Share Increase?		Model 2 Change in Vote Share	
	House	Senate	House	Senate
No. of challenger-themed activities	.012** (.005)	.027* (.015)	.023 (.017)	.028 (.022)
Policy activities	−.003** (.001)	−.009* (.005)	.000 (.004)	−.010 (.007)
Previous vote share	−.10*** (.03)	−.46** (.22)	−.51*** (.08)	−.56*** (.20)
Democrat?	.09 (.27)	−1.71 (1.27)	−.75 (.92)	−3.90 (2.74)
Senior?	−.18 (.28)	1.70 (1.65)	−2.19** (.98)	1.49 (3.14)
Ideological extremity	−.38 (.92)	.297 (4.34)	−2.48 (3.08)	6.84 (10.13)
Constant	7.52 (1.55)	30.29 (14.35)	34.14 (4.96)	37.06 (12.07)
N	366	30	350	29
Pseudo/Adjusted R^2	.17	.68	.13	.25

Note: Cell entries are unstandardized logistic coefficients (for Model 1) and OLS regression coefficients (for Model 2) with standard errors in parentheses.
*** = $p < .01$; ** = $p < .05$; * = $p < .10$.

hypothesis – that engaging in uptake makes legislators safer over time, so those legislators with relatively high uptake levels in one congress should do better in the next election. Exploring the linkages between legislators' uptake levels and subsequent changes in their vote shares can therefore help to further establish the electoral payoff of responsiveness and may also provide additional support for the predictions of the electoral selection hypothesis.

The basic questions of interest are whether uptake levels are related to increases or decreases in legislators' vote shares in the next election and, if so, the magnitude of these changes. The dependent variables in the two sets of models in Table 7.3 reflect these questions. In the first models, the dependent variable is dichotomous, coded 1 if the legislator earned a higher vote share in the next election and 0 otherwise. In the House sample, approximately two-thirds of legislators saw an increase in their vote shares and one-third saw a decrease. Among senators, half improved their vote shares and half suffered a decline. In the second models, the dependent variable is a "vote share change score," measured as each legislator's percentage of the two-party vote in election 1 subtracted from his or her vote share in election 2. A positive vote share change score means that the legislator improved his or her margin, and a negative score indicates that the vote share went down. The values of this variable in the House sample range from –27 (i.e, the representative's vote share dropped by 27 points from the previous election) to 25, with a mean score of 3.04. In the Senate sample, this measure ranges from −23 to 20, with a mean score of −.81.

The primary independent variable of interest in both sets of models is uptake, measured as the total number of challenger-themed activities undertaken by each legislator. The models incorporate the control variables discussed earlier in the win–loss analysis, including previous vote share, volume of policy activity, party, seniority, ideological extremity, and a series of dummy variables for the various election years. Model 1 includes all legislators who ran in the general election (i.e., omitting retirees and the three representatives who lost their primary bids). In Model 2, where the focus is on the linear association between uptake and vote share change, the analysis is limited to those who faced major party opposition in the general election.[5]

The results for the first models show a clear electoral effect of uptake – the higher a legislator's level of responsiveness in the term, the more likely he or she is to see an increase in vote share in the next election. As expected, prior vote share is negatively related to future performance, so those legislators with especially high vote shares in the first election are likely to see their margins go down in the second. Because I am interested in the effect of uptake on change in vote shares (rather than raw performance), this serves as an important control. Finally, we see that the overall volume of activity undertaken by legislators is associated with a decline in vote shares in the next election. This finding makes the positive effect of uptake activities on vote shares even more impressive, offering confirming evidence that the content of the activity undertaken by legislators may contribute more to their reelection efforts than its volume.

The second set of models explores whether uptake influences the magnitude of these changes in vote share. Although the coefficients on uptake in both the House and Senate models are positive, neither set of results

---

[5] For the House, this excludes the sixteen representatives who ran unopposed. In the Senate, it omits John Warner, who faced an independent challenger in the 1990 election and so saw an inordinately large decrease in the second race, where he faced a major party challenger.

suggests a systematic relationship between responsiveness and the amount of change. Why might this be the case? One explanation is that those legislators coming into an election with relatively low vote shares simply have more room for improvement than those who enjoyed large margins of victory in the past, so the same amount of uptake could have a differential impact on vulnerable and safer members' performance. OLS regression analysis, which assumes a constant linear effect, does not enable me to capture this dynamic. It is possible to investigate this possibility, though, by breaking out the samples by the vulnerability groups discussed previously and rerunning the analyses. When this is done for the Senate sample, I find that the results for Model 2 are invariant across vulnerability levels, with relatively safe and relatively vulnerable members receiving similar benefits from uptake. In the House, however, I uncover a different result. Vulnerable members are more likely than their safe colleagues to reap electoral benefits by engaging in it. The coefficient on uptake for vulnerable members is .081 ($p < .05$), considerably larger than the coefficient for all members. This result means that an increase of about twelve to thirteen uptake activities can raise the vote shares of vulnerable members by a point. Uptake doesn't just help vulnerable members more because they are closer to the win–lose dividing line; it also has a larger impact on their vote shares. In essence, then, there is an interaction between uptake levels and vulnerability, with more vulnerable legislators getting more bang for their buck from uptake. I address some possible explanations for this effect later, but first I explore the impact of legislators' different choices about the location and timing of their uptake on their vote shares.

The Impact of Uptake Choices on Electoral Success

An important question that as of yet remains unanswered is *how* legislators' uptake influences their electoral prospects. Is it simply raw levels of uptake that are important or do legislators' decisions about when and where to engage in it matter as well? To illustrate why this might matter, imagine two legislators who each performed about 100 challenger-themed activities in their terms but differed in their patterns of responsiveness. Legislator A introduced many measures on his challenger's themes, cosponsored and spoke about even more, and spread this activity evenly throughout the term. Legislator B spent the first portion of the term focusing almost entirely on her own issue interests and waited until right before the next election to respond to her challenger's issues. When she did take up these issues, she made many cosponsorships and floor statements but

TABLE 7.4   *Varying Electoral Impact of Different Uptake Decisions*

	House		Senate	
	Did Vote Increase?	Vote Share Change	Did Vote Increase?	Vote Share Change
By activity				
Introduction uptake	.452*	.629	.140*	.134*
	.251	(.845)	(.081)	(.067)
Cosponsorship uptake	.012**	.026	.031*	.038
	(.006)	(.019)	(.019)	(.040)
Floor statement uptake	.101**	.167	.021	.003
	(.040)	(.120)	(.036)	(.095)
By timing				
Early in term	.016**	.028	.053*	.044
	(.008)	(.024)	(.031)	(.029)
Late in term	.029*	.056	.031	.017
	(.015)	(.044)	(.026)	(.067)

Note: Cell entries reflect unstandardized regression coefficients on uptake (OLS for the vote share change analyses and logistic for the vote increase analyses) with standard errors in parentheses.

*** = $p < .01$; ** = $p < .05$; * = $p < .10$.

devoted very few of her introductions to her challenger's priorities. Will these legislators receive the same benefits from their 100 uptake activities or will Legislator A's consistent responsiveness on more difficult activities yield a greater payoff?

To answer this question, I simply replicated the analyses presented in Table 7.3, where total uptake was the primary independent variable, but varied the particular measure of uptake used. Instead of uptake across all activities, I separated out uptake on introductions,[6] cosponsorships, and floor statements. Similarly, rather than looking at overall uptake during the term, I compared the relative impact of early uptake versus uptake undertaken later in the term.[7] The results of these analyses are

[6] In the House, the measure of uptake on introductions is a dummy variable coded 1 if the representative made any challenger-themed introductions and 0 otherwise. This is used rather than a count because of the large proportion (nearly half) who make no challenger-themed introductions at all and because of the small range on this measure. However, similar results are obtained using the count measure.

[7] In these analyses, I use the same divisions that were used in Chapter 6. Thus, for the House, uptake in the first year of the term is counted as "early," while second-year uptake is "late." For the Senate, challenger-themed activities performed in the first two congresses following an election are designated as early uptake, while activities performed in the last congress are late uptake.

presented in Table 7.4. In the interest of saving space, and for ease of comparison, I do not report the full results for all twenty specifications, and instead present only the coefficients on the uptake measure from each model.

These analyses yield some very interesting findings. Most importantly, we see substantial differences between the chambers. In the House, high levels of uptake significantly increase the probability of doing better in the next election, regardless of whether this responsiveness occurs early or late in the term or is concentrated on introductions, cosponsorships, or floor statements. In the Senate, the electoral benefits of uptake are more contingent on timing and location. Early uptake is related to higher vote shares in the next election, but last-minute responsiveness does not appear to pay off in this way. This may be because challengers' decisions to run generally take place in the year or two before the next election, so that uptake after that time cannot dissuade strong challengers from running (though it could still have a direct payoff). The finding also accords with more anecdotal discussions of legislators' strategies. For example, Fenno (1996) interviewed Wyche Fowler's (D-GA) pollster in the aftermath of his 1992 defeat by Paul Coverdell and asked why Fowler had not highlighted a particular theme in his campaign. The pollster explained that Fowler had not paid enough attention to it early in the term to do so. His assertion that "You can't save all your salesmanship for the last year" (190) is certainly supported by these results.

The findings in Table 7.4 also indicate that uptake on introductions and cosponsorships has an electoral payoff for senators, but that making a large number of floor statements on the challenger's themes does not bring about this reward. Moreover, high levels of uptake on introductions not only increase senators' probability of doing better in the next election, they also influence the magnitude of this increase. Every challenger-themed bill or resolution introduced results in a .13 point increase in vote share in the next election, so an increase of about seven to eight uptake introductions can raise vote share by 1 point. Because senators typically introduce about 225 measures, uptake has the potential to have a large impact on their margins.

These results demonstrate that the electoral effects of uptake are fairly robust, and when they vary, they do so in a manner that accords with earlier findings about the dynamics of responsiveness and with the broader theory of uptake. In the House, where uptake levels are lower and not as much variation exists in timing and activity choices, the primary difference between responsive and unresponsive legislators is in the overall volume of uptake, and for them, it is the raw level of responsiveness that matters for reelection. In the Senate, where overall uptake levels are higher, what distinguishes responsive and unresponsive legislators are both their levels of uptake *and* their choices about when and where to exhibit this behavior. Accordingly, in that chamber, we observe differential benefits based on these choices. A critical finding here is that the strategies that pay off the most are also those that are used more often by safer, higher-uptake senators. So, not only do they make the right choice in engaging in high levels of uptake in the first place, they choose to concentrate it where it can do them the most good. This finding brings the electoral selection hypothesis full circle – safer senators owe their electoral security, at least in part, to past responsiveness, are savvy in their uptake strategies in office, and are rewarded in the next election, where they increase their vote shares and become even safer.

Uptake and Electoral Opposition

Thus far, my focus has largely been on the direct effect of uptake on vote shares. However, uptake could also have important indirect effects if it influences the presence and quality of the opposition that legislators face. The vote share analyses do offer some insight into these questions; we can assume, for instance, that the smaller the winner's vote share, the greater the level of competition. Addressing this question directly is useful, though, because of the insight it can offer into the effects of uptake and because of its potential normative implications. Uncontested races or races that attract only weak challengers are often interpreted by reformers as a sign of a problem with the system. If reduced competition is instead the result of responsive behavior on the part of elected officials, this offers a more positive interpretation – that the lack of quality opposition serves as an indicator of the incumbent's good performance in office.

I begin by estimating the impact of incumbents' uptake activities on the probability that their races will be contested. Senators rarely have the luxury of running unopposed, but in the House, this occurs more frequently. Of the 366 representatives in the sample who ran in the next general election, 16 faced no opposition at all. More common, of course, is a lack of opposition in primary elections. In both chambers, incumbents sometimes face unwanted competition in their primaries, forcing them to devote resources to these races and possibly divert them from the general election campaign.[8] Of the legislators in the sample who chose to stand for reelection, seventy-six representatives (~20 percent) and twelve senators (~40 percent) faced a primary challenge. What are the predictions about the impact of uptake on opposition? For general election opposition, we might hypothesize that higher levels of responsiveness should increase the probability of running unopposed. For primary election opposition, the expectation about the impact of uptake is a bit more complicated. If primary challengers enter races because they fear that their incumbent copartisans' performance in office will cause them to lose to the general election challenger, then legislators who are highly responsive to their past challengers' issues may be less likely to face opposition. On the other hand, if this attention to the challengers' issues results in less attention to their own party's core interests, then they might be more likely to face a challenger who criticizes them on this point.

In Table 7.5, I present the results of a series of logistic regression specifications designed to investigate these questions. The dependent variable in the first model is a dummy for general election opposition in the House (1 = opposition; 0 = no opposition). In the second and third models, the dependent variable is a dummy for primary opposition in the House and Senate.[9] The measure of uptake used here is "early uptake," since uptake that occurs after a challenger's decision to run cannot influence that choice. Other independent variables include the volume of early-in-the-term policy activities, party, ideological extremity, seniority, and a series of dummy variables for the different cross sections (which in the interest of saving space are not reported). In the primary opposition analyses, I also include an indicator of whether or not the legislator faced a primary challenge in the previous election to control for variation in the tendency of district/state party organizations to field challengers. This choice necessitates a slightly different measure of seniority than was used in previous analyses. Legislators who were in the first term faced different patterns of primary competition in their first race (i.e., the race that put them into office) than returning legislators. If I don't take this into

---

[8] The literature on the impact of divisive primaries generally concludes that such primaries harm candidates, though there is considerable debate about the magnitude of this effect and whether incumbents and challengers are affected differently (see, for example, Bernstein 1977; Born 1981; Kenney 1988).

[9] Legislators from states like Washington and Louisiana with so-called blanket or jungle primaries, where candidates from both parties run in the same primary, are coded as having primary opposition only if they were challenged by a copartisan.

TABLE 7.5 *Effect of Uptake on General and Primary Election Opposition*

	House General	House Primary	Senate Primary
No. of challenger-themed activities	.022	.000	−.034[*]
	(.033)	(.008)	(.020)
Policy activities	.004	.002	.006
	(.005)	(.002)	(.005)
Previous vote share	−.07	−.02	.21[*]
	(.05)	(.03)	(.11)
Democrat?	.55	.03	−1.68
	(.64)	(.31)	(1.38)
Senior/new?	−.81	.51	−1.36
	(.58)	(.32)	(1.74)
Ideological extremity	2.37	2.36[**]	−12.94[*]
	(2.23)	(1.09)	(7.16)
Challenged in last primary?	—	1.06[***]	4.20[**]
		(.33)	(2.12)
Constant	4.39	−2.71	−11.77
	(2.80)	(1.77)	(7.54)
N	366	369	30
Percent correctly predicted	95.6	79.7	80.0
Pseudo R^2	.19	.12	.60

Note: Cell entries are unstandardized logistic regression coefficients with standard errors in parentheses.
[***] $= p < .01$; [**] $= p < .05$; [*] $= p < .10$.

account, the "last primary" dummy variable is confounded with the effect of being new. As such, I opt to use a dummy variable for "new" as the measure of seniority here.

The dependent variables are all coded such that a negative coefficient on the uptake variable means that high levels of responsiveness reduce the probability of opposition. The results indicate that, for the House, levels of uptake do not have an appreciable effect on the probability of a primary or general election challenger. This conclusion holds even after the sample is broken out by vulnerability levels and the analyses rerun. In the Senate, however, there is a systematic relationship. All other things being equal, the more uptake engaged in by a senator, the *less* likely he or she will be to face a primary challenge. Since these challenges require some expenditure of time and resources and may influence general election outcomes, the ability to ward them off through responsiveness is an important benefit of uptake.

Responsiveness and Challenger Quality

Of course, avoiding a challenge completely may be a tall order, even for the most responsive legislators. However, even if uptake levels aren't directly related to the presence or absence of a challenge, they may have an influence on the quality of the opposition that legislators face. Because nearly all senators and the vast majority of representatives do run in contested races, this is perhaps a more interesting area of inquiry. Previous research on candidate emergence has concluded that higher-quality challengers are more likely to run when they perceive the incumbent as weak (see, for example, Canon 1993; Jacobson and Dimock 1994; Jacobson and Kernell 1983), so we may see a systematic relationship between legislators' levels of responsiveness and the quality of their challengers. Given the choice, most legislators would not want to face a quality challenger, and so may use strategies like uptake to remedy their issue weaknesses and discourage these potential challengers from running.

What makes for a quality challenger? There is a large literature in legislative studies concerning the measurement of challenger quality (see, for example, Bond, Covington, and Fleisher 1985; Lublin 1994; Squire 1989, 1992), but most scholars agree that the most important indicator is a challenger's prior political experience. Those who have held office before have proven themselves capable of running a campaign, are generally better able to raise money, have a higher level of name recognition, and may enjoy more credibility in the eyes of voters.

To explore the relationship between uptake and challenger quality, I first coded the quality of the challengers faced by the sampled legislators in the next election. Those who had held any elective office in the past were coded as "quality challengers," while those without experience were designated "nonquality challengers." By this definition, 115 of the 366 representatives who ran for reelection and won their primary bids faced quality challengers in the general election, as did 18 of the 30 senators. To determine whether uptake levels are related to the probability of facing a quality challenger, I conducted a series of logistic regression analyses, using challenger quality as the dependent variable and uptake and the controls used in previous analyses as independent variables. The measure of uptake is once again early uptake. The one new variable in these analyses is a control in the House specifications for whether or not the sitting president at the time of the next election was a copartisan of the representative. This is included to control for differences in the quality of challengers and the performance of the president's party in

TABLE 7.6 *Uptake and the Quality of Competition*

	House		Senate	
	Model 1	Model 2	Model 3	Model 4
No. of challenger-themed activities	−.012	−.026*	.032	−.008
	(.008)	(.016)	(.021)	(.018)
Policy activities	.001	.003	.002	.007
	(.002)	(.003)	(.007)	(.006)
Previous vote share	−.07***	—	−.45**	−.25
	(.03)		(.21)	(.15)
Democrat?	−.61**	−.94	3.58	2.50
	(.29)	(.65)	(2.29)	(1.47)
Senior?	−.06	−1.59**	1.98	−.19
	(.28)	(.73)	(2.35)	(1.44)
Ideological extremity	−1.13	−1.65	−7.69	2.28
	(.91)	(1.87)	(7.73)	(4.58
Same party as president?	.06	.94	—	—
	(.27)	(.63)		
Constant	3.89	.25	22.38	8.67
	(1.16)	(.98)	(11.33)	(8.37)
N	350	89	30	30
% correctly predicted	68.9	63.6	86.7	83.3
Pseudo R^2	.09	.20	.78	.67

Note: Cell entries reflect logistic regression coefficients with standard errors in parentheses.
*** = $p < .01$; ** = $p < .05$; * = $p < .10$.

midterm versus presidential-year elections. This variable is not included for the Senate models because the party of the president was constant for all reelection years for the senators in the sample (i.e., Bill Clinton was president during the 1994, 1996, and 1998 election cycles).

The results of these analyses are presented in Table 7.6. A negative coefficient on uptake in these models indicates that high levels of responsiveness reduce the probability of facing an experienced challenger. The specifications in Models 1 and 3 examine the impact on uptake for the entire House and Senate samples, and indicate that there is no systematic relationship between uptake and the quality of a challenger. Once again, though, there may be more subtle effects. We saw in earlier analyses that vulnerable representatives who engage in uptake get more of a payoff from it than safer representatives. The assumptions about competition implicit in the strategic motivation theory discussed in previous chapters are that engaging in uptake helps legislators to remedy their issue weaknesses, enabling them to inoculate themselves against critiques from future opponents and perhaps even to discourage strong challengers from running in the next election. Because they should be viewed as easier targets, vulnerable legislators may be subjected to more surveillance by possible challengers, so their behavior in office could have more of an impact than that of safer representatives on the decision making of these potential candidates. If higher uptake levels lead vulnerable legislators to face weaker challengers, but have no effect on the opposition faced by safer legislators, this could explain the relationships we see between responsiveness and vote shares for both groups.

In the Senate, the N is too small to reliably conduct such an analysis, but in the House, it is possible to test whether uptake impacts the quality of vulnerable members' challenges. When the analysis is limited to those who fall in the most vulnerable group and the specification rerun, I find, as illustrated in Model 2, that there is a significant relationship. Vulnerable legislators who engage in high levels of uptake are less likely to face an experienced challenger than their less responsive peers. Thus, there is indeed evidence that engaging in uptake helps these representatives to ward off strong challenges in the future.

One final issue remains to be addressed – the potential impact of the prestige of a challenger's prior experience (rather than just the presence of experience). A challenger with previous experience as a congressperson or in a statewide office like governor is likely a higher-quality candidate than one whose experience was more local in nature, perhaps serving in the state legislature or as a county commissioner or mayor.[10] While the vast majority of experienced challengers in House races had only local experience, nearly half of the senators who were challenged by a candidate with experience faced a very experienced challenger, one who had served either as a congressperson or as a statewide official. Do we see a difference in results if we examine the impact of uptake on the probability that senators will face a very experienced challenger?

As shown in Model 4, where the dependent variable is coded 1 if the legislator faced a high-quality challenger and 0 otherwise, the answer is no. For senators, uptake does not appear to be related to the quality of future challengers (though, as demonstrated previously, it is related to the vote share incumbents receive relative to these challengers). This could be because even inexperienced Senate challengers often have high profiles,

---

[10] There are, of course, exceptions to this rule. A big-city mayor may be known by more people and have a better-financed campaign organization than the typical congressperson. Nonetheless, in most cases, this distinction applies.

so prior experience may not correlate as strongly with quality. Among the inexperienced challengers in the sample are Oliver North, Dottie Lamm (the wife of a former governor and a prominent columnist in Colorado), Hugh Rodham (Hillary Clinton's brother), and Mitt Romney (the son of the former governor of Michigan, who is himself the current governor of Massachusetts). The celebrity of these candidates may help them to raise money and enjoy the name recognition typically afforded only to politically experienced candidates.

The general conclusion to be reached about the impact of uptake on opposition is that the effect is neither overwhelming in magnitude nor constant across legislators, but that it does exist. Responsive senators are able to forestall primary election challenges, and vulnerable representatives with high levels of uptake are less likely than their lower-uptake peers to face experienced challengers in their next election. By reducing the amount of competition legislators face, uptake can help them to achieve their electoral goals.

This conclusion parallels the broader one to be drawn from the analyses in this chapter. The claim that activity in office promotes reelection may seem intuitive but, as discussed previously, concrete evidence that reelection-oriented behavior indeed yields an electoral impact has been hard to find. This may be because the effects of responsiveness are contingent on a variety of factors, including the status of individual legislators, their patterns of behavior, and the chamber of Congress in which they serve. Given the complexity of these contingencies, it is useful to summarize the main effects uncovered in these analyses.

First, and most importantly, for all representatives and senators, whether safe or vulnerable, engaging in uptake increases the probability of performing better in the next election, providing a clear incentive for reelection-oriented legislators to demonstrate responsiveness to their challengers' campaign critiques. Equally importantly, although the size and significance of the effect vary, there is absolutely no evidence to support the claim that uptake is somehow detrimental to reelection.

Second, of all the legislators studied, vulnerable representatives are perhaps the most affected by uptake. For them, the magnitude of its effect on their vote shares is strong enough to significantly influence the likelihood of winning or losing. These benefits may come indirectly, as they face lower-quality challengers, or directly, as they themselves run better campaigns, or perhaps as some combination of the two. And, along with their safer peers, they stand to gain from any type of uptake and so need not be particularly concerned about timing or activity choice.

Third, senators also reap electoral benefits from uptake, but the evidence suggests that their choices about how to demonstrate their responsiveness are as important as their overall levels of uptake. They get the most direct payoff from uptake on introductions and from responsiveness undertaken early in the term. In this sense, high-quality uptake appears to yield more benefits than relatively easy uptake. This finding dovetails with the patterns uncovered in the previous chapter about variation in uptake across activities and across time. Safer, higher-uptake senators also make the best decisions about how to allocate their challenger-themed activities.

These results support the more general claim that legislators understand that uptake can help them and behave accordingly, linking their responsiveness to their electoral considerations. This is evident in the individual variation analyses presented in Chapter 5, in the findings regarding patterns in uptake and between-chamber differences in Chapter 6, and in the vote shares and strategic retirement analyses undertaken here. Thus, the impact of uptake on reelection may not be large, but it is on par with the effects found for legislative voting, and is stronger than those found for other studies of raw introduction and cosponsorship activity. In short, there is considerable reason to conclude that legislators are correct in their belief that uptake can benefit them. To borrow Mayhew's terminology, high levels of uptake are not the hallmark of fools or saints but of "skilled politicians going about their business" (1974, 37).

8

Uptake and Public Policy

The analyses to this point have demonstrated that congressional campaigns have a clear legacy in the content of legislators' agendas in office. Challengers' issue priorities in these campaigns are regularly taken up by winning representatives and senators in their bill, resolution, and amendment introductions and cosponsorships, and in their statements on the floor. While the degree of responsiveness varies across individuals and, to a lesser extent, across legislative activities and across time, uptake itself is a widespread phenomenon. Moreover, not only do legislators behave as if they believe that this behavior will pay off for them, there is evidence that it actually does. High-uptake legislators tend to face less competition in the next election and do better at the polls than their lower-uptake peers. These findings provide strong support for the two basic claims underlying the theory of uptake – that legislators' experiences as candidates shape their subsequent behavior in office, and that this responsiveness to campaigns is motivated, at least in part, by their desire to be reelected.

What have yet to be examined are the policy implications of these linkages between legislators and their campaigns – in particular, how much downstream impact legislators' uptake behavior has on the content of the laws passed by Congress. Given uptake's considerable influence on the congressional agenda, it is reasonable to assume that we will observe traces of this influence in later stages of the policy process. Thus, although uptake is defined and measured at the individual level, its implications extend beyond its impact on the behavior and electoral fortunes of individual legislators to have a potentially important legacy in public policy.

However reasonable this claim may seem, it is important to note that it is in direct contrast with much of the conventional wisdom on legislative behavior. It is a common, if usually tacit, assumption in the literature on the subject that any activity that yields an electoral payoff for legislators must be undertaken for strategic reasons rather than sincere ones and hence should have less of a policy impact than more substantively-oriented behaviors. Uptake, like many other activities that prove advantageous for legislators' reelection efforts, is thus susceptible to the critique that it is solely symbolic, useful, perhaps, for credit-claiming, but without any lasting effects on policy. From this perspective, uptake is, at best, an irrelevant activity and, at worst, perhaps even detrimental to the lawmaking process because it diverts legislators' attention from supposedly more serious matters.[1]

This dichotomous view of legislative behavior has come under increasing fire in recent years, most notably from scholars of legislative participation. Hall (1996), for example, is highly critical of the temptation to "distinguish between two sorts of activities – those which are substantive and serious and those which are legislatively superfluous or symbolic," which he argues "ought to be strongly resisted" on both conceptual and practical grounds (25). Most obviously, the claim that a given behavior can serve either strategic or substantive purposes, but not both, seems overly simplistic. Even if it were true, it is virtually impossible to identify criteria to reliably categorize activities themselves in this manner (Hall 1996, 26). Among the legislators who cosponsor a particular bill, some might have chosen to sign on as part of a sincere desire to see it passed into law, others might have done so with the sole intention of claiming credit, and still others might have decided that cosponsoring it would satisfy both their policy and electoral goals. The same activity can therefore have multiple meanings to the legislators who undertake it. And, if the bill eventually passes, all of the cosponsors are linked to this policy outcome, regardless of whether or not they intended it to have an impact.

In short, because legislators' motives can be complicated, because their behavior does not always allow us to reliably infer these motives, and, perhaps most importantly, because the eventual policy importance of an activity may be largely independent of individual legislators' intentions, it would be short sighted to conclude a priori that a reelection-promoting activity like uptake must be unimportant for policy. At the same time, it would be premature to claim a strong policy impact. It is

---

[1] In fact, it is often argued that legislators' reelection-oriented behavior, if left unfettered, can be deleterious to policy, resulting in swollen budgets and disjointed policy. For a further discussion, see Mayhew (1974) or Arnold (1990).

certainly true that some activities have more of an influence on policy than others, so the finding that challengers' campaigns are reflected in the content of legislators' agendas does not guarantee that they will have a tangible effect on public policy. The main point is that uptake's policy relevance (or lack thereof) should not be seen as a foregone conclusion or as the subject of a theoretical debate, but as an important empirical question meriting further investigation. The goal of this chapter is to address this issue, exploring the nature and extent of the downstream influence of individual legislators' uptake behavior.

Keeping Hall's caveats about conceptualization and measurement in mind, I begin my investigation by theorizing about what uptake patterns would look like if the assumptions discussed earlier were true and legislators approached uptake as a solely reelection-oriented activity. Thus, I assume that they are savvy enough to recognize the potential electoral benefits of this responsiveness, but that they are unconcerned about any policy effects their behavior might have and perhaps even wish to limit them. Furthermore, they have substantive interests in other issues and want to pay attention to them as well. Given these incentives and constraints, how might we expect legislators to behave? One option they might choose would be to limit their uptake to less resource-intensive activities so that they can devote their scarce introductions to their other interests. Alternatively, the greater credit-claiming payoffs of introductions might induce them to sponsor some bills or resolutions on their challengers' themes but to pursue them with less intensity than their other introductions, perhaps neglecting activities that could promote passage (i.e., gathering cosponsors and pushing for a hearing) but that also require time and resources.

If such strategies were widespread, the end result would be a number of systematic and important differences between uptake activities and other activities. It is likely that challenger-themed introductions would be disadvantaged in the legislative process, receiving less attention from their sponsors, dying earlier than most other measures, and ultimately passing into law at lower rates. My approach to investigating the potential policy implications of uptake is to determine the extent to which the available evidence supports this account. As such, I ask three interrelated questions about the importance of uptake activity and its legacy in public policy. First, how seriously do legislators pursue their challenger-themed measures? Second, how well do these measures fare at various stages of the legislative process? Finally, what is the lasting legacy of the uptake behavior of the legislators I study? I approach this last question in several different ways, looking at the salience of uptake introductions, the policy impact of those introductions that did get passed into law, and the amount of uptake activity associated with the most important legislation enacted in each congress.

Legislators' Attention to Their Uptake Activities

The findings discussed in Chapter 6 regarding the location of uptake provide the first evidence in favor of the claim that it does indeed have an important influence on policy. Of the three types of activities studied here, introductions have the most direct connections to policy, as introduced bills and resolutions have the potential to become law. Cosponsorships and floor statements, while related to the probability that a bill or resolution will progress through the legislative process, are less directly linked to policy outcomes (Krutz 2000). If we found very high uptake rates for cosponsorships and floor statements but substantially lower ones for introductions, we might conclude that uptake, while useful for credit-claiming, had only tenuous ties to policymaking. However, as discussed previously, the opposite is true. Legislators devote comparable, and sometimes significantly higher, proportions of their introduction activity to uptake. There is no evidence, then, that legislators' attention to their challengers' priorities is relegated to those activities that are the least policy-relevant.

Of course, this does not mean that legislators make these introductions with the expectation, or even the desire, to see them become law. Given that very few introduced bills or resolutions ever reach this stage, no reasonable legislator can assume passage when introducing a piece of legislation. It is even possible that legislators introduce challenger-themed measures because they are conducive to strong claims to credit, but actually prefer that they *not* become law. Such legislators might simply place their challenger-themed bills in the hopper and then walk away, leaving them to founder while they devote their attention to other matters.

The basic question of interest is whether legislators somehow treat their challenger-themed introductions differently from those they make on other issues. What might indicate such behavior? In his study of legislative entrepreneurship in the House, Wawro (2000) argues that legislators' sponsorship of bills is a useful way of measuring their levels and areas of entrepreneurship because serving as a sponsor for a measure usually entails doing more than writing it (or, more often, having it written) and then formally introducing it. Primary sponsors of legislation are also responsible for "gathering and communicating information, coalition building, and shepherding legislation through the House" (27). Importantly, though, sponsorship does not require performing these tasks, so legislators enjoy considerable discretion in deciding how intensely to pursue their various introductions. The amount of entrepreneurial attention paid to a bill therefore provides a good indicator of the sponsor's interest in it.

Two measures of legislators' interest in their introduced measures are particularly amenable to this kind of analysis – whether or not cosponsors were gathered for a bill or resolution (and, if so, how many) and whether or not it was introduced "by request." The former measure is straightforward; the more effort a sponsor puts into pushing a bill or resolution, the more cosponsors it should receive. The latter measure requires a bit more explanation. In both the House and the Senate, members can introduce a piece of legislation by request, which indicates that the introduction is "in compliance with the suggestion of another person" (Johnson 2003, 8). Introducing by request is a way for legislators to distance themselves from a measure, so it is unlikely that they would introduce bills they care about in this manner. If legislators introduce a high proportion of their uptake bills or resolutions by request, this would suggest a lack of interest in these measures.

To investigate differences between legislators' challenger- and non-challenger-themed introductions, I first determined the cosponsorship and by request status of every measure in the sample. To permit reliable comparisons between the two groups, only policy-relevant introductions were included in the analysis (i.e., omitting governmental operations measures). Overall, cosponsorship is fairly routine, occurring for approximately two-thirds of all policy-relevant bills and resolutions. The issue to investigate is whether cosponsorship rates vary across members' challenger-themed and non-challenger-themed measures. Because the appropriate comparison is *within* individual legislators' activities, I use a series of paired *t*-tests to compare cosponsorship patterns on uptake introductions versus all other introductions. The results of these analyses are presented in Table 8.1. Model 1 for the House and Senate shows the comparisons for all legislators in the sample who introduced at least one challenger-themed measure and one non-challenger-themed measure.[2] As indicated,

---

[2] This choice is necessary to have a basis for comparison. The analyses in Table 8.1 include all of the Senate sample and the majority of the House sample. The results hold, however, when the entire House sample is included and independent samples *t*-tests are used to investigate aggregate differences between challenger- and non-challenger-themed introductions.

ABLE 8.1   *Do Challenger-Themed Bills Receive Less Attention from Their*
ponsors?

Comparison	Model 1 All Legislators		Model 2 No Overlap	
	House	Senate	House	Senate
Mean no. of cosponsors				
Challenger-themed	18.7	6.4	15.5	4.6
Non-challenger-themed	18.8	6.4	17.7	6.4
	$t = -.05$	$t = .004$	$t = -.63$	$t = -1.07$
Percent of measures that have cosponsors				
Challenger-themed	67.2%	67.9%	69.2%	58.8%
Non-challenger-themed	68.5%	68.4%	70.9%	64.0%
	$t = -.43$	$t = -.14$	$t = -.29$	$t = -.64$
Percent of measures introduced by request				
Challenger-themed	14.0%	1.9%	—	—
Non-challenger-themed	11.2%	4.6%	—	—
	$t = .35$	$t = -1.65^{**}$		
N	220	51	70	30

Note: Cell entries are means and *t* values from a series of paired samples *t*-tests comparing the
behavior of legislators on their challenger-themed and non-challenger-themed introductions.
*** $= p < .01$; ** $= p < .05$; * $= p < 0.10$.

in none of the comparisons do challenger-themed bills and resolutions
receive less attention than other introductions. They are just as likely to
receive cosponsors and have, on average, no fewer cosponsors than other
introductions.

Model 2 for each chamber presents the results of the comparisons when
the analysis is limited to those legislators for whom there was no overlap
at all between their campaign themes and their challengers' themes. This
provides a much stricter basis for comparison since, in the "all legislators" analysis, some of the challenger-themed measures were also related
to the legislators' own priorities. Once again, however, the results demonstrate no difference in sponsors' treatment of their challenger- and non-
challenger-themed introductions.

Compared to cosponsored introductions, by request introductions are
a much rarer phenomenon, with only about 1 percent of bills introduced
this way. In fact, the vast majority of legislators introduce no measures by
request. Because of this, the comparisons in Table 8.1 are limited to those
legislators who introduced at least one bill or resolution by request.[3] These

---

[3] Thirteen representatives and sixteen senators meet this criterion. Due to the low *N*'s, I did
not perform the "no overlap" analysis.

results indicate that those who do engage in by request introductions are no more likely to introduce their challenger-themed measures in this manner. In the House, by request rates average 14 percent for challenger-themed measures and 11 percent for those that are non-challenger-themed ($t = .35$). For senators, these figures are 1.9 percent for challenger-themed measures and 4.6 percent for non-challenger-themed measures ($t = -1.65$). As such, to the extent that attention from sponsors is related to the probability that a piece of legislation will pass, uptake introductions should have the same likelihood as any other introduced measure of having a policy impact.

How Uptake Measures Fare in the Legislative Process

How can we assess more precisely the extent of this impact? Regardless of the origin of an introduction, its probability of becoming law is slight at best because most introduced legislation fails to progress very far. In the 105th Congress, for example, only about 10 percent of introduced measures were reported out of their committees, and, of these, about half were eventually passed into law. Of course, assuming that an introduction matters for policy only if it can be traced to a specific outcome largely ignores what we know about how legislative work is done. Introduced legislation that fails to become law can still have a posthumous influence, impacting policy in a number of ways. It may pique other legislators' interest in the topic, leading to additional introductions, may "soften up" the relevant policy constituency to encourage future agenda access for the issue (Kingdon 1984), or may simply expand the scope of deliberation and discussion, giving a voice to minority interests (Hall 1996). As Hall (1996) puts it, "the view that position-taking and other forms of symbolic action are irrelevant politically simply because they are inconsequential legislatively is difficult to justify unless one's sole concern is the prediction of outcomes, not the practice of representation" (29).

It nonetheless seems reasonable to assume that the further an introduced bill progresses through the legislative process, the more likely it is to have this type of indirect effect. For example, bills that get a hearing or a vote on the floor will usually attract more attention and interest than those that die in committee. Investigating the legislative fate of challenger-themed bills thus provides a way of estimating their effect on the broader congressional agenda and on policymaking. Because uptake-based introductions appear to be treated no differently by their sponsors than other bills and resolutions, we should expect that these measures would be just as likely as any others to progress through the legislative process. It is possible, though, that sponsors treat these measures similarly but that other members do not. Challenger-themed measures may be directly disadvantaged if other legislators do not view them as serious attempts by the sponsor or disadvantaged indirectly if, given that they are generally outside the sponsors' areas of expertise, they are less skillfully written or framed. Fortunately, determining what actually happens to these challenger-themed measures is a straightforward and easily testable empirical issue. In an investigation that parallels the sponsor-treatment analysis discussed previously, I compared for each chamber the proportion of challenger- and non-challenger-themed introductions that were successful at each of four stages in the legislative process.[4] With each successive stage, the introduced bill or resolution progresses closer to becoming law, and the fate of the measure moves further from the control of the sponsoring legislator.

The first stage studied is whether or not the bill or resolution received a hearing in committee.[5] Hearings are not required for a measure to progress, but they serve as an indicator of the amount of interest the committee had in it and also as a predictor of how likely it is to be passed.[6] The second stage is whether the bill or resolution was reported out of committee, a necessity for later action, and the stage at which most measures die. The third and fourth stages concern broader legislative support for the bill or resolution – whether it passed a floor vote in the sponsor's chamber, and whether it went on to pass in the other chamber, get signed by the president (or vetoed and then overridden), and become law.

Figure 8.1 illustrates the fates of the challenger-themed introductions for the sample. The most obvious finding is the precipitous dropoff from introductions to legislative action. The 1,306 introduced measures generated 229 hearings (a handful were the subject of multiple hearings),

---

4 Once again, since governmental operations bills can't be challenger-themed (because of the coding scheme), they are omitted from this analysis, leaving only those bills identified earlier as policy-relevant. To permit reliable comparisons, I also limit this analysis to those introduced measures that, if passed, have the force of law. This includes all bills and joint resolutions but excludes simple and concurrent resolutions.
5 I used the Congressional Universe databases available through Lexis-Nexis to determine whether bills received hearings or not. Data on bills' and resolutions' progression through the other three stages studied here were obtained through the Policy Agendas Project's bill introductions data.
6 For bills introduced by the legislators in the House sample, 36% of those that eventually became law received hearings compared to only 11% of those that failed.

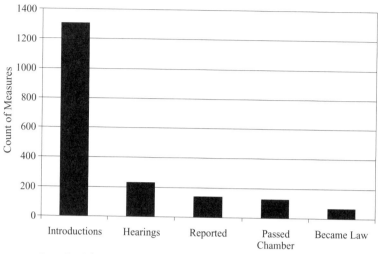

FIGURE 8.1   Legislative Fates of Uptake Introductions.

140 were reported out of committee, 128 went on to a vote and passed in the chamber of origin, and 66 of these eventually became law. Thus, relatively few proceeded very far in the legislative process. For the purposes of assessing the potential policy impact of uptake, the important question is whether or not this pattern differs for non-challenger-themed introductions. Do they succeed at higher rates or at about the same rate as uptake introductions?

The results of a series of independent samples *t*-tests designed to answer this question are presented in Table 8.2. As shown, there are few differences in the fates of these two groups of bills, and when they do exist, the difference is actually in favor of those that are challenger-themed. For instance, in the House of Representatives, challenger-themed bills are more likely to receive a hearing in committee than those on a topic other than the sponsor's challenger's priorities. Individual members do have the ability to encourage hearings for their favored legislation, so this may be the result of sponsors pushing for this on their challenger-themed bills. A prominent and visible hearing can be a boon to legislators in the quest to claim credit, so they may be especially eager to promote this as part of their uptake activity. This difference between uptake measures and other introductions ceases, however, when we examine later stages of the legislative process. Challenger- and non-challenger-themed bills are reported out of committee, pass their votes on the House floor, and become law at the same rates.

TABLE 8.2 *Comparing the Fates of Challenger- and Non-Challenger-Themed Bills*

	House	Senate
Hearing?		
Challenger-themed	14.31%	14.59%
Non-challenger-themed	9.86%	12.30%
	$t = 3.15^{***}$	$t = 1.67^{*}$
Reported?		
Challenger-themed	8.13%	12.97%
Non-challenger-themed	6.89%	13.55%
	$t = 1.05$	$t = -.63$
Passed by chamber?		
Challenger-themed	7.42%	11.59%
Non-challenger-themed	7.56%	9.39%
	$t = -.12$	$t = 1.79^{*}$
Law?		
Challenger-themed	3.36%	6.33%
Non-challenger-themed	3.85%	4.40%
	$t = -.56$	$t = 2.20^{**}$
Number of bills		
Challenger-themed	566	742
Non-challenger-themed	2,830	2,885

Note: Cell entries are percentages of challenger-themed and non-challenger-themed bills that were successful at each stage of the legislative process. The percentages for these two groups are then compared using a series of independent samples t-tests.
$^{***} = p < .01$; $^{**} = p < .05$; $^{*} = p < .10$.

In the Senate, the situation is slightly different. Challenger- and non-challenger-themed introductions are equally likely to be reported out of committee, but challenger-themed bills and resolutions are more successful at other stages of the process. They are more likely to get hearings, more likely to pass their chambers of origin, and more likely to become law. There is no clear explanation for this difference, though it is possible that the higher-quality challengers who generally run against incumbent senators are skilled at identifying and highlighting issues that resonate with constituents and other legislators. Therefore, bills on their themes are more likely to succeed in the legislative process. It should be noted, though, that this difference is substantively very slight.

Uptake introductions thus succeed at about the same rate as all other measures. Based on the frequency with which they are the subject of CQ

Almanac "key votes," they are also just as likely to attract attention and interest from fellow legislators and outside observers. A key vote is one of about sixty to sixty-five roll calls per Congress (typically sixteen per chamber per year) that the editors of *CQ* judge to be "a matter of major controversy . . . a matter of presidential or political power . . . [or] a matter of potentially great impact on the nation and lives of Americans." Across the 101st–105th Congresses, there were 293 key votes on bills and resolutions representing 230 unique measures. Forty-one of the 230 votes were on bills and resolutions introduced by the representatives and senators in my sample, and over one-fifth of these were challenger-themed. To put this in perspective, members of the sample introduced 13,051 policy-relevant measures, of which 2,358 were challenger-themed and 10,693 were non-challenger-themed. About .4 percent of their challenger-themed introductions generated key votes, as did .3 percent of their non-challenger-themed introductions. Thus, just as with the other stages of the legislative process, there are no important differences between legislators' uptake measures and their other measures.[7]

There is simply no evidence, then, that challenger-themed activity has less impact on public policy than other activities, dealing a severe blow to the claim that it is merely symbolic behavior. To the contrary, uptake can have a substantial effect on the content of policy. The legislators in the House and Senate samples introduced 270 policy-relevant bills that eventually became law, about one-quarter of which were challenger-themed.[8] In the 101st through 105th Congresses, sixty-six new laws can be traced to uptake activity on the part of the sample.[9] These uptake laws were not limited to a handful of policy areas but have a wide scope. As illustrated in Figure 8.2, twelve of the seventeen issue categories are

[7] In this analysis and those to follow, the appropriate comparison is between legislators' challenger- and non-challenger-themed measures rather than between the sample's challenger-themed measures and all other measures introduced or passed during this time period. This is because the bills and resolutions introduced by legislators not in the sample include both uptake measures and nonuptake measures. However, since I do not have data on their campaign themes, I cannot classify these measures into one category or the other.

[8] If all of these challenger-themed bills were on issues that had also been highlighted by the winning legislator (i.e., if there was overlap in the choice of campaign themes), then we might conclude that few of these laws are the result of uptake itself. However, for the Senate sample, where I have information on both the challenger's and winning candidate's campaign themes for all legislators, the majority of the laws originated from sponsors for whom the issue was only the challenger's.

[9] And, of course, if I were able to investigate the behavior of all legislators across this time period, this number would be substantially larger.

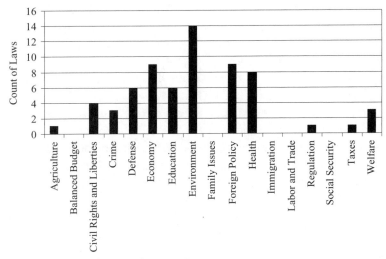

FIGURE 8.2   Uptake Laws by Issue Category.

represented, many with multiple laws. They run the gamut in terms of subject matter, including measures to guard against terrorism, to increase funding for the public health service, to regulate savings and loans, to protect rivers, to support veterans' affairs, to advance charter schools, to promote technology education, to prevent child abuse, to encourage national community service programs, to fund hospice care, to guard international human rights, to preserve national forests, to change rules regarding private mortgage insurance, and to increase rural economic development. This diversity in topics suggests that the potential policy impact of uptake is widespread.

The Policy Content of Uptake Laws

To get a more concrete sense of this impact, it is useful to explore a few of these laws, investigating their content and importance, as well as how they fit into their sponsors' uptake strategies. Take, for instance, two important education measures passed in the 105th Congress, H.R.2616, which dealt with charter schools, and H.R.1853, which focused on vocational/technical education. Both of these laws originated as uptake introductions by Representative Frank Riggs (R-CA). Riggs first came to Washington following the 1990 election as one of forty-four freshman representatives in the 102nd Congress. He lost his first bid for reelection in 1992 but retook the seat in 1994 with 53 percent of the vote. In the 1996 election, he won once again by a similar margin but came under harsh criticism from his challenger, Michela Alioto, who argued that he had not been attentive enough to health care, the environment, and education (Greenblatt and Elving 1996, 2974). While the environment had already been raised as a campaign theme by his 1994 election challenger, health care and education were new issues. Riggs's record provided Alioto with some ammunition for her critiques; he had prioritized none of these issues in his own campaign (his own themes were agriculture, crime, defense, and labor and trade issues) and had devoted relatively little attention to them in his previous term, performing only thirteen activities on health and nine on education.

When he returned to Congress, he significantly increased his attention to these issues, undertaking twenty-two health activities and forty-one education activities, including ten bill introductions. Of these, H.R.2616 and H.R.1853 eventually became law. H.R.2616 amended the Elementary and Secondary Education Act of 1965 to "improve and expand charter schools." This law increased federal funding for public charter schools, encouraged states to raise standards for these schools (because states that established and implemented such standards would receive additional funds), and provided federal money to conduct studies to evaluate their successes and failures (Katz 1997).

H.R.1853 was equally important, reauthorizing the Carl D. Perkins Vocational and Applied Technology Education Act of 1990, the major vocational and technical education program at the federal level. It granted $1.3 billion to the program for fiscal year 1998 with additional funding through 2002. It also recalculated the formula for allocating this money to states (to target more directly those with younger populations who would be most likely to make use of vocational and technical education), increased the proportion of funding the states would have to send to localities, and maintained "tech-prep" education for high school students as a separate program with independent funding (Cassata 1997).

Riggs's uptake activity thus left an undeniable trace on education policy, and its effect is far from unique. Indeed, it is matched in magnitude by Senator Nancy Kassebaum's (R-KS) uptake on health policy. Kassebaum won the 1990 election to her third term in office handily, beating challenger Dick Williams by 48 points (74 percent to 26 percent). However, as discussed in Chapter 1, she was criticized on a number of issues, including her "insufficient attention to health-care" (Benenson 1990, 3310). Williams had evidence to back up this critique, as Kassebaum had made only a single bill introduction on health care in the previous term. Her response to this challenge was impressive; in the next term, she performed 187 activities on health care, including 26 introductions (24 bills and 2 resolutions). Both resolution introductions and two of the bill introductions became law. While the resolutions (S.J.Res.127 and S.J.Res.251, both in the 102nd Congress) were more symbolic in nature, designed to raise public awareness of Huntington's Disease, the bills had a more tangible policy impact. S.1044, passed into law in the 104th Congress, amended the Public Health Service Act, authorizing the secretary of health and human services to make grants to develop and fund health centers for "medically under-served populations," with a particular focus on reducing infant mortality. It also initiated a program to provide insurance for loans made by private lenders to these health centers. S.641, which also became law in the 104th Congress, reauthorized the Ryan White Care Act of 1990, the federal government's "key AIDS program" for treatment and support of human immunodeficiency virus (HIV) and acquired immune deficiency syndrome (AIDS) patients (MacPerson 1995, 947). Among its provisions were an appropriation of $633 million to the program for the next fiscal year, a change in the allocation of benefits to provide more equitable distribution of funding between cities and rural areas, and, as part of a bipartisan effort between Kassebaum and Edward Kennedy (D-MA), an amendment that required states receiving funding to offer voluntary HIV testing to pregnant women (Fraley 1995).[10]

While it would be an overstatement to claim that similar policies would not have passed had Riggs and Kassebaum not introduced these particular bills, it is clear that uptake activity can have an influence on the shape of public policy. Indeed, across this time period, challengers' critiques of winners' records on a variety of issues found their way into law. For example, Representatives Bill Emerson (R-MO), Robert Lagomarsino (R-CA), and Brian Bilbray (R-CA) were all lambasted by their challengers for their weak environmental records. Emerson's challenger, Russ Carnahan, highlighted in particular his appearance on the "Dirty Dozen" list put out by Environmental Action (Cook 1990, 3327). In the next Congress, Emerson responded by introducing measures to expand the Mark Twain National Forest; to establish the Greer Spring Special Management Area, restricting timber harvesting, mining, hunting and fishing, and vehicular access; and to provide for management of the Eleven

---

[10] This provision was the source of considerable controversy, as a number of other senators, led by Jesse Helms (R-NC), wanted to make such testing mandatory.

Point Wild and Scenic River Corridor. One of these measures, H.R.3604 (which received bipartisan cosponsorship support from Missouri's congressional delegation), became law, as did Lagomarsino's La Padres Condor Range and River Protection Act (H.R.2556, 102nd Congress) and Bilbray's measure to amend the Clean Air Act to prohibit the entry of foreign vehicles that did not comply with emissions standards (H.R.8, 105th Congress).

Another common target of uptake was defense, particularly policies related to military personnel. Representative Mike Espy's (D-MS) 1988 challenger, Jack Coleman, accused him of being "against defense, against America and against Americans" (Bragdon 1988, 2913). Espy responded in his next term with twenty-six defense measures, including a resolution introduction (H.J.Res.566, designating a "National Military Families Recognition Day") that became law. Representatives George Sangmeister (D-IL) and Henry Bonilla (R-TX) faced similar situations. They both unseated incumbents who claimed that if their opponents were to win, less attention would be paid to military and defense issues of interest to their constituencies. Perhaps to prove them wrong, both representatives introduced measures on these topics in the next term. Sangmeister's (H.J.Res.575), which honored veterans of the Korean War, became law in the 101st Congress, and Bonilla's (H.R.821), which extended the option for burial in national cemeteries to retired members of the Armed Services reserves, became law in the 103rd.

The Importance of Uptake Laws

These laws all provide strong evidence of the tangible effects of uptake on public policy. At the same time, though, it is clear that their legacies vary in importance. In all likelihood, Kassebaum's introduction of the Ryan White Care Act had more of an impact than her measure to declare a Huntington's Disease awareness month, and Bonilla's defense measure mattered more for policy than Espy's. Therefore, as the final stage of the analysis, I employ some outside indicators of the importance of legislation that enable me to make comparative assessments of the status of uptake laws. As always, the question of interest is whether legislators' uptake laws are somehow less important than their other laws.

The CQ key vote classification provides one possible measure of importance, but is not necessarily the most appropriate because it is an indicator of the attention and controversy surrounding a vote rather than the policy impact of a law. Although this may often serve as a good proxy for importance, it is not true in all cases. Perhaps more importantly, many key votes are on measures that fall short of becoming law. Of all the measures introduced by the sample that were the subject of key votes, only six were enacted into law. Thus, although none of these were challenger-themed, this does not provide enough evidence to form a conclusion about the relative policy importance of uptake.

More promising methods are those that focus specifically on the laws themselves. The best-known approach was developed by Mayhew (1991) in his work on the effects of divided government. He suggests combining end-of-session appraisals by journalists about the most important enactments in a congress with retrospective judgments by policy specialists in each area on the effects of the laws. Unfortunately, this method is tenable only for laws that were passed long enough ago to evaluate their long-term effects, which is not the case for many of the congresses studied here. An alternative method, which is more appropriate for my sample, is suggested by Jones and Baumgartner (2005) in their work on the dynamics of governmental agenda-setting. They propose weighting statutes by the amount of coverage they receive in the *CQ Almanac*, with those laws receiving the most coverage judged as the most important.[11]

Their procedures yield a list of 576 "most important laws" passed between 1948 and 1998. Of these, 123 fall within the 101st through 105th Congresses, constituting about 5 percent of the 2,324 statutes passed during this time. An inspection of the data reveals that ten of these laws were introduced by members of my samples, and three of these were challenger-themed. Thus, of the 270 laws for the sample, 66 of which were challenger-themed and 204 of which were non-challenger-themed, 4.5 percent of the challenger-themed laws qualify as "most important" (3 of 66), slightly more than the 3.4 percent of non-challenger-themed laws (7 of 204) that attained this status.

Moreover, these findings provide only a partial assessment of the policy impact of uptake activities. Focusing only on the bill and resolution introductions that become law neglects the potential policy importance of other activities like cosponsorships, floor statements, and amendments. These activities should be considered because they can influence the probability that a piece of legislation will pass, and can also shape the specific provisions of a law. As such, it is useful to turn the importance question around to ask how much uptake activity is related to the laws identified

---

[11] This procedure began by ranking each law by lines of CQ coverage and then adjusting to account for undercoverage between 1948 and 1961. See Jones and Baumgartner (2005).

as important by Jones and Baumgartner (2005), regardless of whether they originated as uptake introductions. For the 123 most important laws in the 101st–105th Congresses, I find a total of 456 associated uptake activities (a median of 4 activities per law), with less than 15 percent of these laws devoid of any uptake activity. Legislators' uptake behavior thus leaves its trace on all types of laws, from the most symbolic to the most important.

In sum, it would be a mistake to assume that because uptake pays off for legislators, it must therefore be irrelevant for lawmaking. As demonstrated by the analyses in this chapter, legislators pay just as much attention to their challenger-themed introductions as to all other measures in their portfolios. These uptake introductions are just as likely (and, in the case of the Senate, slightly more likely) to become law as any other introduction made in Congress, and the uptake laws that get passed are wide-ranging in topic and at least occasionally mark important changes in policy. Uptake can therefore be seen as a win–win situation. For individual legislators, it helps to promote reelection, and for the polity as a whole, it brings important issues to the congressional agenda and can lead to more responsive public policy.

9

Elections, Governance, and Representation

The dual nature of Congress has long been one of its defining features. Because it functions both as a policymaking body and as a representative body, legislators must successfully balance the substantive tasks of making law with the more symbolic tasks of cultivating good relationships with their constituents in their districts or states (Davidson and Oleszek 1996). Moreover, the reelection imperative requires that they regularly persuade constituents, potential challengers, and other political actors of their accomplishments in each of these arenas by organizing and running successful campaigns. Thus, as Fenno reminds us, representatives and senators spend their careers "moving between two contexts, Washington and home, and between two activities, governing and campaigning" (1989, 119).

This duality is reflected in research on legislative studies, with the continued development of theoretically rich and methodologically rigorous literatures on these two contexts and two activities. By and large, however, these literatures have been separate, with studies focusing on legislators' activities in Washington *or* their behavior as candidates on the campaign trail *or* their home styles in their constituencies. What is missing is a similarly nuanced literature on the linkages *between* the two contexts and two activities. For example, little attention has been paid to how legislators' experiences as candidates shape their behavior as policymakers, an omission that is particularly surprising when we consider that electoral connection theories are central to our understanding of the motivations underlying legislative behavior. As discussed in Chapter 1, this bifurcation can be attributed to the "Two Congresses" division in legislative studies, which treats the electoral and legislative arenas as analytically separable, assuming that legislators' behavior as lawmakers and their behavior as candidates can be studied as distinct phenomena.

In contrast to this traditional approach to analyzing legislative behavior, the investigation of uptake undertaken here has explicitly connected electoral and legislative politics, demonstrating how the two are linked through the issue agendas of candidates in campaigns and legislators in office. My theory of the uptake process posited that these linkages between agendas occur because of the strategic choices made by challengers and by winning legislators. In short, challengers have an incentive to identify salient issues that the incumbent has previously neglected and to prioritize these issues in their campaigns. Winners are motivated to respond to these signals and act on their challengers' issues in office in order to remedy their weaknesses and promote their future reelection prospects. They therefore use campaigns as a source of information about changes they should make in the content of their issue agendas in the following congress, and, after returning to office, take up and incorporate these issues into their legislative activity.

The findings in this book have demonstrated the value added of this approach. Foremost among these is a greater understanding of these linkages themselves, including the factors that influence individual uptake levels, the nature of legislators' decisions about where and when to engage in this behavior, and the impact of this activity on legislators' electoral fortunes and on collective public policy outputs. Uptake has been shown to be a widespread, measurable, and predictable phenomenon that offers new insight into the electoral connection in Congress. From the perspective of uptake, a linkage between elections and legislative behavior doesn't just mean that legislators are forward-looking and choose their activities with future electoral contests in mind, or that vulnerable and safe legislators behave differently from one another (though the evidence presented here supports both of these hypotheses), but that the specific content of legislators' prior challengers' campaigns shapes the content of their subsequent activity in office.[1]

These conclusions about uptake also bear on a number of important and enduring questions in the broader literature on American politics. However, before discussing these implications, it is useful to review the

---

[1] Scholars like Fenno (1996) and Hershey (1984) have hypothesized that campaigns should influence winners' behavior, but the concrete details of how and why this occurs have not been studied.

most important findings from this investigation. They can be summarized as follows:

Congressional Campaigns Have a Clear Influence on the Content of Legislators' Agendas in Office

Legislators adjust the issue content of their activity following campaigns, with all legislators engaging in at least some uptake of their challengers' themes into their legislative activity. As such, the issues highlighted by challengers inform the content of individual legislative agendas and, in turn, the nature of the aggregate congressional agenda. In the 101st through 105th Congresses, the members of the House and Senate samples studied here introduced 2,358 challenger-themed bills, resolutions, and amendments, made 18,320 cosponsorships on measures relating to their challengers' priority themes, and spoke about them on the floor 3,860 times. Campaigns therefore matter greatly from an institutional perspective because they have a legacy in the content of legislative activity.

The Extent of This Legacy Serves as an Indicator of Legislative Responsiveness

Uptake varies considerably across legislators and also, to a lesser extent, across legislative activities and across time. Some legislators devote very little of their attention to uptake, while others are very active on their challengers' issues. Uptake levels thus reflect the amount of responsiveness a legislator demonstrates to salient issues.

Individual Uptake Levels Are Influenced by Past Electoral Vulnerability and in Turn Affect Future Electoral Prospects

Individual variation in uptake is systematically related to legislators' levels of electoral vulnerability. However, this relationship is more complicated than is usually recognized. Uptake is a strategic activity – many legislators behave as if they understand that acting on their challengers' themes will help them in their reelection efforts, and so engage in uptake at levels that correspond to their ability, willingness, and need to do so. Moreover, the results presented in Chapter 7 indicate that it does indeed yield tangible electoral payoffs. Legislators who engage in high levels of uptake do better in the next election than their less responsive peers. Over time, then, those legislators who are very responsive should make themselves safer, while their less responsive peers should remain vulnerable. From a cross-sectional perspective, we therefore see a negative relationship between vulnerability and uptake (with, of course, the exception of a small group of the very safest members of the House of Representatives, who show less uptake than their moderately safe colleagues).

Electoral Safety Does Not Necessarily Lead to a Lack of Accountability

Instead, the causal arrow may go the other way. Considered over the long term, legislators' levels of electoral security are, at least in part, reflections of their past responsiveness. Safe legislators are safe because they have performed their jobs well. High reelection rates for incumbents are not necessarily indicative of a problem because electoral replacement is *not* a requirement for responsiveness.

Uptake Is Higher in the Senate Than in the House of Representatives

Contrary to the conventional wisdom about legislative responsiveness, senators demonstrate higher levels of uptake than do House members. This is likely due to a number of factors, including the existence of structures and norms in the Senate that support a generalist approach to legislative work, longer terms that allow legislators in that chamber to engage in more activity overall, and the greater electoral vulnerability of Senate incumbents, which provides a stronger incentive for uptake. Neglecting to consider how these differences may influence legislators' ability and willingness to be responsive can therefore lead to incorrect predictions about when and where we should see the highest levels of responsiveness.

More generally, this finding underscores the need for congressional scholars to avoid limiting their analyses to a single chamber. The majority of studies of legislative behavior focus on either the House or the Senate, but not both. In many cases, this is a reasonable choice, if the activity of interest is limited to one chamber or the other (e.g., the introduction of tax bills in the House or treaty ratifications in the Senate) or if data availability prohibits the study of both chambers. In other cases, however, understanding how representatives behave may not allow us to infer reliably how senators behave, and vice versa. Instead, differences in the structures of these institutions and in the incentives they provide to members may result in differences in the behavior of legislators within them. Understanding this variation can provide a more nuanced understanding of legislative behavior within the chambers, as well as a more accurate conception of when institutional differences do and do not matter.

Individual Uptake Decisions Have Downstream Consequences for Public Policy

That uptake is strategic does not mean that it is solely symbolic. Legislators pursue their challenger-themed activities with the same intensity as the other activities in their portfolios, and these measures are just as likely as any other introduced legislation to be passed into law. Uptake decisions thus leave their mark on the types of policies that government makes, so individual responsiveness and collective public policy outcomes are linked.

Implications of Uptake

The study of uptake clearly offers new insight into the ways in which electoral and legislative politics are connected to one another. However, as should be clear from this discussion, the implications of uptake extend beyond just understanding these linkages. The findings that legislators respond to their challengers, that this behavior varies systematically, and that traces of individual uptake decisions can be found in public policy bear on a number of broader questions relating to democratic accountability. In particular, the uptake process expands our understanding of the dynamics of legislative representation and of the role of campaigns and elections in promoting responsiveness. These may seem like areas of inquiry where a focus on the relationship between campaigns and legislative activity would be most natural, but connections of this type remain largely unexplored. To demonstrate the analytical leverage uptake provides in understanding these phenomena, I begin by briefly summarizing the traditional approach to their study and then describe the value added of including uptake.

Rethinking Responsiveness

Concerns about representation and responsiveness lie at the core of popular and scholarly debates about the health of the American political system, and rightly so. In modern democracies such as our own, democratic government is necessarily representative government, so the extent to which elected officials faithfully reflect the interests of their constituents is a major criterion in assessing legitimacy. Although democratic theorists have discussed at length the nuances of representation, the basic requirements are straightforward. Citizens must have concerns or preferences about public policy problems, legislators must have the ability to learn about these and act on them, and there must be a mechanism through which constituents can hold legislators accountable for their actions. Elections are theorized to serve as the linchpin in these systems, providing a motivation for responsiveness and a means for ensuring it. As such, a primary focus in political science research has been to determine how well these ideals are realized in contemporary American politics.

The answer that has emerged from a half century of empirical research on representation is a somewhat discouraging one. While most studies have identified a relationship between the preferences of legislators and the preferences of their constituents, the general conclusion is that the relationship is fairly weak – that "the strength of this connection varies across issue dimensions and is never overwhelmingly large" (Jacobson 2001, 238). This relative lack of what Miller and Stokes (1963) termed "policy congruence" is usually attributed to the failure of voters and legislators to conform to the textbook models envisioned for them. The majority of citizens know little about the details of public policy, pay scant attention to what their representatives do in office, and hold only tenuous opinions about what actions government should take (Delli Carpini and Keeter 1996; Neuman 1986; Zaller 1992). For their part, legislators have been found to be attentive to their constituents but not necessarily responsive to their policy preferences. Instead, they are often accused of focusing instead on satisfying the particularistic interests of their districts or states, potentially overburdening the budget with pork (Bickers and Stein 1996).

In the eyes of critics, the situation is exacerbated by the fact that elections do not appear to enforce responsiveness. Incumbent legislators, the argument goes, enjoy so many advantages that it is very difficult for challengers to unseat them even if they are poor representatives.[2] More generally, in practice campaigns and elections seldom live up to their promise as the focus of debate and deliberation on important issues. Candidates, incumbents and challengers alike, are criticized for emphasizing style over substance and, when they do focus on issues, are accused of talking past one another. From this perspective, the prospects for representation seem fairly dim.

However, this conclusion is based on a very narrow conception of representation and responsiveness, one that focuses entirely on the

---

[2] Of course, it is not true that legislators can behave however they want and still win reelection. For example, Jacobson and Dimock (1994) demonstrate that the worst offenders in the House banking scandal suffered at the polls. Nonetheless, very seldom are legislators voted out of office solely as a result of their voting records.

congruence of issue positions. It assumes that the only way that legislators can respond to the policy interests of their constituents is through the roll call votes they cast on the floor of the House or Senate. Taking a broader view of legislative behavior reveals that this type of preference-based responsiveness comprises only a single dimension of policy representation. Indeed, it is fairly easy to generate a number of other standards (of which uptake is one) that might be used to determine whether or not legislators demonstrate responsiveness to the concerns of their districts or states.

Thus, while congruence is clearly a meaningful standard for assessing representational linkages, it is not the only one. Exploring other avenues for policy responsiveness could therefore yield a more optimistic, and certainly more complete, picture of the nature and quality of representation. Nonetheless, for scholars studying legislative representation, responsiveness and congruence have come to be almost synonymous with one another. As Mansbridge (2003) describes it, "In the field of United States legislative studies, the democratic norms regarding representation have often been reduced to one criterion: Does the elected legislator pursue policies that conform to the preferences of voters in the legislator's district?" (525).

Given that other normative standards and empirical measures are possible, why has policy congruence become the point of departure in almost all studies of legislative representation? Fenno argues that the "complexity of the subject seems to have dictated an incremental literature" (1996, 337), a point that certainly seems applicable here. Also, given the somewhat surprising conclusions from the early studies, there has a been a tendency in later research to try to "rescue" a congruence-based conception of representation. Perhaps, some scholars have argued, the relatively weak linkages we observe are artificially dampened as the result of conceptual and methodological problems in how we measure congruence (e.g., Achen 1978) or preferences (Kuklinski 1977; Sullivan and Uslaner 1978). Or perhaps we observe only tenuous cross-sectional relationships between legislators' and constituents' policy positions because legislators are forward-looking, anticipating their districts' or states' interests (Arnold 1990). Others have argued that we observe low levels of congruence because we look for it in the wrong place – at the dyadic rather than the collective level. The question to ask, these scholars claim, is not whether individual legislators reflect their constituents' positions in their roll call voting, but whether Congress, as a whole, reflects and responds to changes in public opinion (Erikson et al. 2002; Weissberg 1978).

The theory underlying uptake suggests a very different approach: that to more fully understand the dynamics of representation, we need to expand our definition of what constitutes legislative responsiveness. The inclusion of an agenda-based notion like uptake offers several distinct analytical advantages over solely preference-based models. First, in many situations, it accords more closely with what we know about how citizens and legislators approach politics. It doesn't require that citizens have clearly defined policy positions on dozens of issues that they have to communicate to their elected representatives. Instead, all that is needed is for there to be a set of problems or issues that the people of the district or state would like to see addressed by their legislator and a challenger available to filter these concerns and highlight them as campaign issues. Because legislators demonstrate agenda-based responsiveness by addressing the underlying issue concerns raised by challengers rather than by adopting their favored solutions, it is generally a more politically feasible option for them. Uptake allows legislators to respond to the concerns of their constituents while retaining control over the specifics of how those concerns will be addressed. As such, it may also address the critique that elected officials pay *too much* attention to (often mercurial) public opinion, "pandering" to the results of polls rather than demonstrating true leadership (Jacobs and Shapiro 2000).

Second, using legislative agendas to study representation and responsiveness draws our focus away from roll call voting and toward other types of legislative behavior that take up more of legislators' time and hence may more adequately reflect their priorities (Hall 1996; Schiller 2000). Roll call voting is only one of a large number of activities engaged in by legislators, so it should not be the sole focus of our research efforts. Including the content of their introductions, cosponsorships, and floor statements as a potential locus of responsiveness offers a more inclusive view of legislative behavior. If we do not consider the content of agendas when assessing representational linkages, we miss out on a crucial component of the representative process. As demonstrated here, legislators design their agendas with reelection and representational considerations in mind, so political scientists should approach them that way as well.

In addition to these practical advantages of including agendas, there are also more fundamental theoretical reasons to consider them. Although they have not been the focus of much empirical work on representation, democratic theorists imbue agendas with great importance in assessing democratic legitimacy. Dahl (1989), for example, argues that setting the agenda and deciding policy outcomes constitute the two basic stages of the policymaking process, and so he claims that a political system cannot be considered democratic unless some measure of popular control exists at both stages (107). A government may adhere to citizens' preferences on every matter it addresses, but if the choice of matters is limited and impervious to change, its status as a democracy is compromised. A truly democratic system should thus show evidence of responsiveness at the decision stage as well as at the agenda-setting stage. At the individual level, responsive legislators should demonstrate both congruence with the opinions of their constituents in their voting and uptake of salient issues in their agendas.

Reconceiving the Role of Campaigns and Elections

By focusing our attention on the ways in which electoral challenges influence the subsequent behavior of legislators, uptake also gives a new role to campaigns and elections in the representative process. In short, campaigns are important because they shape the content of congressional agendas, leaving a downstream legacy in legislative politics and public policy. The potential for an institutional legacy of this sort is usually left out of the ongoing debates about the influence of campaigns, which have focused almost entirely on the impact that they might or might not have on citizens' attitudes, turnout decisions, and vote choices. The results presented here indicate that these debates, while important, are fundamentally incomplete. Because campaigns influence winners, they clearly matter, even if no voter's mind was ever changed by a candidate's appeal or if no campaign ever persuaded a citizen to turn out (or not) on Election Day.

More specifically, uptake underscores the need to reassess the role that challengers play in campaigns. The traditional view is that challengers are influential in the political process to the extent that they win their races and replace less responsive incumbents or, at the least, to the extent that they pose a significant threat of doing so and thus encourage responsible behavior on the part of legislators. Uptake is perfectly compatible with these views, but it suggests that they are not necessary conditions for challengers to have an influence. Because winning legislators are concerned about their future electoral prospects and because responding to their previous challengers' issues can help them to promote their reelection goals, they will engage in uptake of these themes. As such, challengers can be important regardless of how well they do at the polls,[3] and, indeed, the

---

[3] In fact, since safer senators engage in more uptake than their vulnerable colleagues, it is paradoxically the case that, for that chamber, the worse a challenger does at the polls, the more impact he or she has on the agenda.

true extent of most challengers' influence is visible only *after* the election. Put simply, losers matter.

This is not a new point. It echoes Schattschneider's (1960) argument that those on the losing end of the current status quo have the incentive, and, if they are strategic and lucky, the power, to introduce new issues and new cleavages into politics. This ability to influence the agenda is critical because those who play a role in this process choose those issues on which the government will be active and, perhaps equally important, those issues that will not receive attention (Bachrach and Baratz 1962; Walker 1977). As Schattschneider viewed it, control over these choices was "the supreme instrument of power. . . . He who determines what politics is about runs the country because the definition of the alternatives is the choice of conflicts and the choice of conflicts allocates power" (1960, 66). Although it would be an overstatement to claim that challengers' campaign choices determine the agenda, it is clear that they have some influence over it. To neglect this impact leads to an incomplete understanding of the ways in which campaigns, and challengers in those campaigns, shape democratic politics.

Conclusions

The study of uptake makes two significant contributions to research on American politics. First, it provides a fresh perspective on a number of old puzzles and questions about the representative process. As illustrated previously, understanding how congressional elections influence legislative behavior extends electoral connection theories beyond the idea that legislators are forward-looking and generally reelection-oriented, pushes the literature on campaign effects beyond "the dominant notion that campaigns are worth studying only to explain electoral outcomes" (Fenno 1996, 336), and advances our conception of legislative responsiveness beyond policy congruence.

Second, and, equally important, the findings about uptake raise a number of new and intriguing questions about elections and policymaking. For example, it is a common refrain of third-party candidates in presidential elections that, while they may not have won the election, they forced the major parties to listen to their arguments and adopt some of their proposals. Such claims are often dismissed as mere rationalizations for poor performance at the polls, but the results presented here suggest that there could be considerable validity to them. Extending the study of uptake to settings beyond Congress thus promises to be a fruitful avenue for future research.

More generally, uptake demonstrates the value of exploring the institutional impact of campaigns, particularly as they are related to issue agendas. Building on the insights developed here to address phenomena ranging from promise-keeping by winning legislators to the processes through which legislators translate their agendas in office into campaign appeals to the impact of party platforms on subsequent policymaking can further our understanding of the role played by campaigns while, at the same time, contributing to the growth of literature in legislative studies that focuses on activities beyond roll call voting.

The major substantive conclusion to emerge from the study of uptake is a simple one. Legislators' experiences as candidates are inextricably linked to their activity as legislators, so the two should not be analyzed in isolation from one another. They are both components of legislative responsiveness, which is best thought of as a process, and a long one at that. It begins in campaigns as candidates learn about the salience of issues and their strengths and weaknesses on them; continues throughout winning legislators' terms in office, influencing not just how they vote but also the content of legislation they introduce, cosponsor, and speak about on the floor; goes on to inform their career decisions and future electoral prospects; and leaves a tangible trace on public policy outputs. By approaching campaigns and legislative work as interrelated stages of the broader democratic process, we learn more about these stages themselves, as well as the ways in which they are linked. In short, to fully understand the dynamics of the Two Congresses, we must think about them as legislators do, as one Congress.

Appendix

House and Senate Samples

1988 Election/101st House

State	Winning Legislator	Winner's Party	Challenger
AK	Don Young	R	Peter Gruenstein
CA	C. Christopher Cox	R	Linda Lenney
CA	Robert Lagomarsino	R	Gary Hart
CO	Dan Schaefer	R	Martha Ezzard
FL	Harry Johnston	D	Ken Adams
GA	Newt Gingrich	R	David Worley
HI	Patricia Saiki	R	Mary Bitterman
IA	Fred Grandy	R	Dave O'Brien
ID	Richard Stallings	D	Dane Watkins
IL	George Sangmeister	D	Jack Davis
IL	Glenn Poshard	D	Patrick Kelley
IL	Jerry Costello	D	Robert Gaffner
IL	Robert Michel	R	G. Douglas Stephens
IN	Jim Jontz	D	Patricia Williams
IN	John Hiler	R	Thomas Ward
KS	Jim Slattery	D	Phil Meinhardt
LA	Clyde Holloway	R	Faye Williams
MD	Constance Morella	R	Peter Franchot
MD	Roy Dyson	D	Wayne Gilchrest
MI	Carl Pursell	R	Lana Pollack
MI	Howard Wolpe	D	Cal Allgaier
MI	Robert Davis	R	Mitch Irwin
MN	Arlan Stangeland	R	Marv Hanson

(*continued*)

State	Winning Legislator	Winner's Party	Challenger
MO	Bill Emerson	R	Wayne Cryts
MO	Jack Buechner	R	Robert Feigenbaum
MO	Mel Hancock	R	Max Bacon
MS	Larkin Smith	R	Gene Taylor
MS	Mike Espy	D	Jack Coleman
MS	Mike Parker	D	Thomas Collins
MT	Ron Marlenee	R	Richard O'Brien
NC	David Price	D	Tom Fetzer
NC	Howard Coble	R	Tom Gilmore
NC	James McClure Clarke	D	Charles Taylor
NC	Stephen Neal	D	Lyons Gray
NE	Peter Hoagland	D	Jerry Schenken
NH	Charles Douglas	R	Jim Donchess
NH	Robert C. Smith	R	Joseph Keefe
NJ	Frank Pallone	D	Joseph Azzolina
NM	Steven Schiff	R	Tom Udall
NV	Barbara Vucanovich	R	James Spoo
NV	James Bilbray	D	Lucille Lusk
NY	Bill Paxon	R	David Swarts
NY	George Hochbrueckner	D	Edward Romaine
NY	Guy Molinari	R	Jerome O'Donovan
NY	James Walsh	R	Rosemary Pooler
NY	Louise Slaughter	D	John Bouchard
NY	Nita Lowey	D	Joseph DioGuardi
OH	Thomas Luken	D	Steve Chabot
OK	James Inhofe	R	Kurt Glassco
OR	Denny Smith	R	Mike Kopetski
PA	Don Ritter	R	Ed Reibman
PA	Peter Kostmayer	D	Ed Howard
SC	Butler Derrick	D	Henry Jordan
SD	Tim Johnson	D	David Volk
TX	Bill Sarpalius	D	Larry Milner
TX	Greg Laughlin	D	Mac Sweeney
UT	James Hansen	R	Gunn McKay
UT	Wayne Owens	D	Richard Snelgrove
WA	John Miller	R	Reese Lindquist
WA	Jolene Unsoeld	D	Bill Wight

1990 Election/102nd House

State	Winning Legislator	Winner's Party	Challenger
AK	Don Young	R	John Devens
AL	Bill Dickinson	R	Faye Baggiano
AL	Bud Cramer	D	Albert McDonald
CA	Al McCandless	R	Ralph Waite
CA	Calvin Dooley	D	Charles Pashayan
CA	Frank Riggs	R	Douglas Bosco
CA	George E. Brown	D	Bob Hammock
CA	John Doolittle	R	Patricia Malberg
CA	Robert Lagomarsino	R	Anita Ferguson
CO	David Skaggs	D	Jason Lewis
CO	Wayne Allard	R	Dick Bond
CT	Gary Franks	R	Toby Moffett
CT	Rosa DeLauro	D	Thomas Scott
DE	Thomas Carper	D	Ralph Williams
FL	Craig James	R	Reid Hughes
FL	Jim Bacchus	D	Bill Tolley
GA	Ben Jones	D	John Linder
GA	Doug Barnard	D	Sam Jones
GA	Newt Gingrich	R	David Worley
HI	Neil Abercrombie	D	Mike Liu
IA	Jim Nussle	R	Eric Tabor
ID	Larry LaRocco	D	C.A. Smyser
ID	Richard Stallings	D	Sean McDevitt
IL	Frank Annunzio	D	Walter Dudycz
IL	George Sangmeister	D	Manny Hoffman
IL	John W. Cox	D	John Hallock
IN	Jim Jontz	D	John Johnson
IN	Timothy Roemer	D	John Hiler
KY	Carl Perkins	D	Will Scott
KY	Romano Mazzoli	D	Al Brown
LA	Clyde Holloway	R	Cleo Fields
LA	Jim McCrery	R	Foster Campbell
MD	Wayne Gilchrest	R	Roy Dyson
ME	Thomas Andrews	D	David Emery
MI	David Bonior	D	Jim Dingerman
MI	David Camp	R	Joan Dennison
MI	Howard Wolpe	D	Brad Haskins
MN	Jim Ramstad	R	Lewis DeMars
MO	Bill Emerson	R	Russ Carnahan
MO	Joan Kelly Horn	D	Jack Buechner

(*continued*)

State	Winning Legislator	Winner's Party	Challenger
MS	Gene Taylor	D	Sheila Smith
MT	Pat Williams	D	Brad Johnson
NC	Charles Taylor	R	James Clarke
NC	David Price	D	John Carrington
ND	Byron Dorgan	D	Ed Schafer
NE	Bill Barrett	R	Sandra Scofield
NE	Peter Hoagland	D	Ally Milder
NH	Bill Zeliff	R	Joseph Keefe
NH	Dick Swett	D	Chuck Douglas
NJ	Dick Zimmer	R	Marguerite Chandler
NJ	Robert Andrews	D	Daniel Mangini
NV	Barbara Vucanovich	R	Jane Wisdom
NV	James Bilbray	D	Bob Dickinson
NY	Bill Paxon	R	Kevin Gaughan
NY	George Hochbrueckner	D	Francis Creighton
OH	Charles Luken	D	J. Blackwell
OH	David Hobson	R	Jack Schira
OH	John Boehner	R	Gregory Jolivette
OK	James Inhofe	R	Kurt Glassco
OR	Mike Kopetski	D	Denny Smith
RI	John Reed	D	Trudy Coxe
RI	Ronald Machtley	R	Scott Wolf
SC	Liz Patterson	D	Terry Haskins
TX	Bill Sarpalius	D	Dick Waterfield
TX	Chet Edwards	D	Hugh Shine
TX	Greg Laughlin	D	Joe Dial
TX	Jack Brooks	D	Maury Meyers
TX	Jim Chapman	D	Hamp Hodges
TX	John Bryant	D	Jerry Rucker
UT	Bill Orton	D	Karl Snow
UT	Wayne Owens	D	Genevieve Atwood
VA	D. French Slaughter	R	David Smith
VA	James Moran	D	Stan Parris
VT	Bernard Sanders	I	Peter Smith
WA	John Miller	R	Cynthia Sullivan
WA	Jolene Unsoeld	D	Bob Williams
WI	Toby Roth	R	Jerome Van Sistine
WV	Harley Staggers	D	Oliver Luck
WV	Nick Rahall	D	Marianne Brewster

1992 Election/103rd House

State	Winning Legislator	Winner's Party	Challenger
AK	Don Young	R	John Devens
AL	Spencer Bachus	R	Ben Erdreich
AR	Jay Dickey	R	W.J. McCuen
AZ	Karan English	D	Doug Wead
CA	Anthony Beilenson	D	Tom McClintock
CA	Elton Gallegly	R	Anita Ferguson
CA	Howard McKeon	R	James Gilmartin
CA	Jane Harman	D	Joan Flores
CA	Ken Calvert	R	Mark Takano
CA	Michael Huffington	R	Gloria Ochoa
CA	Richard Lehman	D	Tai Cload
CA	Steve Horn	R	Evan Braude
CA	Vic Fazio	D	H.L. Richardson
CO	David Skaggs	D	Brian Day
CT	Rosa DeLauro	D	Tom Scott
FL	C.W. Bill Young	R	Karen Moffitt
FL	Charles Canady	R	Tom Mims
FL	E. Clay Shaw	R	Gwen Margolis
FL	Earl Hutto	D	Terry Ketchel
FL	Karen Thurman	D	Tom Hogan
FL	Michael Bilirakis	R	Cheryl Knapp
FL	Sam Gibbons	D	Mark Shape
FL	Tillie Fowler	R	Mattox Hair
GA	Don Johnson	D	Ralph Hudgens
GA	Jack Kingston	R	Barbara Christmas
GA	John Linder	R	Cathey Steinberg
GA	Nathan Deal	D	Daniel Becker
IA	Jim Ross Lightfoot	R	Elaine Baxter
ID	Larry LaRocco	D	Rachel Gilbert
ID	Michael Crapo	R	J.D. Williams
IL	Dan Rostenkowski	D	Elias Zenkich
IL	Donald Manzullo	R	John Cox
IL	George Sangmeister	D	Robert Herbolsheimer
IL	Lane Evans	D	Ken Schloemer
IL	Philip Crane	R	Sheila Smith
IL	Richard Durbin	D	John Shimkus
IL	William Lipinski	D	Harry Lepinske
IN	Frank McCloskey	D	Richard Mourdock
IN	Steve Buyer	R	Jim Jontz
KS	Dan Glickman	D	Eric Yost
MA	Gerry Studds	D	Daniel Daly
MA	Martin Meehan	D	Paul Cronin

(continued)

State	Winning Legislator	Winner's Party	Challenger
MA	Peter Torkildsen	R	Nicholas Mavroules
MD	Albert Wynn	D	Michele Dyson
MD	Roscoe Bartlett	R	Thomas Hattery
MD	Steny Hoyer	D	Lawrence Hogan
MD	Wayne Gilchrest	R	Tom McMillen
ME	Olympia Snowe	R	Patrick McGowan
ME	Thomas Andrews	D	Linda Bean
MI	Bob Carr	D	Dick Chrysler
MI	Joseph Knollenberg	R	Walter Briggs
MN	Collin Peterson	D	Bernie Omann
MN	Rod Grams	R	Gerry Sikorski
MS	Gene Taylor	D	Paul Harvey
MT	Pat Williams	D	Ron Marlenee
NC	Charles Taylor	R	John Stevens
NC	Tim Valentine	D	Don Davis
NE	Peter Hoagland	D	Ronald Staskiewicz
NJ	Christopher Smith	R	Brian Hughes
NJ	Herbert Klein	D	Joseph Bubba
NJ	William Hughes	D	Frank LoBiondo
NV	Barbara Vucanovich	R	Pete Sferrazza
NY	Carolyn Maloney	D	Bill Green
NY	Gary Ackerman	D	Allan Binder
NY	George Hochbrueckner	D	Edward Romaine
NY	Jack Quinn	R	Dennis Gorski
NY	Maurice Hinchey	D	Bob Moppert
NY	Nita Lowey	D	Joseph DioGuardi
NY	Peter King	R	Steve Orlins
NY	Rick Lazio	R	Thomas Downey
NY	Sherwood Boehlert	R	Paula DiPerna
NY	Susan Molinari	R	Sal Albanese
NY	Thomas Manton	D	Dennis Shea
OH	Martin Hoke	R	Mary Oakar
OH	Sherrod Brown	D	Margaret Mueller
OK	James Inhofe	R	John Selph
OR	Elizabeth Furse	D	Tony Meeker
TX	Charles Wilson	D	Donna Peterson
TX	Henry Bonilla	R	Albert Bustamante
TX	Michael Andrews	D	Dolly McKenna
TX	Pete Geren	D	David Hobbs
TX	Ronald Coleman	D	Chip Taberski
VA	Leslie Byrne	D	Henry Butler
WA	Maria Cantwell	D	Gary Nelson
WI	Scott Klug	R	Ada Deer
WI	Tom Petri	R	Peggy Lautenschlager
WY	Craig Thomas	R	Jon Herschler

1994 Election/104th House

State	Winning Legislator	Winner's Party	Challenger
AL	Bud Cramer	D	Wayne Parker
AR	Jay Dickey	R	Jay Bradford
AZ	J. D. Hayworth	R	Karan English
AZ	Matt Salmon	R	Chuck Blanchard
CA	Anthony Beilenson	D	Rich Sybert
CA	Brian Bilbray	R	Lynn Schenk
CA	Frank Riggs	R	Dan Hamburg
CA	Jane Harman	D	Susan M. Brooks
CT	Gary Franks	R	James H. Maloney
CT	Sam Gejdenson	D	Edward W. Munster
FL	Charles Canady	R	Robert Connors
FL	David Weldon	R	Sue Munsey
FL	Joe Scarborough	R	Vince Whibbs Jr.
FL	Karen Thurman	D	Don Garlits
FL	Sam Gibbons	D	Mark Sharpe
GA	Charlie Norwood	R	Don Johnson
HI	Neil Abercrombie	D	Orson Swindle
IA	Greg Ganske	R	Neal Smith
IA	Jim Nussle	R	Dave Nagle
IA	Jim Ross Lightfoot	R	Elaine Baxter
IA	Tom Latham	R	Sheila McGuire
ID	Helen Chenoweth	R	Larry LaRocco
IL	Ray LaHood	R	G. Douglas Stephens
IL	William Lipinski	D	Jim Nalepa
IN	David McIntosh	R	Joseph Hogsett
IN	John Hostettler	R	Frank McCloskey
IN	John Myers	R	Michael M. Harmless
IN	Mark Souder	R	Jill L. Long
KS	Sam Brownback	R	John Carlin
MA	Peter Blute	R	Kevin O'Sullivan
MA	Peter Torkildsen	R	John F. Tierney
MD	Bob Ehrlich	R	Gerry L. Brewster
MD	Steny Hoyer	D	Donald Devine
MI	Bart Stupak	D	Gil Ziegler
MI	Dale Kildee	D	Megan O'Neill
MI	Lynn Rivers	D	John A. Schall
MI	Sander Levin	D	John Pappageorge
MN	Bill Luther	D	Tad Jude
MN	Gil Gutknecht	R	John C. Hottinger
MO	Harold Volkmer	D	Kenny Hulshof
MO	Mel Hancock	R	James R. Fossard

(continued)

State	Winning Legislator	Winner's Party	Challenger
MS	Roger Wicker	R	Bill Wheeler
MT	Pat Williams	D	Cy Jamison
NC	Charles Taylor	R	Maggie Lauterer
NC	David Funderburk	R	Richard Moore
NC	Richard Burr	R	A. P. Sands
ND	Earl Pomeroy	D	Gary Porter
NE	Jon Christensen	R	Peter Hoagland
NH	Charles Bass	R	Dick Swett
NJ	Bill Martini	R	Herb Klein
NJ	Frank LoBiondo	R	Louis Magazzu
NJ	Frank Pallone	D	Mike Herson
NY	Carolyn Maloney	D	Charles Millard
NY	Louise Slaughter	D	Renee F. Davison
NY	Maurice Hinchey	D	Bob Moppert
NY	Michael Forbes	R	George J. Hochbrueckner
OH	Frank Cremeans	R	Ted Strickland
OH	Robert Ney	R	Greg L. DiDonato
OH	Sherrod Brown	D	Gregory White
OH	Steve Chabot	R	David Mann
OH	Steven LaTourette	R	Eric D. Fingerhut
OR	Elizabeth Furse	D	Bill Witt
OR	Jim Bunn	R	Catherine Webber
PA	Jon Fox	R	Marjorie Mezvinsky
PA	Phil English	R	Bill Leavens
RI	Patrick Kennedy	D	Kevin Vigilante
SD	Tim Johnson	D	Janet Berkhout
TN	Ed Bryant	R	Harold Byrd
TN	Van Hilleary	R	Jeff Whorley
TN	Zach Wamp	R	Randy Button
TX	Henry Bonilla	R	Rolando L. Rios
TX	Ken Bentsen	D	Gene Fontenot
TX	Ronald Coleman	D	Bobby Ortiz
TX	William Thornberry	R	Bill Sarpalius
UT	Enid Greene	R	Karen Shepherd
VA	Lewis Payne	D	George Landrith III
VA	Norman Sisisky	D	George Sweet
VA	Owen Pickett	D	Jim Chapman
VA	Thomas Davis	R	Leslie L. Byrne
VT	Bernard Sanders	I	John Carroll
WA	George Nethercutt	R	Thomas S. Foley
WA	Jack Metcalf	R	Harriet A. Spanel
WA	Randy Tate	R	Mike Kreidler
WA	Rick White	R	Maria Cantwell
WY	Barbara Cubin	R	Bob Schuster

1996 Election/105th House

State	Winning Legislator	Winner's Party	Challenger
AK	Don Young	R	Georgianna Lincoln
AL	Bob Riley	R	T. D. Little
AL	Bud Cramer	D	Wayne Parker
AL	Robert Aderholt	R	Robert Wilson
AR	Marion Berry	D	Warren Dupwe
AR	Victor Snyder	D	Bud Cummins
AZ	J. D. Hayworth	R	Steve Owens
CA	Brad Sherman	D	Rich Sybert
CA	Brian Bilbray	R	Peter Navarro
CA	Cal Dooley	D	Trice Harvey
CA	Ellen Tauscher	D	Bill Baker
CA	Frank Riggs	R	Michela Aliota
CA	George E. Brown	D	Linda Wilde
CA	Steve Horn	R	Rick Zbur
CA	Vic Fazio	D	Tim Lefever
CA	Walter Capps	D	Andrea Seastrand
CO	David Skaggs	D	Pat Miller
CO	Diana DeGette	D	Joe Rogers
CO	Robert Schaffer	R	Guy Kelley
CT	Sam Gejdenson	D	Edward Munster
FL	Allen Boyd	D	Bill Sutton
FL	David Weldon	R	John Byron
FL	Jim Davis	D	Mark Sharpe
FL	Robert Wexler	D	Beverly Kennedy
GA	Charlie Norwood	R	David Bell
GA	Cynthia McKinney	D	John Mitnick
GA	Sanford Bishop	D	Darrel Ealum
GA	Saxby Chambliss	R	Jim Wiggins
IA	Leonard Boswell	D	Mike Mahaffey
ID	Helen Chenoweth	R	Dan Williams
IL	Jerry Weller	R	Clem Balanoff
IL	John Shimkus	R	Jay Hoffman
IL	Lane Evans	D	Mark Baker
IL	Rod Blagojevich	D	Michael Flanagan
IL	Thomas Ewing	R	Laurel Prussing
IN	Ed Pease	R	Robert Hellmann
IN	John Hostettler	R	Jonathan Weinzapfel
IN	Julia Carson	D	Virginia Blankenbaker
IN	Lee Hamilton	D	Jean Leising

(continued)

State	Winning Legislator	Winner's Party	Challenger
KS	Jim Ryun	R	John Frieden
KS	Todd Tiahrt	R	Randy Rathbun
KS	Vince Snowbarger	R	Judy Hancock
KY	Anne Northup	R	Mike Ward
KY	Edward Whitfield	R	Dennis Null
KY	Ron Lewis	R	Joe Wright
KY	Scotty Baesler	D	Ernest Fletcher
LA	John Cooksey	R	Francis Thompson
MA	John Tierney	D	Peter Torkildsen
MA	William Delahunt	D	Edward Teague
MD	Robert Ehrlich	R	Connie DeJuliis
MD	Steny Hoyer	D	John Morgan
MI	Dale Kildee	D	Patrick Nowak
MI	Deborah Stabenow	D	Dick Chrysler
MI	Lynn Rivers	D	Joe Fitzsimmons
MN	Bruce Vento	D	Dennis Newinski
MN	Collin Peterson	D	Darrell McKigney
MN	David Minge	D	Gary Revier
MN	Gil Gutknecht	R	Mary Rieder
MN	William "Bill" Luther	D	Tad Jude
MO	James Talent	R	Joan Horn
MO	Kenny Hulshof	R	Harold Volkmer
MT	Rick Hill	R	Bill Yellowtail
NC	David Price	D	Fred Heineman
NC	Mike McIntyre	D	Bill Caster
NE	Jon Christensen	R	James Davis
NH	Charles Bass	R	Deborah Arnesen
NH	John Sununu	R	Joseph Keefe
NJ	Mike Pappas	R	David Del Vecchio
NJ	Steve Rothman	D	Kathleen Donovan
NJ	William Pascrell	D	Bill Martini
NV	Jim Gibbons	R	Thomas Wilson
NV	John Ensign	R	Bob Coffin
NY	Jack Quinn	R	Francis Pordum
NY	Maurice Hinchey	D	Sue Wittig
NY	Michael Forbes	R	Nora Bredes
OH	Dennis Kucinich	D	Martin Hoke
OH	Steve Chabot	R	Mark Longabaugh
OH	Steven LaTourette	R	Tom Coyne
OH	Ted Strickland	D	Frank Cremeans
OK	Tom Coburn	R	Glen Johnson
OK	Wes Watkins	R	Darryl Roberts
OR	Darlene Hooley	D	Jim Bunn

State	Winning Legislator	Winner's Party	Challenger
PA	Jon Fox	R	Joseph Hoeffel
PA	Paul McHale	D	Bob Kilbanks
SC	John Spratt	D	Larry Bigham
SD	John Thune	R	Rick Weiland
TN	Bart Gordon	D	Steve Gill
TN	Van Hilleary	R	Mark Stewart
TN	Zach Wamp	R	Charles Jolly
TX	Charles Stenholm	D	Rudy Izzard
TX	Chet Edwards	D	Jay Mathis
TX	Jim Turner	D	Brian Babin
TX	Kay Granger	R	Hugh Parmer
TX	Ken Bentsen	D	Dolly McKenna
TX	Martin Frost	D	Ed Harrison
TX	Nick Lampson	D	Steve Stockman
TX	Pete Sessions	R	John Pouland
TX	Ron Paul	R	Charles Morris
UT	Chris Cannon	R	Bill Orton
UT	Merrill Cook	R	Ross Anderson
VT	Bernard Sanders	I	Susan Sweetser
WA	George Nethercutt	R	Judy Olson
WA	Jack Metcalf	R	Kevin Quigley
WA	Linda Smith	R	Brian Baird
WA	Richard "Doc" Hastings	R	Rick Locke
WA	Rick White	R	Jeffrey Coopersmith
WI	David Obey	D	Scott West
WI	Mark Neumann	R	Lydia Spottswood
WI	Ron Kind	D	Jim Harsdorf
WI	Scott Klug	R	Paul Soglin
WY	Barbara Cubin	R	Pete Maxfield

1988 Election/101st–103rd Senates

State	Winning Legislator	Winner's Party	Challenger
AZ	Dennis DeConcini	D	Keith DeGreen
CA	Pete Wilson	R	Leo McCarthy
FL	Connie Mack	R	Buddy MacKay
MA	Edward Kennedy	D	Joseph Malone
MI	Donald Riegle	D	Jim Dunn
MN	David Durenberger	R	Hubert Humphrey III
MO	John Danforth	R	Jay Nixon
NE	Bob Kerrey	D	David Karnes
NJ	Frank Lautenberg	D	Pete Dawkins
NY	Patrick Moynihan	D	Robert McMillan
OH	Howard Metzenbaum	D	George Voinovich
TX	Lloyd Bentsen	D	Beau Boulter
VA	Charles Robb	D	Maurice Dawkins
WA	Slade Gorton	R	Mike Lowry

1990 Election/102nd–104th Senates

State	Winning Legislator	Winner's Party	Challenger
CO	Hank Brown	R	Josie Heath
IL	Paul Simon	D	Lynn Martin
KS	Nancy Kassebaum	R	Dick Williams
KY	Mitch McConnell	R	Harvey Sloane
MA	John Kerry	D	Jim Rappaport
MI	Carl Levin	D	Bill Schuette
MN	Paul Wellstone	D	Rudy Boschwitz
NC	Jesse Helms	R	Harvey Gantt
NE	Jim Exon	D	James Daub
NJ	Bill Bradley	D	Christine Todd Whitman
OK	David Boren	D	Stephen Jones
OR	Mark Hatfield	R	Harry Lonsdale
TN	Al Gore	D	William Hawkins
TX	Phil Gramm	R	Hugh Parmer
VA	John Warner	R	Nancy Spannaus

1992 Election/103nd–105th Senates

State	Winning Legislator	Winner's Party	Challenger
AZ	John McCain	R	Claire Sargent
CO	Ben Nighthorse Campbell	D	Terry Considine
CT	Christopher Dodd	D	Brook Johnson
FL	Bob Graham	D	Bill Grant
GA	Paul Coverdell	R	Wyche Fowler
IA	Charles Grassley	R	Jean Lloyd-Jones
IL	Carol Moseley-Braun	D	Richard Williamson
IN	Daniel Coats	R	Joseph Hogsett
KS	Bob Dole	R	Gloria O'Dell
KY	Wendell Ford	D	David Williams
MD	Barbara Mikulski	D	Alan Keyes
MO	Christopher Bond	R	Geri Rothman-Serot
NC	Lauch Faircloth	R	Terry Sanford
NV	Harry Reid	D	Demar Dahl
NY	Alfonse D'Amato	R	Robert Abrams
OH	John Glenn	D	Mike DeWine
OK	Don Nickles	R	Steve Lewis
OR	Bob Packwood	R	Les AuCoin
PA	Arlen Specter	R	Lynn Yeakel
SC	Ernest Hollings	D	Tommy Hartnett
WA	Patty Murray	D	Rod Chandler
WI	Russ Feingold	D	Bob Kasten

References

Abramowitz, Alan I. 1980. "A Comparison of Voting for U.S. Senator and Representative in 1978." *American Political Science Review* 74(3): 633–40.

Abramowitz, Alan I. and Jeffrey A. Segal. 1992. *Senate Elections*. Ann Arbor: University of Michigan Press.

Achen, Christopher H. 1977. "Measuring Representation: Perils of the Correlation Coefficient." *American Journal of Political Science* 21(4): 805–15.

Achen, Christopher H. 1978. "Measuring Representation." *American Journal of Political Science* 22(3): 475–510.

Ahuja, Sunil. 1994. "Electoral Status and Representation in the United States Senate." *American Politics Quarterly* 22(1): 104–18.

Ainsworth, Scott H. and Thad E. Hall. 2001. "Ties That Bind: Participation and Coordination in the U.S. Congress." Paper presented at the annual meeting of the Midwest Political Science Association, Chicago.

Ansolabehere, Stephen and Shanto Iyengar. 1995. *Going Negative: How Attack Ads Shrink and Polarize the Electorate*. New York: Free Press.

Arnold, R. Douglas. 1990. *The Logic of Congressional Action*. New Haven, CT: Yale University Press.

Arnold, R. Douglas. 2004. *Congress, the Press, and Political Accountability*. Princeton, NJ: Princeton University Press.

Bachrach, Peter and Morton Baratz. 1962. "Two Faces of Power." *American Political Science Review* 56(4): 947–52.

Baker, Ross K. 1989. *House and Senate*. New York: W. W. Norton & Company.

Bauer, Raymond, Ithiel de Sola Pool, and Lewis Anthony Dexter. 1963. *American Business and Public Policy*. New York: Atherton Press.

Baumgartner, Frank R. and Bryan D. Jones. 1993. *Agendas and Instability in American Politics*. Chicago: University of Chicago Press.

Baumgartner, Frank R. and Bryan D. Jones, eds. 2002. *Policy Dynamics*. Chicago: University of Chicago Press.

Baumgartner, Frank R., Bryan D. Jones, and Michael C. MacLeod. 2000. "The Evolution of Bureaucratic Institutions." *Journal of Politics* 62(2): 321–49.

Bendor, Jonathan and Terry M. Moe. 1985. "An Adaptive Model of Bureaucratic Politics." *American Political Science Review* 79(3): 755–74.

Benenson, Bob. 1988. "Election Guide 1988: New York Outlook." *CQ Weekly*, October 15, 1988, 2926.

Benenson, Bob. 1990. "Election 1990: Kansas Outlook." *CQ Weekly*, October 13, 1990, 3310.

Bernstein, Robert A. 1977. "Divisive Primaries Do Hurt: U.S. Senate Races, 1956–1972." *American Political Science Review* 71(2): 540–45.

Bernstein, Robert A. 1988. "Do U.S. Senators Moderate Strategically?" *American Political Science Review* 82(1): 237–41.

Bernstein, Robert A. 1989. *Elections, Representation, and Congressional Voting Behavior: The Myth of Constituency Control*. Englewood Cliffs, NJ: Prentice Hall.

Bianco, William T. 1994. *Trust: Representatives & Constituents*. Ann Arbor: University of Michigan Press.

Bickers, Kenneth N. and Robert M. Stein. 1996. "The Electoral Dynamics of the Federal Pork Barrel." *American Journal of Political Science* 40(4): 1300–26.

Birkland, Thomas A. 1997. *After Disaster: Agenda Setting, Public Policy, and Focusing Events*. Washington, DC: Georgetown University Press.

Bohman, James. 1996. *Public Deliberation: Pluralism, Complexity, and Democracy*. Cambridge, MA: MIT Press.

Bond, Jon R. 1985. "Dimensions of District Attention Over Time." *American Journal of Political Science* 29(2): 330–47.

Bond, Jon, Cary Covington, and Richard Fleisher. 1985. "Explaining Challenger Quality in Congressional Elections." *Journal of Politics* 47(2): 510–29.

Born, Richard. 1981. "The Influence of House Primary Election Divisiveness on General Election Margins, 1962–76." *Journal of Politics* 43(3): 640–61.

Brady, David W., Brandice Canes-Wrone, and John F. Cogan. 2000. "Differences Between Winning and Losing Incumbents." In *Change and Continuity in House Elections*, ed. David W. Brady, John F. Cogan, and Morris Fiorina. Stanford, CA: Stanford University Press.

Bragdon, Peter. 1988. "Election Guide 1988: Mississippi Outlook." *CQ Weekly*, October 15, 1988, 2912–14.

Bullock, Charles S. 1973. "Committee Transfers in the United States House of Representatives." *Journal of Politics* 35(1): 85–120.

Burden, Barry C. and David C. Kimball. 2002. *Why Americans Split Their Tickets: Campaigns, Competition, and Divided Government*. Ann Arbor: University of Michigan Press.

Cain, Bruce, John Ferejohn, and Morris Fiorina. 1987. *The Personal Vote: Constituency Service and Electoral Independence*. Cambridge, MA: Harvard University Press.

Campbell, Angus, Philip Converse, Warren Miller, and Donald Stokes. 1960. *The American Voter*. New York: Wiley.

Campbell, James E. 1982. "Cosponsoring Legislation in the U.S. Congress." *Legislative Studies Quarterly* 7(4): 415–22.

Canes-Wrone, Brandice, David W. Brady, and John F. Cogan. 2002. "Out of Step, Out of Office: Electoral Accountability and House Members' Voting." *American Political Science Review* 96(1): 127–40.

Canon, David T. 1993. "Sacrificial Lambs or Strategic Politicians? Political Amateurs in U.S. House Elections." *American Journal of Political Science* 37(4): 1119–41.

Carsey, Thomas M. 2000. *Campaign Dynamics: The Race for Governor.* Ann Arbor: University of Michigan Press.

Cassata, Donna. 1997. "Vocational Program Gets Panel OK." *CQ Weekly,* June 14, 1997, 1378–9.

Cnudde, Charles F. and Donald J. McCrone. 1966. "The Linkage Between Constituency Attitudes and Congressional Voting Behavior: A Causal Model." *American Political Science Review* 60(1): 66–72.

Cobb, Roger W. and Charles D. Elder. 1983. *Participation in American Politics: The Dynamics of Agenda-Building.* Boston: Allyn and Bacon.

Cook, Rhodes. 1990. "Election 1990: Missouri Outlook." *CQ Weekly,* October 13, 1990, 3326–7.

Dahl, Robert A. 1989. *Democracy and Its Critics.* New Haven, CT: Yale University Press.

Davidson, Roger H. and Walter J. Oleszek. 1996. *Congress and Its Members,* 5th edition. Washington, DC: CQ Press.

Deckard, Barbara Sinclair. 1976. "Electoral Marginality and Party Loyalty in House Roll Call Voting." *American Journal of Political Science* 20(3): 469–81.

Delli Carpini, Michael X. and Scott Keeter. 1996. *What Americans Know about Politics and Why It Matters.* New Haven, CT: Yale University Press.

Downs, Anthony. 1972. "Up and Down with Ecology: The Issue Attention Cycle." *The Public Interest* 28(2): 38–50.

Duncan, Phil. 1988. "Indiana 5: Jontz vs. Williams A Standout in the Heartland." *CQ Weekly,* October 29, 1988, 3102.

Duncan, Phil, ed. 1993. *CQ's Politics in America.* Washington, DC: Congressional Quarterly.

Elling, Richard C. 1982. "Ideological Change in the U.S. Senate: Time and Electoral Responsiveness." *Legislative Studies Quarterly* 7(1): 75–92.

Erikson, Robert S. 1971. "The Electoral Impact of Congressional Roll Call Voting." *American Political Science Review* 65(4): 1018–32.

Erikson, Robert S. 1978. "Constituency Opinion and Congressional Behavior: A Reexamination of the Miller–Stokes Representation Data." *American Journal of Political Science* 22(3): 511–35.

Erikson, Robert S., Michael B. MacKuen, and James A. Stimson. 2002. *The Macro Polity.* New York: Cambridge University Press.

Erikson, Robert S. and Gerald C. Wright. 1993. "Voters, Candidates, and Issues in Congressional Elections." In *Congress Reconsidered,* 5th edition, ed. Lawrence Dodd and Bruce Oppenheimer. Washington, DC: CQ Press.

Eulau, Heinz and Paul D. Karps. 1977. "The Puzzle of Representation: Specifying Components of Responsiveness." *Legislative Studies Quarterly* 2(3): 233–54.

Fenno, Richard F. 1973. *Congressmen in Committees.* Boston: Little, Brown.

Fenno, Richard F. 1978. *Home Style.* Boston: Little, Brown.

Fenno, Richard F. 1989. *The Making of a Senator: Dan Quayle.* Washington, DC: CQ Press.

Fenno, Richard F. 1996. *Senators on the Campaign Trail: The Politics of Representation.* Norman: University of Oklahoma Press.

Fiorina, Morris P. 1973. "Electoral Margins, Constituency Influence, and Policy Moderation: A Critical Assessment." *American Politics Quarterly* 1(4): 479–98.

Fiorina, Morris P. 1974. *Representatives, Roll Calls, and Constituencies*. Boston: D. C. Heath.

Fowler, Linda L., Scott R. Douglass, and Wesley D. Clark, Jr. 1980. "The Electoral Effects of House Committee Assignments." *Journal of Politics* 42(1): 307–19.

Fraley, Colette. 1995. "Senate Votes to Reauthorize Ryan White AIDS Program." *CQ Weekly*, July 29, 1995, 2277–8.

Franklin, Charles H. 1991. "Eschewing Obfuscation? Campaigns and the Perception of U.S. Senate Incumbents." *American Political Science Review* 85(4): 1193–1214.

Freedman, Paul and Kenneth Goldstein. 1999. "Measuring Media Exposure and the Effects of Negative Campaign Ads." *American Journal of Political Science* 43(4): 1189–1208.

Greenblatt, Alan and Robert D. Elving. 1996. "Election Preview: California." *CQ Weekly*, October 19, 1996, 2974.

Gronke, Paul. 2000. *The Electorate, the Campaign, and the Office: A Unified Approach to Senate and House Elections*. Ann Arbor: University of Michigan Press.

Groseclose, Timothy and Keith Krehbiel. 1994. "Golden Parachutes, Rubber Checks, and Strategic Retirements from the 102nd House." *American Journal of Political Science* 38(1): 75–99.

Hale, Jon F. 1987. "The Scribes of Texas: Newspaper Coverage of the 1984 U.S. Senate Campaign." In *Campaigns in the News: Mass Media and Congressional Elections*, ed. J. P. Vermeer. New York: Greenwood Press.

Hall, Richard L. 1996. *Participation in Congress*. New Haven, CT: Yale University Press.

Hart, Roderick P. 2000. *Campaign Talk: Why Elections Are Good for Us*. Princeton, NJ: Princeton University Press.

Herrnson, Paul S. 1998. *Congressional Elections*, 2nd edition. Washington, DC: CQ Press.

Hershey, Marjorie Randon. 1984. *Running for Office: The Political Education of Campaigners*. Chatham, NJ: Chatham House Publishers.

Hill, Kim Quaile and Patricia A. Hurley. 1999. "Dyadic Representation Reappraised." *American Journal of Political Science* 43(1): 109–37.

Hinckley, Barbara. 1980. "House Re-Elections and Senate Defeats: The Role of the Challenger." *British Journal of Political Science* 10(4): 441–60.

Holbrook, Thomas M. 1996. *Do Campaigns Matter?* Thousand Oaks, CA: Sage Publications.

Hurley, Patricia A. 1982. "Collective Representation Reappraised." *Legislative Studies Quarterly* 7(1): 119–36.

Hurley, Patricia A. and Kim Quaile Hill. 2003. "Beyond the Demand-Input Model: A Theory of Representational Linkages." *Journal of Politics* 65(2): 304–26.

Idelson, Holly. 1990. "Election 1990: Washington Outlook." *CQ Weekly*, October 13, 1990, 3354.

Iyengar, Shanto and Donald R. Kinder. 1987. *News That Matters*. Chicago: University of Chicago Press.

Jacobs, Lawrence R. and Robert Y. Shapiro. 2000. *Politicians Don't Pander: Political Manipulation and the Loss of Democratic Responsiveness.* Chicago: University of Chicago Press.

Jacobson, Gary C. 1996. "The 1994 House Elections in Perspective." *Political Science Quarterly* 111(2): 203–23.

Jacobson, Gary C. 2001. *The Politics of Congressional Elections*, 5th edition. New York: Longman.

Jacobson, Gary C. and Michael A. Dimock. 1994. "Checking Out: The Effects of Bank Overdrafts on the 1992 House Elections." *American Journal of Political Science* 38(3): 601–24.

Jacobson, Gary C. and Samuel Kernell. 1983. *Strategy and Choice in Congressional Elections*, 2nd edition. New Haven, CT: Yale University Press.

Jewell, Malcolm E. 1983. "Legislator–Constituency Relations and the Representative Process." *Legislative Studies Quarterly* 8(3): 303–37.

Johannes, John R. 1984. *To Serve the People: Congress and Constituency Service.* Lincoln: University of Nebraska Press.

Johannes, John R. and John C. McAdams. 1981. "The Congressional Incumbency Effect: Is It Casework, Policy Compatibility, or Something Else? An Examination of the 1978 Election." *American Journal of Political Science* 25(3): 512–42.

Johnson, Charles. 2003. *How Our Laws Are Made.* Washington, DC: Government Printing Office.

Jones, Bryan D. 1973. "Competitiveness, Role Orientations, and Legislative Responsiveness." *Journal of Politics* 35(4): 924–47.

Jones, Bryan D. 1994. *Reconceiving Decision-Making in Democratic Politics.* Chicago: University of Chicago Press.

Jones, Bryan D. 2001. *Politics and the Architecture of Choice: Bounded Rationality and Governance.* Chicago: University of Chicago Press.

Jones, Bryan D. and Frank R. Baumgartner. 2005. *The Politics of Attention: How Government Prioritizes Problems.* Chicago: University of Chicago Press.

Jones, Bryan D., Frank R. Baumgartner, and Jeffery C. Talbert. 1993. "The Destruction of Issue Monopolies in Congress." *American Political Science Review* 87(3): 657–71.

Kahn, Kim Fridkin. 1991. "Senate Elections in the News: Examining Campaign Coverage." *Legislative Studies Quarterly* 16(3): 349–74.

Kahn, Kim Fridkin and Patrick J. Kenney. 1999. *The Spectacle of U.S. Senate Campaigns.* Princeton, NJ: Princeton University Press.

Kaplan, Dave. 1988. "Election Guide 1988: South Dakota Outlook." *CQ Weekly*, October 15, 1988, 2942.

Kaplan, Dave. 1990. "Election Guide 1990: Montana Outlook." *CQ Weekly*, October 13, 1990, 3327.

Katz, Jeffrey L. 1997. "GOP School Plans Get Retooling." *CQ Weekly*, December 13, 1997, 3062–5.

Kenney, Patrick J. 1988. "Sorting Out the Effects of Primary Divisiveness in Congressional and Senatorial Elections." *Western Political Quarterly* 41(4): 765–77.

Kessler, Daniel and Keith Krehbiel. 1996. "Dynamics of Cosponsorship." *American Political Science Review* 90(3): 555–66.

King, David C. 1997. *Turf Wars: How Congressional Committees Claim Jurisdiction*. Chicago: University of Chicago Press.

Kingdon, John W. 1968. *Candidates for Office: Beliefs and Strategies*. New York: Random House.

Kingdon, John W. 1984. *Agendas, Alternatives, and Public Policies*. Boston, MA: Little, Brown.

Kingdon, John W. 1989. *Congressmen's Voting Decisions*. New York: Harper & Row.

Krasno, Jonathan S. 1994. *Challengers, Competition, and Reelection: Comparing Senate and House Elections*. New Haven, CT: Yale University Press.

Krasno, Jonathan S. and Donald Philip Green. 1988. "Preempting Quality Challengers in House Elections." *Journal of Politics* 50(4): 920–36.

Krutz, Glen S. 2000. "Congressional Leaders and the Winnowing of Legislation." Paper presented at the annual meeting of the American Political Science Association, Washington, DC.

Kuklinski, James H. 1977. "District Competitiveness and Legislative Roll-Call Behavior: A Reassessment of the Marginality Hypothesis." *American Journal of Political Science* 21(3): 627–38.

Kuklinski, James H. 1978. "Representativeness and Elections: A Policy Analysis." *American Political Science Review* 72(1): 165–77.

Kuklinski, James H. and Richard C. Elling. 1977. "Representational Role, Constituency Opinion, and Legislative Roll-Call Behavior." *American Journal of Political Science* 21(1): 135–47.

Lazarsfeld, Paul F., Bernard Berelson, and Hazel Gaudet. 1944. *The People's Choice: How the Voter Makes Up His Mind in a Presidential Campaign*. New York: Duell, Sloan, and Pearce.

Long, J. Scott. 1997. *Regression Models for Categorical and Limited Dependent Variables*. Thousand Oaks, CA: Sage Publications.

Lublin, David I. 1994. "Quality, Not Quantity: Strategic Politicians in U.S. Senate Elections, 1952–1990." *Journal of Politics* 56(1): 228–41.

MacPherson, Peter. 1995. "Senate Panel OKs Ryan White Act." *CQ Weekly*, April 1, 1995, 947–8.

Mann, Thomas E. 1978. *Unsafe at Any Margin: Interpreting Congressional Elections*. Washington, DC: American Enterprise Institute.

Mann, Thomas E. and Raymond E. Wolfinger. 1980. "Candidates and Parties in Congressional Elections." *American Political Science Review* 74(3): 617–32.

Mansbridge, Jane. 2003. "Rethinking Representation." *American Political Science Review* 97(4): 515–28.

Marcus, George E. and Michael B. MacKuen. 1993. "Anxiety, Enthusiasm, and the Vote: The Emotional Underpinnings of Learning and Involvement During Presidential Campaigns." *American Political Science Review* 87(3): 672–85.

Matthews, Donald R. 1960. *U.S. Senators and Their World*. Chapel Hill: University of North Carolina Press.

Mayhew, David R. 1974. *Congress: The Electoral Connection*. New Haven, CT: Yale University Press.

Mayhew, David R. 1991. *Divided We Govern: Party Control, Lawmaking, and Investigations, 1946–1990*. New Haven, CT: Yale University Press.

McCombs, Maxwell E. and Donald L. Shaw. 1972. "The Agenda-Setting Function of Mass Media." *Public Opinion Quarterly* 36(2): 176–87.

McCrone, Donald J. and James H. Kuklinski. 1979. "The Delegate Theory of Representation." *American Journal of Political Science* 23(2): 278–300.

McCrone, Donald J. and Walter J. Stone. 1986. "The Structure of Constituency Representation: On Theory and Method." *Journal of Politics* 48(4): 956–75.

Miller, Warren E. and J. Merrill Shanks. 1996. *The New American Voter*. Cambridge, MA: Harvard University Press.

Miller, Warren E. and Donald E. Stokes. 1963. "Constituency Influence in Congress." *American Political Science Review* 57(1): 45–56.

Moss, Bill. 1992. "He Has Drive, But No Fuel." *St. Petersburg Times*, October 28, 1992, 1B.

Neuman, W. Russell. 1986. *The Paradox of Mass Politics: Knowledge and Opinion in the American Electorate*. Cambridge, MA: Harvard University Press.

Nie, Norman H., Sidney Verba, and John R. Petrocik. 1976. *The Changing American Voter*. Cambridge, MA: Harvard University Press.

Ornstein, Norman J., Thomas E. Mann, and Michael J. Malbin. 1990. *Vital Statistics on Congress, 1989–1990*. Washington, DC: Congressional Quarterly.

Ornstein, Norman J., Thomas E. Mann, and Michael J. Malbin. 1992. *Vital Statistics on Congress, 1991–1992*. Washington, DC: Congressional Quarterly.

Ornstein, Norman J., Thomas E. Mann, and Michael J. Malbin. 1994. *Vital Statistics on Congress, 1993–1994*. Washington, DC: Congressional Quarterly.

Ornstein, Norman J., Thomas E. Mann, and Michael J. Malbin. 1996. *Vital Statistics on Congress, 1995–1996*. Washington, DC: Congressional Quarterly.

Ornstein, Norman J., Thomas E. Mann, and Michael J. Malbin. 1998. *Vital Statistics on Congress, 1997–1998*. Washington, DC: Congressional Quarterly.

Page, Benjamin I. and Robert Y. Shapiro. 1992. *The Rational Public: Fifty Years of Trends in Americans' Policy Preferences*. Chicago: University of Chicago Press.

Page, Benjamin I., Robert Y. Shapiro, Paul W. Gronke, and Robert M. Rosenberg. 1984. "Constituency, Party, and Representation in Congress." *Public Opinion Quarterly* 48(4): 741–56.

Parker, Glenn R. 1980. "Sources of Change in Congressional District Attentiveness." *American Journal of Political Science* 24(1): 115–24.

Patterson, Thomas. 1993. *Out of Order*. New York: Random House.

Pitkin, Hanna. 1967. *The Concept of Representation*. Berkeley, CA: University of California Press.

Polsby, Nelson W. and Eric Schickler. 2002. "Landmarks in the Study of Congress Since 1945." *Annual Review of Political Science* 5: 333–67.

Ragsdale, Lyn and Timothy E. Cook. 1987. "Representatives' Actions and Challengers' Reactions: Limits to Candidate Connections in the House." *American Journal of Political Science* 31(1): 45–81.

Riker, William H. 1986. *The Art of Political Manipulation*. New Haven, CT: Yale University Press.

Salisbury, Robert H. and Kenneth A. Shepsle. 1981. "U.S. Congressman as Enterprise." *Legislative Studies Quarterly* 6(4): 559–76.

Schattschneider, E. E. 1960. *The Semisovereign People*. New York: Holt, Rinehart and Winston.

Schiller, Wendy J. 1995. "Senators as Political Entrepreneurs: Using Bill Sponsorship to Shape Legislative Agendas." *American Journal of Political Science* 39(1): 186–203.

Schiller, Wendy J. 2000. *Partners and Rivals: Representation in U.S. Senate Delegations.* Princeton: Princeton, NJ: University Press.

Sellers, Patrick J. 1998. "Strategy and Background in Congressional Campaigns." *American Political Science Review* 92(1): 159–71.

Shapiro, Catherine R., David W. Brady, Richard Brody, and John A. Ferejohn. 1990. "Linking Constituency Opinion and Senate Voting Scores: A Hybrid Explanation." *Legislative Studies Quarterly* 15(4): 599–622.

Shaw, Eugene F. 1977. "The Interpersonal Agenda." In *The Emergence of American Political Issues: The Agenda-Setting Function of the Press*, ed. Donald Shaw and Maxwell McCombs. St. Paul, MN: West Publishing.

Simon, Adam F. 2002. *The Winning Message: Candidate Behavior, Campaign Discourse, and Democracy.* New York: Cambridge University Press.

Sinclair, Barbara. 1989. *The Transformation of the U.S. Senate.* Baltimore: Johns Hopkins University Press.

Spiliotes, Constantine J. and Lynn Vavreck. 2002. "Campaign Advertising: Partisan Convergence or Divergence?" *Journal of Politics* 64(1): 249–61.

Squire, Peverill. 1989. "Challengers in U.S. Senate Elections." *Legislative Studies Quarterly* 14(4): 531–47.

Squire, Peverill. 1992. "Challenger Quality and Voting Behavior in U.S. Senate Elections." *Legislative Studies Quarterly* 17(2): 247–63.

Stimson, James A., Michael B. MacKuen, and Robert S. Erikson. 1995. "Dynamic Representation." *American Political Science Review* 89(3): 543–65.

Stone, Walter J. 1979. "Measuring Constituency–Representative Linkages: Problems and Prospects." *Legislative Studies Quarterly* 4(4): 623–39.

Stone, Walter J. 1982. "Electoral Change and Policy Representation in Congress: Domestic Welfare Issues from 1956–1972." *British Journal of Political Science* 12(1): 95–115.

Sullivan, John L. and Eric M. Uslaner. 1978. "Congressional Behavior and Electoral Marginality." *American Journal of Political Science* 22(3): 536–53.

Talbert, Jeffrey C., Bryan D. Jones, and Frank R. Baumgartner. 1995. "Nonlegislative Hearings and Policy Change in Congress." *American Journal of Political Science* 39(2): 383–406.

Wahlke, John C. 1971. "Policy Demands and System Support: The Role of the Represented." *British Journal of Political Science* 1(3): 271–90.

Walker, Jack. 1977. "Setting the Agenda in the U.S. Senate: A Theory of Problem Selection." *British Journal of Political Science* 7(4): 423–45.

Wattenberg, Martin P. and Craig Leonard Brians. 1999. "Negative Campaign Advertising: Demobilizer or Mobilizer?" *American Political Science Review* 93(4): 891–99.

Wawro, Gregory. 2000. *Legislative Entrepreneurship in the U.S. House of Representatives.* Ann Arbor: University of Michigan Press.

Weissberg, Robert. 1978. "Collective vs. Dyadic Representation in Congress." *American Political Science Review* 72(2): 535–47.

Weissberg, Robert. 1979. "Assessing Legislator–Constituency Policy Agreement." *Legislative Studies Quarterly* 4(4): 605–22.

Westlye, Mark C. 1991. *Senate Elections and Campaign Intensity.* Baltimore: Johns Hopkins University Press.

Wilson, Rick K. and Cheryl D. Young. 1997. "Cosponsorship in the U.S. Congress." *Legislative Studies Quarterly* 22(1): 25–43.

Wright, Gerald C. and Michael B. Berkman. 1986. "Candidates and Policy in United States Senate Elections." *American Political Science Review* 80(2): 567–88.

Zaller, John R. 1992. *The Nature and Origins of Mass Opinion.* New York: Cambridge University Press.

Zaller, John R. 1998. "Politicians as Prize Fighters: Electoral Selection and Incumbency Advantage." In *Party Politics and Politicians*, ed. John Geer. Baltimore: Johns Hopkins University Press.

Index